IN THE DAYS
OF THE
SECOND TEMPLE

THE TOWER OF DAVID
Really the Tower of Phasael built by Herod.

IN THE DAYS OF THE SECOND TEMPLE

By JACOB S. GOLUB, Ph. D.

Librarian Emeritus
Jewish Education Committee of New York

NEW YORK

The Union of American Hebrew Congregations

Eleventh Printing, Revised 1955

PRINTED IN THE UNITED STATES OF AMERICA

DEDICATED
TO
MY WIFE

EDITOR'S INTRODUCTION

The continuity and enrichment of Jewish life in America as elsewhere is largely dependent on an adequate system of Jewish education. In the development of a well founded American Jewish school many factors enter, but one of the most important is the improvement of the course of study.

The elaboration of an adequate course of study for our schools requires a first hand study and investigation of the Jewish past. Jewish scholarship must necessarily form the basis of an enriched curriculum. But of equal importance with Jewish scholarship is the development of an educational methodology that will translate the results of scholarship into classroom material.

To date our text book literature cannot as yet boast of even a single series of Jewish history books for children that will meet the requirements of recent educational theory and practice. History for children is usually an abbreviated text compressed from more extended works written for adults, often without even the element of simplicity which should be a characteristic of children's literature. The period of the Second Commonwealth in particular has been almost entirely neglected so that there is practically no book for this period suited to the needs of children in the elementary schools.

"In the Days of the Second Temple" by Dr. Jacob S. Golub is an attempt to treat of this neglected period in Jewish History. For this reason alone it fulfills a much felt need. The chief value of this new text, however, is to be found in the method pursued by the author, a teacher and supervisor of Jewish Schools for many years. He has had the opportunity to experiment with his own material before publication. The result is not merely a history but a new Jewish history based on sound pedagogic theory and deeply rooted in experience with children.

The basic idea underlying this book is the utilization of the problem approach to the study of Jewish history. The problem is the beginning of thought and therefore a stimulus which leads to learning. While in general education, problems and projects as a means of education are no longer new, in Jewish education they have hardly been attempted. Instead of teaching history as a series of unrelated facts the author has organized the entire story of the Second Commonwealth around seven questions or problems. In the attempt to answer the questions the pupil is stimulated not only to acquire knowledge but what is even more important, to think, to form judgments. The raw material of history assumes new life as it becomes related to life.

The author has succeeded in including the most important historical events of the period in spite of the fact that the particular organization which he followed necessitated the exclusion of some events. His emphasis on the present and his constant comparison with it help to make history real and living in contrast with most

history textbooks which give an impression of a dead
past.

To help both teacher and pupil to test achievement
a series of questions and exercises have been appended
to each section. Projects including map work for the
pupil have been arranged, and an adequate bibliography
for each section has been added for pupil and teacher.
In addition, the Union of American Hebrew Congregations has spared no effort to make the appearance of the
book attractive as far as type, cover, illustrations and
maps are concerned.

The failure of most textbooks in Jewish history in
the past has been partly due also to their constant
emphasis on wars, political events, succession of kings
and memorization of dates. In this book all of these
are rightly relegated to the background. The center of
gravity is clearly placed on the social religious life of
the period and on the development of Jewish ideals.

The editor is confident that herewith the Union of
American Hebrew Congregations is presenting to the
children in our Jewish Schools a textbook which will
mark a new departure in the writing of Jewish history
for children and will lead to an intelligent understanding of the most inspiring story in the history of peoples.

EMANUEL GAMORAN

NOTE TO ELEVENTH PRINTING, REVISED

The response throughout the country to *In the Days of the Second Temple* by Dr. Jacob S. Golub has been such as to justify our issuing many printings, and a revised edition on the occasion of the eleventh printing. We made changes in view of the establishment of the new State of Israel. A basic change has been made in Section III, formerly called "The Last Independent State." The new State of Israel obviously made it necessary to change this title to "The Second Independent State" and to do a basic revision in that section. This the author has done.

We are grateful to the many rabbis, educators, and teachers who have given us concrete evidence of their appreciation of this series of history texts.

E.G.

TO THE TEACHER AND ADULT READER

The writer of a book for children hardly owes any apology or explanation to his possible adult readers. It may be presumptuous on his part to assume that he will have adult readers at all. Yet in view of the paucity of Jewish historical literature that is popularly readable, this book may fall into the hands of maturer readers than the writer contemplated and to them as well as to the teacher a word of explanation is due.

The author is not a professional historian, but a worker in the field of Jewish education. This text is offered, therefore, mainly as a contribution to selection and pedagogic organization of a period of Jewish history rather than to original historical research. Wherever, therefore, scholars clash in the interpretation of facts or situations, it was deemed most advisable to accept the traditional view. Thus the edict of Cyrus, the number of returned exiles, etc., is assumed as described in the Book of Ezra though the biblical accounts themselves offer more than enough grounds to question the coherence of the narrative. Anyone who would investigate these problems is referred to more scholarly works.

In similar manner the adult reader may take issue with attempts at interpretation of the facts which the author has consciously introduced. The teaching of history must concern itself with both processes, acquisition of facts and applying or interpreting them through comparison or through passing of judgment. The adult generally prefers to draw his own conclusions and it is well that he should. But the child is not equally capable. The adult, too, has a richer basis of experience for weighing both sides of a controversy which a child has not. Thus the adult may feel that there is something to be said for the Hellenists, that probably not all the Hassidim were heroes nor that all the Sadducees will forever be damned. The child, however, must be given a complete reaction to the situation. Children's history cannot be pure science, an excursion into fact finding, but an applied science, a method of arriving at conclusions about social values, a means of judging contemporary situations through more dispassionate criteria formed over the perusal of the past. And if the writer has assumed any one point of view he has left room for many other possible sources of interpretation through the questions appended for discussion.

Nothing further need be said about the organization of the book beyond what is already told in the editor's introduction. The writer has attempted to include aids to concrete understanding in the form of pictures and maps, with only limited success. Unfortunately, the period in question does not afford sufficient material remains that can be interpreted by children. Most of the archaeological finds are ruins which give an impression of decay rather than of grandeur. Many art illustrations, therefore, have been used, which by their nature are of limited historical worth. Still, even the scant offering is more than has been hitherto attempted.

The writer wishes to acknowledge gratefully valuable assistance which he received in the preparation of this text. Dr. Emanuel Gamoran was responsible for the suggestion of treating this period and for stimulating the completion of the work. Dr. William Rosenau of Baltimore has read the manuscript carefully and offered valuable suggestions which were gratefully incorporated. To my erstwhile colleague, Dr. I. Keyfitz, of the College of Jewish Studies of Chicago, I am indebted for a critical reading of the manuscript, to Mrs. U. S. Schwartz of Chicago for most helpful revision in style, and to my wife, for many patient hours of re-reading and criticism and for testing the material in use before publication.

J. S. G.

Cincinnati, Ohio
February, 1929

CONTENTS

Judean State crushed by Chaldea—Why did the Babylonian Captives desire to return to their homeland—
How did longing for return begin—How the exile
came to an end—Nation overwhelmed with troubles
—Prophets again awaken hope, the Temple completed
—New hardships lead Judeans to despair—Ezra, the
saviour of his people—Nehemiah, the great governor
—How were the reforms of Ezra and Nehemiah made
permanent—How other people influenced the Jews.

SECTION II

The Maccabean Wars—How did the Greeks interfere with the life of the Jewish people—Why was the
festival of Chanukah instituted—How did the Jews
defend their religion—How armed rebellion began—

LIST OF MAPS

LIST OF ILLUSTRATIONS

SECTION I

After Bendemann

"By the Rivers of Babylon, There We Sat Down, Yea, We Wept"

Psalm 137.

HOW DID OUR ANCESTORS REËSTABLISH THEIR STATE AFTER THEIR EXILE?

JUDEAN STATE CRUSHED BY CHALDEA

THE earlier story of our people, we thought, had marked the end of the Jewish state. Nebuchadnezzar, one of the world's great conquerors, had led his victorious Chaldeans [1] through the whole of Syria, including Judea. Judea was first made a dependent nation which might still have its kings, but would be obliged to pay tribute to Babylon (597 B.C.E.). The Judean king proving rebellious, his capital was destroyed together with the sacred Temple, and Judea became a royal province. Gedalia ben Ahikam, a Judean, was appointed royal governor by Nebuchadnezzar (586 B.C.E.).

After the first invasion (597 B.C.E.), Nebuchadnezzar, thinking that without its leaders the nation would remain faithful, had taken captive to Babylon many princes, members of the nobility, and other men of importance. When, eleven years later, the Judeans again rose in rebellion, Nebuchadnezzar was determined on removing every man of any importance at all. In the great deportation (586 B.C.E.), the larger part of the

---

[1] people of Chaldea

Jewish nation either perished in the war or was led away to distant Babylon. Aside from those who succeeded in hiding from the invaders, or who fled in voluntary exile to Egypt, there remained only the poor peasants and shepherds scattered in their mountain villages.

But even after their two calamities, some of the Judeans were not yet ready to submit to Babylon. Spurred on by a ruler east of the Jordan, a Judean prince who had escaped the captivity organized a new plot against Babylon. As an outcome of this plot, the governor and the Babylonian garrison were murdered. Many now fearing Babylonian vengeance, fled to Egypt with their followers, taking with them also the prophet Jeremiah.

Thereafter, Judea was not even a separate colony; its lands were annexed to the nearby kingdoms. Philistines from the west, Ammonites and Moabites from the east, and Edomites from the south, gradually took possession of the deserted farms and villages. Palestine as an independent state disappeared from the map, and the Judeans, or as we may now call them, the Jews, apparently passed out of history as a separate nation.

After all that had befallen Judea, the lands surrounding it could surely believe that it would never return to nationhood. The wealth of the land had been carried off as booty;[1] all its able citizens: rulers, teachers, soldiers, artisans,[2] even skilled farmers had

---

[1] plunder taken by victorious soldiers   [2] skilled workers

been taken as prisoners. The poor folk left in Judea could never again reëstablish their independence. The group remaining in Judea did, in fact, prove unable to regain its lost position in the world without outside assistance.

How then did our ancestors succeed in restoring their state? We can readily guess that if the survivors in Palestine were not responsible for the restoration, some of the Babylonian captives must have returned. This is indeed what happened about forty-eight years later (538 B.C.E.), and the rest of this section will tell how it came about.

We shall begin by trying to find out why the Babylonian exiles wished to return to their home-land.

WHY DID THE BABYLONIAN CAPTIVES DESIRE TO RETURN TO THEIR HOME-LAND?

We might attempt a ready guess in answer to this question. The Judeans were in exile, and exile was a fearful thing to men of ancient times. It meant being led away to a strange land, brought to a slave market, and auctioned off—each member of the family to a different master.

When the Temple went up in flames, and, one behind the other, the Judeans were marched in chains between rows of Chaldeans, they felt that free life had ended for them. It would be their lot, they were certain, to serve among the thousands of human beasts of burden.

Not for Economic Reasons

But this is not the answer at all. The Judeans found Nebuchadnezzar was not the cruel conqueror they had feared he would be. He did not sell them as slaves, he did not separate the families, nor did he even take their servants away. On the contrary, he settled them on a fertile land well watered by the river Chebar, and made it possible for them to live comfortably and to prosper. When some of the early exiles sent a letter of complaint to the prophet Jeremiah at Jerusalem, the prophet not only told them they had little to complain about, but even advised them to build homes in Babylon, to pray for the peace of the city, and to look forward to living there for many years.

Strangely enough, it happened that many of the exiles found their condition even better than it had been in Palestine. The soil of Babylon was richer than that of Palestine and yielded more fruit with less labor. Many who had been poor in Palestine, who hadn't the means to buy a field or a garden, and had been obliged to hire out their labor to wealthy landowners, were now given the opportunity to gain an independent estate. In addition, Babylon was a wealthier country, where one might turn to many different trades and occupations. One might become a skilled artisan or even a merchant. Many did, in fact, enter into manufacture and commerce, and within twenty or thirty years, men of great wealth were found among them.

There was as much to make people happy in Babylon as the visiting farmer finds in the big city. Babylon was the greatest city in Asia, where men and merchandise of all the known nations were to be found. Babylonian merchants were wise in worldly matters. In order to keep their accounts, they had invented a form of writing which was borrowed by the Phoenicians who later spread it throughout Europe. They developed systems of bookkeeping, a careful and quite accurate commercial law, and weights and measures which are the foundation for our own. They built magnificent temples and palaces, and their so-called "hanging gardens" were among the wonders of the ancient world. There were also many wise men in Babylon: doctors who healed the sick, writers, and bards who sang and told legends of ancient Babylon—how the world was created, and of the coming of the great flood—astronomers who studied the stars, and who first divided the days into weeks and months.

They Were Religiously Unhappy

There was every reason, apparently, why the Judeans should have been happy in Babylon. Perhaps some of them were—those to whom prosperity, wealth, and greater comfort, were the aims and purposes of life. But most of the Jews were very unhappy. Something was lacking in this gorgeous Babylon; something which was very dear to them. Babylonian life, like all heathen life, was too cruel and selfish. In comparison with their Jewish religion, the religion of Babylon was coarse and savage. The gods were worshipped in drinking festivals; children were often offered as sacrifices;

DAGON

The fish god of the
Philistines.

the king was called a god and was worshipped. All priests prayed for him, the ways of the stars were read for him, the scribes wrote for him, and the singers sang for him. How different it was from the life in Judea where God was the great Heavenly King who ruled justly and lovingly, and was the Father of all, both the poor and the rich. Every Jew knew his God. The prophets spoke God's word in the market place. The Jewish God hated all the pomp and festivity of the Babylonian religion. He would not look upon the blood-stained hands lifted up in prayer.

A desire was kindled in the hearts of the exiles to return home. Somewhere, a Mount Zion which many of them had never seen, was calling them. There they could find their God. There He would await them. The old glories of their first kingdom were told and retold. Their hearts glowed at the thought of the sacred Temple wherein God had dwelt. Lovingly, they recalled every detail of it, every measurement, every part of its plan, its chambers, and its furnishings. They would return to Zion and rebuild their Temple. They would not end their lives in Babylon. The exile to Babylon was a punishment from God for their sinful lives, for their idol worship, and their oppression of the poor. Their prophets had so taught them, and it had come to be. But the prophets had also foreseen the return, and God would surely fulfill the second half of His promise as He had fulfilled the first.

How Did Longing for Return Begin?

The movement for the return to Judea was begun by the prophets of the exile. The fiery orators who had so bravely championed the cause of the people against the oppression of kings and nobles, had their descendants in the great leaders of Babylon. These, however, had a different task before them. Theirs was no longer to scold or to reprove. Their task was to remake dead souls into live spirits; faint-hearted Jews, now more Babylonian than Jewish, had to be made once more into Jews.

A Religious Revolution

As a result of the teaching of these prophets, a great religious change was taking place in Babylon. A long struggle which had gone on among the Judeans for over two hundred years was finally coming to a close. The battle which the prophets had been waging for two centuries was ending at last in a victory for their followers.

ASTARTE

Babylonian goddess of love and fertility. Later brought to Greece and worshipped as Venus.

What was the struggle? It concerned the nature of God. Who is God? Men of all the nations of old could think of their god only as their king. God was their Heavenly King, ruling their country in heaven as their earthly king ruled them below. Like their king on earth, the Heavenly King ruled over His particular kingdom only, and therefore, every land had its own god. If a man left his country to settle in another, he left his god behind, and accepted the god of the new country just as he was obliged to accept the authority of the king of that new land. When two nations went to war, their gods, too, made battle. The strong god of the victorious people became the triumphant ruler of the conquered country.

A New God-Idea

The Jews had shared the same belief about their God. They thought that their God ruled them as Dagon ruled Ashdod or as Chemosh ruled Moab. But it fell to the prophets to declare the great truth that there is one God Who is the ruler of the entire universe. How foreign the idea must have sounded to their generation! One might as readily imagine one king ruling over the whole world. Yet, the prophets continued their teaching. They explained that the victories of one people over another were not the battles between gods. The victories were directed by the God Who is displeased with a nation, and therefore sends another nation against it to mete out His punishment. God would be particularly severe with Israel, for

Israel is His people and therefore, should know Him best. God also sent messengers to warn Israel. These were the prophets, Amos, Hosea, Micah, and Isaiah, who, one after another, repeated the message. If Israel continued to sin in spite of all warnings, God would bring a great calamity upon her. God would scatter Israel among strange peoples till such a time as Israel would seek Him in truth. Then He would be reconciled to Israel, and would lead her back to her own land.

Little by little, some Judeans had accepted the teachings of the prophets. They sought out the word of God as it was written in His Law, and strove to follow it faithfully.

The king and the nobles, however, who had not heeded the advice of the prophets, stirred up wars at great cost to the nation. As a result, Israel was defeated, the Temple was burned with fire, and the people were led away captive to Babylon.

How would Israel act after this disaster? Those Jews who had not accepted the teachings of the prophets could but feel that their God was defeated by the god of Babylon. There was a Jewish nation no more. The god of Babylon now ruled them; he was their god and they were Babylonians.

The majority of the people, however, refused to accept such a belief. How foolish it was to imagine that "Bel" or "Nebo" had conquered their God. They knew why they had suffered defeat, for the prophets had warned them of it—they had angered God, and He had cast them off. Because of their sins Jerusalem was plowed as a field, and the Temple mount lay in ruins.

The many who had only partly heeded the words of the prophets, now accepted their teachings eagerly. They sought out their books and read them with zeal. The prophets had foretold destruction and it had come to pass. But the prophets also foretold a return if Israel pleased God. How can God be pleased? All idols must be cast away. God's laws, revealed through His greatest prophet Moses, must be studied and followed strictly. If Israel would turn to God with all her heart, with all her soul, and with all her might, God would surely remember the remnant of Israel.

Ezekiel—The Comforter of the Exile

The great prophetic teachers who arose in Babylon found a readier ear than their forerunners [1] in Palestine.

The first great prophet to arise in the exile was Ezekiel. He had been a priest, and was brought to Babylon in the first captivity (597 B.C.E.). For ten years after his exile, he followed the happenings at Jerusalem with great anxiety, troubled that Judea had taken no warning from its earlier punishment and had continued to turn from the ways of God. In fiery prophecies he denounced the sinners of Jerusalem, and warned them that the wrath of God would burn fiercely against them. Then the Temple fell and the great Judean captivity was led to Babylon. Judea was crushed and without hope. Ezekiel now turned to comforting the exiles and arousing new hope among them for a

---

[1] those who came before them

return to Palestine. In his famous "Vision of the Dry
Bones," [1] he told the people a very powerful story of
their God who brought to life even scattered bones
which had been lying dried and bleached under the
hot sun for many, many years.

Another fear was in the hearts of the despairing
Israelites. They had been taught according to the
ancient law that God is vengeful [2] and full of anger,
visiting the sins of the fathers upon the children unto
the third and fourth generation.[3] If their fathers had
sinned, and angered God, no amount of repentance on
their part could undo the Lord's wrath.

The prophet Ezekiel undertook to reassure them.
"What mean ye," says the prophet, "that ye use this
proverb in the land, saying, 'the fathers have eaten
sour grapes, and the children's teeth are set on edge?'
—Behold, all souls are Mine; . . . the soul that
sinneth, it shall die." [4]

The practice of the nations at that time was to punish
a man's family as well as the wrongdoer himself for
his misdeeds. If a man had stolen, or murdered, or
even if he could not pay his debts, his whole family
was punished, or they might all be sold as slaves.
Surely, thought the prophet, this is not the law of the
just and merciful God of Israel. Each man must be
rewarded or punished in accordance with his own merit.
"The soul that sinneth, it shall die; the son shall not
bear the iniquity of the father with him, neither shall

---

[1] Ezekiel chap. XXXVII
[2] taking revenge
[3] Exodus chap. XX
[4] Ezekiel chap. XVIII

the father bear the iniquity of the son with him."

In like manner, Israel need not fear that she would suffer for the sins of her fathers. If she were to become a righteous nation once more, God would love her sons as before.

Ezekiel very carefully gathered many of the laws which he feared might be lost. Although the memory of the Temple was cherished by the exiles, its details were being forgotten. Ezekiel, therefore, wrote out a very full description of the Temple so that if it ever was to be rebuilt, the architects would follow the exact model of the earlier one.

The Synagogue

The teachings of Ezekiel were greatly responsible for a religious change. The Jews turned to their religion more strongly than ever before; they studied with new zeal the holy books which they had brought from Judea. At this time the house of prayer must have become very important in their lives. Amidst the strange temples of heathen Babylon, they gathered in their little meeting houses for prayer and for study: sometimes to listen to the scribe, or to read a portion of the holy writings.

Only at the house of prayer could they feel themselves a people apart from those among whom they lived. In it they found courage to cling to their God, and to hope for a new life which was to maintain them not only in Babylon, but throughout the rest of their residence in strange lands.

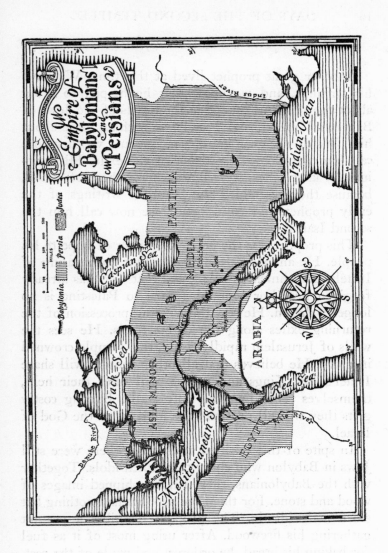

The Empire of Babylonians and Persians

The Unknown Prophet

Another great prophet lived at this time. We have his writings, and we know that he helped to bring about the religious change in the hearts of the Jews of Babylon. Unfortunately, we know nothing more about him. We do not even know his name and we therefore call him the unknown prophet of the exile. His writings, in later times, were mistaken for those of Isaiah, because they resembled the beautiful writings of the early prophet. For convenience, we now call him the second Isaiah.

This prophet was the great messenger of hope to his people. He announces confidently that the measure of Israel's punishment is filled, and that God has already forgiven her. For him the return to Palestine is no longer a dream. He sees the winding procession of the returning exiles along the desert roads. He sees the walls of Jerusalem rapidly rising, the Temple crowned in glory. He believes that all other peoples will share Israel's joy. Kings and princes will offer their help, themselves rebuilding the holy walls. Bearing costly gifts they will all proclaim the majesty of the God of Israel.

In spite of this spiritual awakening, there were still Jews in Babylon who clung to heathen idols. Together with the Babylonians, they still worshipped images of wood and stone. For them the prophet had nothing but scorn and ridicule. The prophet describes a peasant gathering his firewood. After using most of it as fuel for baking his bread, he orders a god made of the rest.

Idol worship did not continue much longer after the unknown prophet's mockery of idol-worshippers.

How the Exile Came to an End
(537 B.C.E.)

As the Jews were becoming more devoted to their religion, and began to dream of returning to their

home-land, they felt the yoke of Babylon becoming ever heavier upon them. The Babylonian kings, too, either angered by the ingratitude of the Jews, or regarding the Jews' refusal to worship their gods as an act of treason, began to oppress and persecute them. The Jews then began to hate Babylon. Eagerly they awaited a deliverance at the hands of Cyrus, the great king of the Medes and the Persians, who was now sweeping everything before him, and was prepared to invade Babylon.

CYRUS
From a bas-relief.

At last the deliverer came. Babylon fell before Persia. The Jews rejoiced.

As the prophet had foretold, so it came to pass. The

decree of King Cyrus rang through the land: "Whosoever there is among you of all His people—his God
be with him—let him go up to Jerusalem, which is in
Judah, and build the house of the Lord, the God of
Israel; He is the God who is in Jerusalem. And whosoever is left in any place where he sojourneth, let
the men of his place help him with silver and with
gold, with goods and with beasts; beside the free-will
offering for the house of God, which is in Jerusalem."
They who loved Zion might now return to the land
of their fathers to rebuild it and to dwell in it, after
fifty years of exile.

The enthusiasm was tremendous. Thousands prepared to give up home and friends in Babylon in order
to return to the old home-land. The total number of
these—men, women and children—is said in the Bible
to have been 42,360. Those who remained behind in
Babylon showered many precious gifts upon the returning exiles—gold, silver, and vessels to be devoted
to the new Temple which was to be built. Many who
could not leave at this time, and hoped to set out later,
gave in advance their share for the holy land. The
king, too, was very generous. He assigned an escort of
a thousand Persian soldiers to guide the pilgrims
safely across the desert, and returned to them all the
Temple vessels which former conquerors had carried
to Babylon.

We can hardly appreciate the heroism of the men
who were prepared to risk life and fortune for no
greater gain than the love of God and of a fatherland
which many of them had never even seen. The jour-

ney lay across a vast desert under a burning sun, inhabited by savage men and beasts. It was like an expedition into a jungle. They were journeying to a land which had probably been overrun by the wandering Bedouin. Whatever was not occupied by strange men, lay in ruins; rank weeds had overgrown the fields, spring torrents had broken up the terraces on the mountain sides and washed the rocks into the fields below. But these were the men who braved all and saved the nation.

Babylon prepared a great farewell for those who were departing. Choruses of singers, with stringed in-

After Schnorr

THE RETURN FROM THE BABYLONIAN EXILE

struments, sang and played songs of parting. Men rejoiced and wept at the same time. Everyone knew that it was a great day for Israel. "When the Lord brought back those that returned to Zion, we were like unto them that dream. Then was our mouth filled with laughter, and our tongue with singing." [1]

Home Again

At last, after several months of weary travel, the band of pioneers was once more in the land of their fathers. The news of their coming had spread; many of their brethren who had been living in hiding in Judea or among the neighboring nations, now came forth to greet those who had returned. It was a happy homecoming. The returned exiles, encamped about the mount where the Temple had stood, were treading the holy dust of Jerusalem. They were in holiday spirit, as people engaged in an exciting adventure usually are.

Their first thought was to restore the nation and the Temple. A prince of the house of David would rule over them once more, and a descendant of Aaron would minister in the new Temple. Zerubbabel, son of Shealtiel, of the royal house of David, was chosen civil ruler, and Jeshua, son of Jozadak, of the priestly family, was appointed high priest.

Under the leadership of these two men the next task was undertaken—the rebuilding of the Temple. In the meantime, an altar was erected which would serve as the centre of worship until the Temple itself would be finished.

---

[1] Psalm CXXVI, v. 1-2

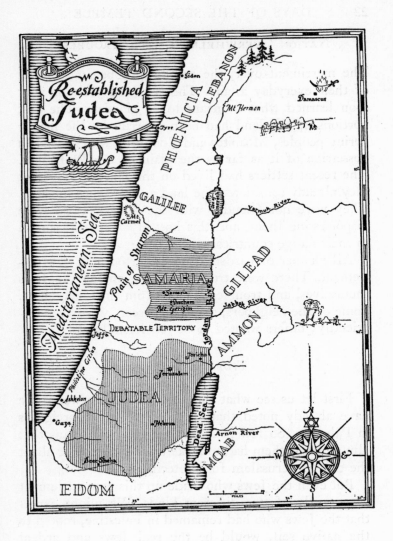

Re-established Judea

Sidon

Tyre

PHŒNICIA

LEBANON

Mt Hermon

Damascus

GALILEE

Yarmuk River

Mt. Carmel

Plain of Sharon

SAMARIA

GILEAD

Mediterranean Sea

Samaria
Shechem
Mt. Gerizim

Jabbok River

DEBATABLE TERRITORY

AMMON

Jaffa

Jericho

Jordan River

Philistine Cities

Jerusalem

Ashkelon

JUDEA

Dead Sea

Gaza

Hebron

Arnon River

MOAB

Beer Sheba

EDOM

MILES

Nation Overwhelmed with Troubles

The merriment over, the people now began to think of their everyday affairs. The returned Judeans very soon learned what it meant to be pioneers. The best portions of the land had been overrun by the neighboring peoples, Moabites and Edomites, who had taken possession of it as far as the plain of the Philistines. The recent settlers had lived on the land so long that they already considered the land as belonging to them. They were not friendly with the Judeans who were dispossessing them, and this hostility naturally spread to their native countries.

All manner of hardships now overtook the new settlement. There were troubles arising among the Jews themselves, and troubles arising from their neighbors. Some of the neighbors, as we have seen, were very unfriendly; others wanted to be too friendly.

Troubles Within

First let us see what the inner difficulties were. We have already noted that there were many foreigners in Palestine. So few in number were the Judeans that almost all of them had to make their homes in or about the city of Jerusalem for protection.

But even the Jews who made up this new settlement were really of two different kinds. We might expect that the Jews who had remained in Palestine, rooted to the native soil, would be the real Jews and ardent patriots. We should imagine that these would be the

© *U. and U.*

THE HOLY ROCK

On the Temple site. At present the famous Mosque of Omar is
built over it.

most zealous for their God and their Law. Strangely
enough, the very opposite was the fact. The Jews who
had remained in Palestine had really given up all hope
of their nation being restored. They were mixed with
the nations among whom they found shelter. They intermarried with them, and they followed many of
their ways, even their methods of worship. The religion of these Judeans was more heathen than had
been the religion of the Jews at the time of the destruction of the Temple.

The pioneers from Babylon, on the other hand, were

the most faithful followers of the teachings of the prophets. They had long wiped out all traces of idol worship from their midst. The Torah was their Law and guide at every step. They had looked forward to setting up a kingdom of God upon the mountain of Zion, and had imagined that the Jews who were privileged to remain in Palestine would be loyal indeed to their religion.

The Babylonian Jews not only had to defend themselves against men of other nations, but they had to fight with their own brothers. They were too few, however, to make headway against the native Jews. Sabbaths and new moons, therefore, were not kept, the priestly portions were not paid, and worship was neglected. The pure religion was fast slipping. The religion of the Samaritans, as well as that of Ammon and Moab, was creeping in. It appeared that this band which had braved everything for its great ideals was to become in time nothing more than another little heathen tribe in the Judean hills. Added to the troubles of civil strife there was further disaster of bad harvests which were followed by famine and pestilence. The sturdiest backs would have broken beneath such burdens.

External Difficulties—Ammon, Moab and Edom

But this was not all; these were only the troubles from within. In addition, there were many troubles from without. We have seen before that the nations living about Palestine would have many reasons for being unpleasant neighbors to the Jews. There were still the Edomites on the southeast, and the tribes of Moab and Ammon which had for many years been under the rule of Jewish kings, and who now saw an opportunity for revenge. On the west were the old Philistines, still as malicious and unfriendly as they had ever been in the days of David and Saul.

The Samaritans

On the north there were peculiar neighbors who, as we have suggested before, were anxious to be too friendly. These neighbors were called Samaritans or Cuthites. The Samaritans, if you remember from your earlier history, were a people who had been brought from Cutha, a city in Assyria, to inhabit the land which formerly belonged to the Northern Kingdom of Israel. The Assyrian kings usually transferred the population of one land to another to prevent new revolts in conquered provinces. In their native country the Cuthites had been idol worshippers. When they were settled in and about Samaria, they felt that according to their own beliefs they must also worship the god of the land in which they had settled. When a number of wild beasts from the jungles invaded the settled provinces and did much damage, the Samaritans considered it a sign that the god of the land was angry. They asked of the Assyrian king, accordingly, that he send a priest of the Israelites to instruct them in their religion.

The Samaritans soon accepted a religion which was

somewhat like the Jewish. But it was the religion which
the more ignorant Israelites had observed a hundred
years before the destruction of the Temple. The Samaritans may have worshipped on the high places, on
tops of mountains where good or evil spirits were believed to dwell. They may still have been worshipping
the golden bulls of Jeroboam when the Israelites returned from Babylon.

We are not told exactly in which ways the Samaritan

© U. and U.

SAMARITAN PASSOVER GATHERING

The Samaritans still gather, as in days of old, to sacrifice the paschal
lamb on Mount Gerizim.

religion differed from the Judean, but it probably was that which it had been during the days when the Temple still stood.

Building of Temple Stopped

When the Judeans were preparing to rebuild the Temple, the Samaritans hoped to be able to take part in the work and later to worship at this Temple with the Jews. They sent an embassy with rich gifts and with an offer of assistance. The very pious Jews, however, said that no one but a Jew could take part in the building of the Temple, and that they would not permit the Samaritans to have any share in it. The Samaritans felt deeply insulted. From possible friends the Samaritans now turned to bitter enemies. If they were to have no share in the Temple, they would see to it that the Temple would not be built. They sent letters to the king of Persia, in which they accused the Jews of wanting to set up an independent kingdom and of breaking from the rule of Persia. The great Cyrus had died, and the king who followed him was not as friendly to the Jews. This king readily believed the Samaritans, and sent back the order that all work cease.

Only the smallest beginning had been made in the building of the Temple, and the city walls had not even been begun. The King's orders, however, had to be obeyed. Enemies from all sides, taking advantage of this unsafe condition, raided and plundered the little Jewish community. Life became unbearable.

Many fled from Jerusalem to a more distant village. The wealthier Jews made alliances with the chiefs and princelings of the Samaritans, the Moabites and the Ashdodites, intermarrying with them to gain security, and the common people followed their example. The Judean heads of families used the Temple materials to build comfortable homes for themselves.

Prophets Again Awaken Hope—the Temple Completed

Fifteen years had gone by, and the Temple was still unbuilt. But these were not altogether years of despair. A community of the faithful still cherished dreams of a restored Jerusalem, and in their midst was reawakened the call of prophecy. Haggai and Zechariah, two of the last prophets of Judea, raised their voices in behalf of the House of God.

The times were troubled. There had been famine and great discontent. The prophets interpreted the famines and attacks from the enemy as a sign of God's anger against the neglect of His home and His city. They called upon the people to rally about Zerubbabel and Jeshua once more, and to seek permission anew for continuing the work on the Temple. A new king was ascending the Persian throne, and the chance of securing permission was believed favorable.

The prophet urged not only the building of the House of God, they demanded that which was a part of the worship of God—righteousness, kindliness to the poor and the needy, the teachings of the prophets of old. They bade the people take heart and not despair because evil men were in authority. They left us the great message which has more than once been the battle cry of the Jew that " 'Not by might, nor by power, but by My spirit,' saith the Lord." [1]

The Temple Rebuilt

As a result of the urging of the prophets, Judean messengers were sent to the Persian court to argue their case and to show that they had received permission from King Cyrus to rebuild their Temple and their city. The messengers succeeded in convincing the king, and the order forbidding the work was revoked. The Temple Mount became the scene of renewed activity. Materials for the Temple were again secured. The rising walls of the Temple filled the nation with enthusiasm. The work of rebuilding lasted four years (519–516 B.C.E.).

There was great rejoicing when this new Temple was ready for dedication. The people gathered as for a great feast. The Levites, in festive garments, sang and prayed. The priests, in their robes of office, offered sacrifices of thanksgiving. A House was once more built for God upon the sacred soil of Zion, as their prophets had foretold.

At the dedication of the Temple, one might have noticed a small group of old men standing aside and taking no part in the festivities. Instead of rejoicing, they wept. These old men were the few who re-

---

[1] Zechariah chap. IV, v. 6

mained of the former inhabitants of Palestine. These had seen the first Temple in all its splendor; this Temple seemed poor and small when compared with the Temple of Solomon. They felt that the old glory would never be restored. But little did these old men know that the second Temple was in time to be of much greater importance to the Jews than Solomon's grand edifice, for this Temple had been built not with a king's gold but with the love and the tears of a whole people. The prophet Haggai well understood the greatness of the event. " 'The glory of this latter house shall be greater than that of the former,' saith the Lord of hosts, 'and in this place will I give peace.' " [1]

New Hardships Lead Judeans to Despair

Barely had the Temple been completed, when the enemies of the Jews again began to accuse them of treason. As proof that they were plotting to gain their independence from Persia, they pointed to the fact that the Jews had chosen a king over themselves—Zerubbabel—of the old royal line. Zerubbabel was deposed; we do not know when or how. The high priest alone remained the ruler. In order to secure peace for themselves, the leaders of the wealthier families again made alliances with the neighboring countries, and intermarried with them.

Year after year the hopes of the pioneers were diminished. The pioneers were old men now. Their gen-

---

[1] Haggai chap. II, v. 9

eration was passing away. Faithfully they had taught
their children, and in their Synagogues the bands of
the faithful still gathered, and clung to their ideals.
The new generation accepted the dream of God's
people, but the dream was only a faint one. In their
innermost hearts even the bravest had given up.

EZRA, THE SAVIOUR OF HIS PEOPLE
(459 B.C.E.)

In the meantime, what was taking place among the
Jews left in Babylon? The religious revival which had
been brought in by Ezekiel and the unknown prophet
was gaining in strength. The noblest families vied with
one another in fulfilling the commands of God.
Eagerly and carefully they followed the precepts of
the Torah. They lived as a people apart from their
neighbors. They observed their Sabbaths and their
feasts. The Law of Moses was their constitution, by
which they lived, and ruled their community. They
taught it to their children, and they studied it diligently themselves.

Copies of the Torah were few and not always accurate. The Law could not be followed unless there
were sufficient scrolls prepared by the most learned
teachers. A man who could copy the scrolls was called
a scribe, and held the position which a rabbi holds
among us today.

The greatest of the scribes, the religious leader of
his community, was Ezra. Today we might call him
the "Chief Rabbi." Ezra had many claims to fame. He

came of a priestly family which had distinguished itself in the service of the Torah for a century and a
half. His great grandfather, Hilkiah, had discovered
the Book of the Law which brought about a religious
awakening in the days of King Josiah. His ancestors
had carried the Law with them to Babylon. It was their
pride and heritage.

Ezra became more distinguished than any of his ancestors. He studied the Torah more thoroughly, and
he understood its meaning more deeply. It is believed
that he was among the first to collect the various writings and to compile the five books of Moses. He taught
the people to live according to the Law which had been
given them for their guidance, that Israel might be a
nation of priests and a holy people. Ezra's soul was
aflame with love for God and the Torah. Faithfully
and joyously he carried out every command of it. His
example was reverently followed by his brethren.

Was it not written in the sacred writings, again and
again, that God would make His glory to shine once
more upon Zion? Was it not written that all the greatness of the old kingdom would be restored a hundred-
fold? God would be Israel's king. His blessings would
fill the land. Israel would know such prosperity as she
had never known.

The struggling remnant in Palestine had failed to
bring the kingdom of God. The righteous were down-
trodden. Half-Jews ruled over the holy land. Worship was neglected. The Torah was not obeyed. There
was injustice in the land, and the cries of the poor and
the oppressed reached as far as Babylon.

Goes to Judea

Ezra anxiously followed the news from Palestine. His heart bled at every report of failure. The faithful were losing courage. Their enemies were too many and too powerful. Something unusual had to be done to save them. Ezra himself would have to set out for the land of Israel.

There was great excitement in Babylon at the news that their religious leader was preparing to leave for Palestine. Many other pious men who were equally concerned with the fate of Palestine prepared to join him. An enlistment began for a company of Palestine settlers. Sixteen hundred persons answered the call.

The whole Babylonian population was greatly roused by Ezra's departure. Jews and non-Jews sent costly gifts for the Temple. The king offered Ezra an escort which Ezra refused. But the king gave him letters of safe-conduct to all the governors on the route between Babylon and Judea.

News of Ezra's coming had reached Judea. His fame had long gone before him. It was a great honor indeed for Palestinian Jews that the leader of Babylon was coming to live among them. The downtrodden gained new hope. Many who had been neglectful of their faith made haste to repent. The whole of Palestine prepared a royal welcome for the distinguished guest.

All through the journey Ezra had been picturing to himself what he would find in Palestine. He felt certain that the reports which reached him must be exaggerated. In the holy land people could not be altogether unmindful of the Torah; conditions could not be as bad as described.

Demands Observance of Torah

What Ezra found in Palestine filled him with deep grief. Corruption and injustice flourished, and the poor were at the mercy of the wealthy landowners. Worship had broken down, Sabbaths were openly violated, and the Sabbatical year was almost forgotten.

Ezra called an assembly of the people. He wished to speak to them but his feelings overcame him. He fell upon his knees and wept. Long and fervently he prayed to God. The assembly was moved. Men raised their voices and wept with him. Then one called out, "Command us, father, and we shall follow you."

Ezra arose and addressed the people: "You have strayed far from the ways of God. You have not kept His Law. Instead of being an example of God among the nations, you are imitating their evil ways. You have intermarried with them in open violation of your Law. Before you can hope to be God's people you must promise to send away your foreign wives, and must swear never more to intermarry with the heathen."

A deathlike silence followed. One after another the heads of the families rose and took the vow as Ezra demanded. Officers were chosen to go among the people to see that the conditions of the oath were carried out fully and conscientiously.

But the people had not foreseen what a dangerous step they were making. When their foreign wives returned home to their native lands, their fellow countrymen could not but look upon this act as a humiliating insult. Among the families which had intermarried with the Jews were some of the leading noblemen of Ammon and Ashdod. The feeling against the Jews became bitter. A cry arose for vengeance. War was soon declared against Judea.

Ezra was no soldier. In war he could not lead. The people were unprepared for war. Also, after the early enthusiasm of Ezra's visit, many Judeans were sorry that they had sent their wives away. Some secretly plotted with the enemies without. Jerusalem was attacked and fell. Its weak fortifications were completely destroyed. Many who feared the vengeance of the enemy or who did not feel safe to remain at Jerusalem left the city. Old conditions were returning. Most of the people forsook Ezra. The few faithful who still clung to him were powerless. The feeling came upon Ezra that perhaps he, too, had failed. His great soul was crushed, but he clung to his faith and hoped that a deliverer might yet come. If he was unworthy of being God's messenger, another might yet be found.

NEHEMIAH, THE GREAT GOVERNOR (422 B.C.E.)

Israel was not to be lost. Again, in the last moments of despair, a new hero arose who turned sorrow into gladness and defeat into victory. This man was also of Babylon, a leader among his brothers. Through his great energy and wisdom, he had succeeded in becoming one of the most important nobles of the land. His official title was "Cup-bearer to the King Artaxerxes." If you call to mind the stories of the old Persian kings, and the constant attempts which were made upon their lives through poison, you will readily see that only the king's most trusted noble was honored with the charge of the king's wine.

Nehemiah was very anxiously following the affairs of his brothers in their newly established land. With great hope he had seen Ezra depart thirteen years before.   He had heard of Ezra's first successes. But now every day brought him word of new failures. He became very sad. He yearned to go to Palestine himself to do what he could for his people. The king noticed how Nehemiah was becoming restless and sorrowful. One day the king asked the reason for his grieving. "How can I be happy," answered Nehemiah, "when the city, the place of my fathers, lies waste as a sepulchre, and the gates thereof are consumed with fire?" Nehemiah begged of the king that he permit him to go to Palestine. The king granted him permission, but on the condition that he return after twelve years. An edict was issued appointing Nehemiah royal governor over the land.

Fortifies Jerusalem

Nehemiah came into Palestine quietly and unannounced. At night, when no one could see him, he went about the city secretly inspecting its broken down for-

After Schnorr

ATTACKED WHILE AT WORK ON THE WALLS
An artist's conception.

tifications and the half-finished Temple.   After he had
spent a few days laying out his plans, he announced
himself to the people as their new governor and
showed them the order of the king. He inspired confidence at once. He called the people together to organize them for the most important task of upbuilding
their walls. The workmen were armed with weapons
and supplied with tools. With one hand they built, and
in the other they had their sword ready against any
sudden attacks. They worked in shifts from early till
late, and set guards by night. Nehemiah and the other

leaders who supervised the work, tell that they did not once undress for bed while the work was in progress. The neighboring enemies who had been in the habit of making raids upon the city suddenly found the people armed against them. Before word could reach the Samaritans and the Moabites of what was happening in Judea, and before these could gather a large army to prevent the work of rebuilding the walls, massive fortifications arose around Jerusalem and the city was now the irresistible fortress which only a large and trained army could hope to attack.

Relieves the Poor

Now that the Jews were safe against their enemies from without, Nehemiah set about to rid the city of the enemies from within. Many of the noble families had once more intermarried with the heathen. Others, heedless of anything else but their own profits, loaned money to the poor at usurious [1] interest, so that when the poor were unable to pay they were prepared to take away their fields, and even to sell them into slavery. It was a dangerous time to risk internal quarrels. The enemies from without were eager to fall upon Jerusalem, and many a Judean was undoubtedly in league with them. Yet Nehemiah braved the danger, and assembling the creditors, he upbraided them. He told them that in Persia wealthy Jews redeemed Jewish slaves from heathen masters, while in Palestine

---

[1] very high rate of interest

wealthy Jews were selling their own brothers into slavery. He declared that he himself would release the poor from all loans which he made to them during his term at Jerusalem. His friends and attendants did likewise. The Judean nobles were shamed into following their example. Nehemiah did even more. Because of the poor harvest he distributed grain to the needy, and he showed his generosity further by not accepting from the people any taxes for his own or for his household's use.

Establishes Reforms of Ezra

Nehemiah's next great concern was for the reëstablishment of both the Temple worship and the government according to the Law of the Torah. Ezra once more came to the fore, and with the aid of Nehemiah his reforms could be carried out. Ezra called a great assembly on the first day of the seventh month. A platform was erected in the market place near the water gate, from which he was to read the Law. Many of the Israelites were hearing for the first time how severe the vengeance of God would be against those who violated [1] the commandments. Repentant, the assembly broke into weeping, but Ezra and Nehemiah quieted them and told them that the occasion was one for gladness. Let them follow the Law and there would be peace in their land.

Ezra and Nehemiah reminded the people that the festival of Succoth, the Feast of Booths, was approach-

---

[1] did not obey

ing. The people were bidden to bring branches and build booths for themselves. The holiday had not been celebrated in this manner since the days of Joshua. How eagerly the Judeans went forth into the mount and fetched branches of wild olive and myrtle, and branches of thick trees!

There was gladness in Israel. Day by day to the end of the feast, the people gathered together to hear Ezra read from the Book of God. A solemn assembly consecrated the last of the seven days. Nehemiah and Ezra then gathered the heads of the people and made a solemn covenant with them. Once more they swore to live according to the Law of Moses. Once more they vowed not to give their daughters in marriage to foreigners; nor would they marry daughters of foreign tribes. For the first time they understood the great danger of intermarriage with foreign nations. The people promised to keep the Sabbath day holy. They also were ready to forego the profits of the seventh year and free their burdened brethren from debts that year. The House of God was not to be neglected. The priests and Levites were to receive their portions as commanded in the Torah. They would pay the yearly tax of one third shekel, the first fruit offerings, the tithes. These obligations were inscribed upon a scroll, and signed and sealed by the heads of the families.

Organizes Local Government

Nehemiah was mindful that he had only a few years to spend in Palestine, and he was eager that everything

be organized properly before he left. Since it was necessary that officers be appointed to rule the people, he
divided the land into districts with local governors in
charge. The city of Jerusalem which was now fortified
with walls was very thinly populated, and it was urgent
that more residents be brought in. Nehemiah decided
to bring a tenth of the country population into the
city. These were chosen by lot from those who could
trace a pure Jewish descent.[1] There were many poor
among them, and for these Nehemiah built houses at
his personal expense.

Nehemiah was particularly concerned for the
Temple service. If that was to continue without inter-
ruption, the priests and Levites must be provided for.
Accordingly, he appointed Levites to collect the tithes,
or tax of one tenth of the grain, from among the
people, and to bring it to the Temple for distribution
among all the priests.

Nehemiah Departs for Persia

When the twelve year period was over, Nehemiah
departed to Shushan, happy in the thought that he
had laid firm foundations for the new Jewish state.
He did not know that there were men plotting to undo
all of his reforms. The head of the opposing party
was none other than Eliashib, the high priest, who may
have felt slighted because Nehemiah followed the ad-

---

[1] Those people who could show that none of their great grand-
fathers or grandmothers had ever married a person forbidden by the
Jewish Law. Records of such marriages, many generations back,
were carefully kept and are called geneologies.

vice of Ezra in religious matters, rather than that of
the high priest. Accordingly, after Nehemiah was
gone, Eliashib declared the covenant which the elders
had signed to be void. His own son married a Samaritan woman, the daughter of the Samaritan chief, San-
ballat. The other priests followed his example. Many
heads of families who were hostile to Ezra and Nehemiah because of their laws against intermarriage which
caused suffering in their homes, or because they could
not collect their usurious debts, joined the party of the
priests.

The pious Jewish farmers in the provinces were
shocked at the treachery of the high priest, and refused
to pay the tithes. The faithful priests now suffered
with the wicked, and they were forced to leave their
posts to seek a livelihood elsewhere. The Temple was
deserted, sacrifices were not offered. A Moabite chieftain, Tobias, whose daughter had married into a noble
Judean family, was lodged within the Temple
grounds.

Once more it seemed that the labors of Ezra had
failed. Even the mighty work of the great governor
Nehemiah would all come to naught.

Nehemiah Returns to Judea

The pious Judeans in their distress may have sent
an embassy to Shushan, for Nehemiah was soon aware
of what was happening in Jerusalem, and obtaining
leave, hurried back to the city. In a short time Nehemiah reëstablished order. He expelled Tobias, the

Moabite, from the Temple, and deposed the high priest. The son of the high priest, refusing to give up his Samaritan wife, was expelled from the land. With him were expelled all other priests who refused to abandon their foreign wives. The loyal priests and Levites were recalled, and the Temple Service was continued. On the Sabbath day the gates of Jerusalem were closed, and guards were posted to keep the foreign merchants from bringing in their wares. At last Sabbath rest was assured.

The party opposed to Nehemiah was broken up after its leaders were expelled. No further opposition is reported during the rest of the days of Nehemiah. At last the hopes of the prophets had been realized. There was a Temple once more in Zion, and Israel was attempting to live according to the Law of "Moses, the Servant of the Lord."

How Were the Reforms of Ezra and Nehemiah Made Permanent?

Difficulties Encountered

The religious changes which Ezra and Nehemiah wished to introduce took many years to become rooted. Many of them had been accepted because of the fear of Nehemiah who was a favorite at the royal court. The very priests were eager to throw these laws aside when they thought it safe to do so, and the common people were not slow to follow their example.

Why did it take so many years for the idea to become accepted? We recognize today that Erza and

Nehemiah labored to preserve the Jewish people. Why were the men of their own generation not prepared to accept them more readily?

We may give three answers to the question. The first is that there must have been a great amount of honest difference of opinion concerning the interpretation of the Law. A second reason is that many a Judean was eager to buy his peace with his neighbors, even at the cost of his religion. The third reason is that the religion and the laws as taught by Ezra and Nehemiah were too democratic [1] for the wealthy families who were ready either to change the Law or to abandon their people. Let us examine each of these reasons more fully.

SEVERITY OF THE LAW

Most parties among the Jews were prepared to accept the Law of Moses as their basic law. The difficulty arose, however, in the explanations of the meaning of the Law. You are well familiar with the early difficulties in the United States, caused by the various interpretations of the Constitution. There were broad-constructionists and strict-constructionists, each insisting that the Constitution meant what they had in mind. In a similar manner, there arose the difficulty of interpreting the Mosaic Law. It clearly stated, for example, that an Ammonite or a Moabite might not be admitted into the fold of Israel. In the Bible the male gender

---

[1] interested in the good of all the people, rather than merely in the welfare of the nobles and large land owners

is used, meaning that an Ammonite or Moabite man
might not become a Jew. Was that prohibition to be
extended to females also? What did the Torah mean
by forbidding labor on the Sabbath? What is labor? Is
chopping wood for exercise labor? Carrying a heavy
load is undoubtedly labor, but is carrying a light load
labor? Is carrying labor?

Many undoubtedly believed that Ezra's interpretations were much too severe. Especially concerning the
Samaritans, there was a strong difference of opinion.
This people was anxious to accept the Law of Moses
and to join with the Jews in the building of the
Temple. The religious leaders of the new Jewish community feared that the Samaritans still retained many
of their heathen practices, though this fear was not
shared by all priests and notables.

Nehemiah's decision to expel some of the priests
from Judea certainly did not help to make his cause
more popular with a large group. It strengthened the
boast of the Samaritans that they now had regular
priests, descendants of the tribe of Aaron, and that
they could worship on Mount Gerizim, which the Bible
calls the "Mountain of the Blessing." They did, in fact,
build a Temple on that mountain to rival the one at
Jerusalem.

HOSTILITY OF NEIGHBORING PEOPLES

The second reason why it was so hard for Nehemiah
to impress his reforms on the Jews was the desire for
peace with their stronger neighbors, which animated

most of the leading Jews of the community. We recall what hardship and danger were created by giving up the foreign wives. Many who were forced to abandon their foreign wives and face the anger of their non-Jewish relatives were naturally opposed to the policy of Ezra and Nehemiah.

DEMOCRACY OF THE LAW

The third reason for Nehemiah's difficulties was that he attempted to enforce the most democratic practices of the Jewish religion. Nehemiah, by his own example, had forced the wealthy landowners to abandon their debts. The law concerning the Sabbatical year was enforced, when all debts had to be cancelled, when there might be no sowing or reaping, but the poor might enter freely and take of what grew without cultivation. The practice of selling Jews into slavery for debt or crime was being abolished. An organized system of charity was being put into operation. The Jewish aristocrats offered strong opposition to such restrictions which did not hamper non-Jewish land-owners.

How the Difficulties Were Overcome

How far Ezra and Nehemiah overcame all these difficulties in their own lives, we do not know. We do know, however, that they laid out the program which later generations followed.

The program of Ezra and Nehemiah may be outlined as follows:

The nation must strive to become a nation of priests, and a holy people. It can do so by following the Law of Moses both as written in the Torah and the Prophets (the written law), and as explained and interpreted by scribe and teacher (the oral law).

In order to follow the Law it is necessary that all Israel know it. They must therefore have opportunity to study it, and they must be urged to do so.

The leaders of the people must treasure the Torah and be able to set a worthy example. The official leaders were the priests, but as experience had shown, these were often unworthy. A priest inherited his rank, and an unfit person might often attain the office, as happens in the history of royalty. The office of the priests was commanded in the Torah, and all honors had to be given it.

But the idea was conceived of entrusting the real leadership to an assembly of elders who represented not merely the priests, but also the learned and the pious. The main body, meeting at Jerusalem, was to act as the legislative and judicial head of the new Jewish state. Smaller assemblies, consisting later of twenty-three persons, were formed for the provinces.

THE POPULAR BODY OF ELDERS—KENESET HAGEDOLAH

Let us begin with the last part of the program, the Keneset Hagedolah, or the Great Synagogue. We know very little about this body. We do not know of how many members it consisted originally. In a short time it must have been limited to seventy, in accordance with the number of elders chosen by Moses. We do not know what the qualifications for membership were. We imagine it must have included the heads of the clans. We are certain of a few facts about this body, however, for we have some of its sayings preserved for us in the "Ethics of the Fathers." These are "Be patient in judgment, and raise up many disciples,[1] and make a fence about the Torah." [2] We can see from these few remarks that they were much concerned with the Torah and with its study, and that leads us to conclude that they were chosen for their learning and piety. We know also of many activities which later generations attributed to the Keneset Hagedolah. Among these are the collection of our earliest prayers, the rules of synagogue worship, and the collecting of the books of the Bible. All these show us that the main concern of this body was with matters of study and worship.

The importance of the Keneset Hagedolah to us today is in the fact that ever since that time the Jewish people in Palestine and elsewhere has always entrusted its leadership to the hands of rabbis and scholars. The Jewish people was perhaps the first to select its leaders by merit rather than by birth, and, as such, it is one of the oldest democratic peoples of the world.

---

[1] pupils, followers
[2] Make the laws even more strict than the Torah calls for so that people would surely not violate the law itself. For example, if one may not handle money on the Sabbath he would be unable to trade on that day.

PROVISIONS FOR STUDY AND SPREAD OF THE TORAH

During that time, the foundation must have been laid for universal education. At the center of it was the local synagogue which served as the Bet Hakneset, the house of assembly. As its name shows, it must have been a house for various sorts of meetings. Not only were prayers recited there, but it housed the school and the court. It was used as a hall for festivals, and as the office for the town charities. The head of the synagogue, the public reader, had to be a person of education, not an hereditary official. All other honors of the synagogue, such as the reading from the Torah Scroll, were reserved for those who could read, and tended again to become a reward for knowledge.

The public reading of a portion of the Torah early became an important part of the service. The Torah was read on the Sabbath and on festival days, and was soon also included on all important days of assembly, as well as on Mondays and Thursdays which were the market days when all the farmers came to town.

One of the earliest reforms ascribed to Ezra was the changing of the script of the Torah [1] from the ancient Hebrew alphabet to the Aramaic. The latter was a much simpler one and could be learned more readily. It is interesting to note that while the rabbis were most careful not to change anything in the Bible, even where the reading was most doubtful, Ezra did, nevertheless, allow himself this great change. Ezra stopped at noth-

---

[1] In modern Palestine, Hebrew, written in the Latin alphabet, is used for commercial purposes, such as in telegrams, etc.

ing which might make for the spread of the Torah. We can judge the wisdom of the step from the effect on the neighbors of the Jews, the Samaritans. These

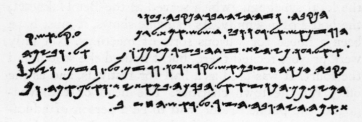

ANCIENT HEBREW WRITING

This writing was found on one of the walls of the Siloam tunnel constructed during the reign of King Hezekiah. It tells of how the tunnel was completed.

denounced the change of the alphabet, and preserved the ancient form to this day. The result was that few, except the priests, ever learned to read their Torah.

What Were the Results of This Spread of Learning?

The spread of learning resulted in a more sincere acceptance of the Torah. The various provisions of the Law for the protection of the poor and the weak were put into practice. Israel became a peace-loving people trusting to the power of the spirit rather than to the sword.

Taxes were high and governors were oppressive. Yet, in spite of all hardships, men studied the older books and wrote many new and beautiful ones. We seldom think of farmers as caring much for literature;

they are too busy working from dawn to sunset. But our early farmer ancestors were of a different sort. Between the days of Ezra and 332 B.C.E., which marks the coming of the Greeks, the following books of the Bible were probably written: Historical books and those of historical fiction, such as Ezra, Nehemiah, Chronicles, Esther, and Ruth; books of prophecy—

Haggai, Zechariah, and Malachi; books of wisdom and philosophy— Job, sections of the Proverbs, and poetry collected and added to the Psalms. The books just mentioned are only those which rabbis in later ages thought fit to include in the Bible as being among the best literature.   It is fair to assume that there were other books written which were not considered fit to be included. An age in which so many great books were written

© U. and U.

THE SAMARITAN CODEX

Containing the Pentateuch and Joshua.   The ancient Hebrew script is still employed.

must have had many readers.

A Comparison with the Samaritans

We might be interested at this point in comparing the Jewish community with that of Samaria. The active

© U. and U.

SHECHEM, BETWEEN GERIZIM AND EBAL

Modern Nablus. Home of surviving Samaritans.

reforms in Judea must have had effect upon the Samaritans, who claimed to follow the Jewish Law also. But the Samaritans appear to have been interested more in the form of the Jewish religion. Sometime after the expelled Judean priests were settled in Shechem, the Samaritans built a temple on Mount Gerizim to rival the Temple at Jerusalem. They could not justify their action from the teachings of the prophets who were always devoted to the thought of Zion. They therefore abandoned the writings of the prophets, and accepted only the Pentateuch [1] with the book of Joshua. The Jews, to stress the difference between themselves

---

[1] the five books of Moses, the Humoshim.

and the Samaritans, included a portion of the prophetic writing to be read every Sabbath and every festival. The Samaritans deprived themselves of this beautiful and inspiring literature. We saw before how they clung to the old script of the Bible which only few could read. They had none of the provisions for study which the Jewish community had. The Samaritans, as a result, are remembered only for the battles they fought. They still exist today, but only in very small numbers. There are but one hundred and twenty families in Nablus, ancient Shechem, and they are as backward as the Palestinian Arabs.[1]

How Other People Influenced the Jews

When the Jewish people adopted the Torah as its constitution, and accepted the principle that one might neither add nor subtract from it, it seemed that the Jewish people would never permit any changes and would never learn from the experiences of other peoples. Yet the history of the Jewish people in every period shows us that they did accept many new teachings from their neighbors and incorporated them into their own beliefs.

When Babylon was conquered by the Persians, the Jews met a people whose religion was in many ways like their own. The Persian religion, like the Jewish, was based on the belief that right conduct pleased God more than costly gifts. There was one important dif-

---

[1] In 1927 great damage was done to the city of Nablus by earthquake. The Jewish settlers and the Zionist organization offered brotherly aid to the Samaritans in their need.

ference, however, between the Jewish and the Persian religions. The Persians believed in two gods: one, Ahura-Mazda, the God of Light, who was forever at war with the other, Ahriman, the God of Darkness and Sin. The pious Persian hoped that in time the God of Light would destroy the God of Darkness, and he therefore joined in battle with the God of Light against the God of Darkness. The good Persian was to live a noble life just as the good Jew was commanded. But the pious Jew would not accept the belief in two gods. The great prophet, the second Isaiah, declares that it is the one God who made light and created darkness, who created the good and evil.

Nevertheless, when the Jews saw the pious Persian going through important ceremonies of purification and bathing before approaching anything holy, they felt that they could do no less toward their own ceremonies. Indeed, they felt that they had to be even more careful than the Persians to touch nothing impure or unclean when approaching their God. As a result we find a great many new laws in which people are commanded to purify themselves upon touching anything unclean or upon approaching holy places. Many of these laws have remained to the present time. You may have noted one or two instances of these as—when a pious Jew washes his hands before saying his prayers, or when persons returning from a funeral wash their hands before entering the house. You may have heard of the Hasidim who take a ceremonial bath before their prayer.

Another thing which the Jews probably learned from

the Persian religion was the belief that there was a heavenly court in which angels had the same positions as ministers of the king have in an earthly court. Such famous names as those of the angels, Gabriel, Michael, Ariel, and Satan, may have had their beginnings at that time. It is suggested also that the idea of a life after death, in which the good are rewarded for their kind deeds, became more prominent in Jewish thought through Persian influence.

SUPPLEMENTARY WORK

MAP EXERCISES

1. On an outline map of Jerusalem show the Temple area and the city walls at the time of Nehemiah.
2. On an outline map of Palestine, locate the neighbors of Judea and the following places:
   Jerusalem, Samaria, Shechem, Hebron, Jaffa, Jordan, Dead Sea, Mediterranean, Mt. Gerizim and Mt. Carmel.

QUESTIONS FOR DISCUSSION AND DEBATE

1. Was Ezra right in demanding that foreign wives be sent away?
2. Were the Jews fair in their dealings with the Samaritans?
3. If the Arabs today were to offer assistance to the Palestinian Jews as the Samaritans did of old, how should their offer be received?
4. Was it necessary for the Babylonian Jews to return to Judea in order to be good Jews?
5. Do the Jews of America hold the same relation to the Jews of the rest of the world as the Babylonian Jews held to those of Judea?
6. Do children and parents suffer for each other's sins?

ADDITIONAL PROJECTS

1. Imagine that you are one of the Babylonians who has returned to Judea with the first group. After ten years you are writing to your relatives in Babylon of what is happening in Judea. Compose the letter.

2. The Samaritan offer to help in the rebuilding of the Temple has just been received. Dramatize a council meeting at which this matter will be fully discussed.
3. At the request of Zerubbabel submit a sketch for the new Temple that is being planned. Use the description found at the end of Ezekiel, as well as the account of Solomon's Temple, and any pictures of the Temple which you can find.
4. Make models of the Temple furniture.
5. Select those laws from Leviticus and Deuteronomy which you would advise Ezra to include in the Jewish constitution.

ADDITIONAL READINGS

FOR TEACHERS

Smith, H. P., *Old Testament History,* chaps. xv–xvii.
Margolis and Marx, *History of the Jewish People,* pp. 109–125.
Graetz, H., *History of the Jews,* I, 329–411.
Josephus, *The Antiquities of the Jews,* Bk. X, chap. ix, Bk. XI, chaps. i–v, vii–viii.
Bevan, E., *Jerusalem Under the High-Priests,* pp. 1–16.
Radin, M., *Jews Among the Greeks and Romans,* chap. 5.
Bailey and Kent, *History of Hebrew Commonwealth,* chaps. xxiii–xxvi.

FOR PUPILS

Harris, M., *People of the Book,* III, 209–270.
Harris, M., *Thousand Years of Jewish History,* pp. 17–24.
Dubnow, S. M., *Outlines of Jewish History,* I, chaps. xiii–xiv.
Magnus, Lady Kate, *Outlines of Jewish History,* pp. 1–12.

SECTION II

"WHOSOEVER IS ZEALOUS OF THE LAW"

After Doré

WHY WE CELEBRATE CHANUKAH

1

THE MACCABEAN WARS

THE first part of the story followed our ancestors back into Palestine. We saw with what struggle and at what great cost they reëstablished themselves in their old home.

We look back upon that period, 2500 years ago, and we ask ourselves: What has remained to us of all the hardships of those early pioneer days? What have our forefathers passed down to us, their descendants, by which we can remember them? Have their deeds, the accidents of their life, their wars, their beliefs, their great men, made any difference to us? Or is their history merely an interesting story to read, like the stories of ancient Rome, Greece, or Babylon?

If we examine our own lives we find ourselves the leaves of a large tree whose roots go deeply into the past. Many facts of our life began to happen two thousand years ago during second Temple days. Why do we live in America, though our ancestors lived in Palestine? Why are we Jews and why are people about us Christians? Which of our ancestors' customs do we still observe? Which of their holidays do we still celebrate? Which of their books do we still read?

Many of these questions will be answered in the

course of our book. This section will select one question: Why do we celebrate the holiday of Chanukah? It seems to be an important festival because it lasts eight days. While some of our other holidays are being forgotten, Chanukah is becoming better known and more celebrated. Every Jewish school has a Chanukah entertainment. There is not a boy or girl in any Jewish school who does not know something about Hannah and her seven sons; about Mattathias, Judas Maccabeus, and the kindling of the menorah.

Here is a brief Chanukah prayer which contains an answer to the question, Why we celebrate Chanukah. It is taken from the "Standard Prayer Book" page 51 f. Read it through carefully.

Al-Hanisim

"We thank Thee also for the miracles, for the redemption, for the mighty deeds, and saving acts, wrought by Thee, as well as for the wars which Thou didst wage for our fathers in days of old, at this season.

"In the days of the Hasmonean, Mattathias son of Johanan the High Priest, and his five sons, when the iniquitous [1] power of Greece rose up against Thy people Israel to make them forgetful of Thy Law, and to force them to transgress [2] the statutes of Thy will, then didst Thou in Thine abundant mercy rise up for them in the time of their trouble. Thou didst plead their cause, Thou didst judge their suit, Thou didst avenge

---

[1] wicked, bad
[2] disobey

their wrong; Thou deliveredst the strong into the hands of the weak, the many into the hands of the few, the impure into the hands of the pure, the wicked into the hands of the righteous, and the arrogant [1] into the hands of them that occupied themselves with Thy Law. For Thyself Thou didst make a great and holy name in Thy world, and for Thy people Israel Thou didst work a great deliverance and redemption, as at this day. And thereupon Thy children came into the oracle of Thy house, cleansed Thy temple, purified Thy sanctuary, kindled lights in Thy holy courts, and appointed these eight days of Chanukah in order to give thanks and praises unto Thy great name."

This is the entire story, but it is told too briefly. It is a good summary, but there is much that needs filling in. How did the Greeks have occasion to interfere with the religion of Palestine? Why did they wish to prevent the Jews from the practice of their religion? What sort of war was waged and who waged it? Let us take up some of these questions, one after another. Our first question will be:

How Did the Greeks Interfere with the Life of the Jewish People?

The conquest of Palestine by Alexander the Great made the Greeks masters over the Jews. When we last told of our ancestors, they were under the rule of Persia. Alexander entered Jerusalem in the year 332 B.C.E., and the Chanukah events took place in 165

---

[1] haughty

B.C.E. We may wonder why we should go back more than one hundred and fifty years to seek for reasons. Yet as we study history, we realize that wars and other disturbances are often the result of anger and hate which have developed over long periods. The generations before us are responsible for many of our difficulties, and we may be sowing the seeds

ALEXANDER THE GREAT

of wars which our great-grandchildren will fight.[1]

When Alexander took possession of Palestine, the Jews believed that they had changed masters for the better. Alexander spared the land, and legend tells that he brought offerings in the Temple. He was very kind to the Jews, and excused them from taxes during the Sabbatical year when there was no planting of

[1] For example, one of the causes of the World War was the war of 1870 between France and Germany, when Germany took away two French provinces. Mistreatment of Orientals may some day be a source of trouble to the United States. What are some of the present sources of conflict in America or Europe which may bring difficulties in the future?

crops. When Alexandria was built (in honor of Alexander), Jews were recognized as citizens equal with the Greeks. Jews who enlisted in Alexander's armies were permitted to practice their religion.[1]

Wars after Alexander's Death. Partition of Empire

But Alexander died within a few years, and then the troubles began. Alexander left no son to inherit his throne, but he left many ambitious generals, each one of whom wished to succeed him. These generals turned their armies upon one another, and long, bloody wars followed.

Look at the next map, and observe the position of Palestine. Alexander's empire was distributed in three continents; in Europe, Asia, and Africa. Syria, the district in which Palestine lay, was in the very center of the Empire.

For over twenty years Palestine was a battle-ground for rival generals. The Jews faced all the horrors of a war in which they had no interest. In addition, they were suspected by each of the sides of favoring the other.[2] After twenty years of warfare, Jerusalem finally fell into the hands of Ptolemy I, ruler of Egypt. Ptolemy surprised the city on the Sabbath when the

---

[1] So greatly did the Jews respect Alexander, that many boys were named after him.

[2] We are strongly reminded of the position of the Jews of Eastern Europe during the World War. The Jews lived on the Russian border between Germany and Austria, where the greatest part of the fighting took place. The Germans treated the Jews as enemy subjects, while the Russians suspected them of favoring Germany because the language of the Jews, Yiddish, resembled the German.

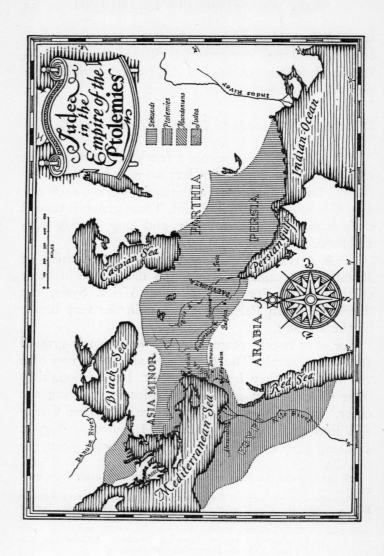

Jews would not fight. He massacred many of the inhabitants and carried thousands with him to Egypt to
be sold as slaves.

The results of the long period of war were that
many families were broken up through death or
through exile. Conditions were very unsettled. The
highways were unsafe, life and property were most
insecure, and the land became greatly impoverished.

Nor did the end of the wars bring peace to the land.
An agreement had been reached between the generals.
The large empire was divided into three parts. One
part embraced the European lands, and will not appear
in our story. The other two parts were divided into the
kingdom of Egypt and the kingdom of the East, which
included Syria and the surrounding lands. Look at
your map once more and decide to which of the
kingdoms Palestine should belong. If you find it
difficult to decide, so did the quarreling kings. The
land was ceded to King Ptolemy I of Egypt. Since
kings did not live in friendship with one another, it
was a sorry omen for Palestine that it was again on the
boundary. It might expect new wars soon.

The Greeks Settle About and Among the Jews

During this entire period a great change was taking
place in the life of Palestine and Syria. Palestine had
been under foreign rule before. Persia had demanded
the payment of taxes, but otherwise it left the land
undisturbed.

Until the coming of the Greeks, the population of

Palestine and Syria had been a uniform one. All the peoples spoke a common language, they looked alike, they dressed alike, and had like homes and like cities. Aside from differences in religion, the nations of Palestine differed from one another only as do American citizens of different states.

The Greeks did not conquer a country merely for its tribute; they meant to settle in it. Greece was not fertile enough to support a large population through agriculture, but it had excellent harbors. The Greeks became a manufacturing and seafaring nation, and earned their livelihood by selling their merchandise in distant lands. Many of their merchants settled permanently in the foreign cities with which they traded, and Greek colonies were therefore to be found in all the Mediterranean lands.

Even before the days of Alexander, Greek merchants had settled in the seacoast cities of Phoenicia and Philistia. With Alexander came a host of new settlers. It was Alexander's custom, later followed by the Romans also, that after a war, large parts of the best lands conquered were distributed among the soldiers. The Greeks were as fond of building new cities as of settling in existing ones.

In a very short time Syria became populated with Greeks. Look at this map and see all the square spots which represent Hellenistic (Grecianized) cities. The old Phoenician, Philistine and Moabite cities were forgetting their language and their religion. The very names of the cities were changed. The old gods were given Greek names. New types of public build-

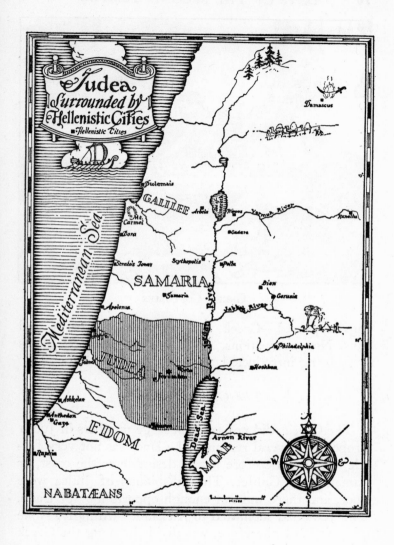

GREEK COSTUMES   © U. and U.

ings appeared—Greek theatres, temples, baths and inns. New occupations, new costumes and new games were being introduced.

The Greeks in Judea

The Greeks did not settle in large numbers in Judea proper for several reasons. The land was not very fertile and was therefore not as desirable as the coast, or Samaria and Galilee. The inhabitants of Judea were poor, and there was not enough opportunity for trade. The Jews had submitted to Alexander willingly. None of their land, therefore, was divided among the Greek veterans as that of Samaria had been. Nor did the Greeks find the Jews as friendly as the surrounding peoples. The Jews looked upon the Greeks as idol worshippers. Judeans could not eat Greek foods or intermarry with Greek families. Jews and Greeks did not therefore meet at friendly gatherings. The Jews were not anxious to learn the language of Greeks. They were proud of their own language and of their great books. In general, the Jews had a suspicion of merchants, as the farmer to this day distrusts the merchant.

But even Judea was not entirely free of Greek influence. Some Greek merchants settled in Judea, and others visited the land from time to time. The merchants introduced many new wares which were known only by their Greek names. Those who traded with the Greek merchants learned a little of their language. In addition, the official language of the government was now Greek.

SUMMARY

We set out to answer how the Greeks interfered in the life of the Jews. Thus far we have seen how Palestine became a part of the Empire of Alexander, and after his death fell to the share of one of his generals; how it suffered through many years of war and finally it remained on the boundary in a state of uncertainty. During this entire time the Greeks were settling in and about Palestine. They were introducing new beliefs and practices into the land. The Greeks were beginning to trade with Judea, and the Jews were becoming more

intimate with them. Let us see how the Greeks interfered further in the life of the Jews.

The Rise of New Sects
HASIDIM (THE PIOUS)—ANTI-GREEK

The Jews had been poor and unhappy under the
kings of Persia. Twenty years of war might hardly
be expected to improve their lot. When a nation suffers, and it sees no hope for better times, new religious
sects usually spring up. People believe that their suffering is the result of their wickedness. They decide
to give up all pleasures and to lead a hard and suffering life in order to obtain forgiveness from God.

During this unsettled period, many persons showed
their desire for a religion of self denial by taking the
oath of the Nazarite. The Nazarites may be compared
with the Christian monks and nuns in later days. Persons who took such an oath swore to give up the drinking of wine and the trimming of their hair. They
fasted frequently and prayed with fervor.

Another evidence of this spirit of severity was
the formation of a new sect called the Hasidim, or the
pious ones. What the differences were between the
Hasidim and the other Jews is not certain. The Hasidim
probably were distinguished by the very strict observance of the Sabbath, even to the point of refusing to
defend themselves from death. They were also known
to observe the dietary laws very rigorously. They
prayed with great devotion. Many of our psalms must
have been written and sung by them, for these psalms

refer to the Hasidim. They believed that theirs was the only true way of life. They despised the Greeks for worshipping idols, and looked with suspicion upon any Jew who followed the Greeks in their habits or who had too frequent dealings with them.

HELLENISTS—PRO-GREEKS

On the small group of wealthy Jews the coming of the Greeks had an opposite effect. They, too, had probably suffered in the war, but they had sufficient wealth left to begin anew. They learned the Greek language, and noted with interest the new ways and manners introduced by the Greeks.

© *U. and U.*
GREEK WRESTLERS

The Greeks possessed many beautiful and comfortable things to make persons happy. They spent their free hours playing games, wrestling, racing on foot or on horse, and throwing the discus. Their very religion was celebrated through athletic games and theatrical performances. The Greeks loved to enjoy life.

A life of pleasure appealed strongly to the young wealthy Jews. The rich young men compared their humble buildings with the Greek temples, their crude wares with the finished Greek products. The Greeks appeared much more refined. Their fellow Jews were simple farmers. The Greeks were the wise men of the world who had travelled far and who had seen much. Surely the Greek knew better how life was to be lived. The young Jew might best learn from him. The young, rich Jews despised the Nazarites who deprived themselves of the good things of life—wines and banquets, singers and dancers. The younger generation of Jews was beginning to dream of becoming Hellenized. The youth of Jerusalem readily took to the new styles. They began to speak Greek, to call themselves by Greek names, and to practice Greek games. The farmers in the villages were too poor or too ignorant to care. The organized Hasidim looked upon them with contempt as sinners.

A MIDDLE PARTY

There were some Jews who would have liked to draw into their religion and into Jewish life what wisdom the Greeks had to offer. They saw before them a highly civilized people who knew much of science, and had produced great philosophers, painters, sculptors, poets and dramatists. The Greeks had many valuable books which the Jews might read and many fine arts to imitate.

Had the land been prosperous and at peace, the two peoples might have lived quietly side by side and learned much from each other. We shall see in a later section how the Jews and Greeks did learn much from one another at Alexandria. In Palestine, unfortunately, the long wars and sufferings had driven people to extremes. The Hasidim had suffered too much at the hands of the Greeks to accept any of their ways.

Why the Hasidim Refused to Be Hellenized

The Jewish Hellenists saw only the hardship and the poverty of their national life. They were mindful only of the demands which their religion made upon them, of all the laws which they had to obey and which made them different from other nations. They were anxious to be like the other peoples about them. The pious Jew, on the other hand, preferred his religion of poverty and privation. He thought it finer to spend his free hours at prayer or at study than at revels or at games. The poor Jew had no time for play. He could hardly earn his livelihood working every hour of the day. And how· absurd must have appeared to them, the idea of honoring the gods with games.

There was still a deeper reason for the Jewish dislike of Greek ways. The Jew thought of the Greek as cruel and selfish. The Greeks considered their games as the most important ends in life. The purpose of the games was to give honor to the strong and the skillful. The Greeks honored the victor. The Jewish religion aimed rather at bringing comfort to the weak and the needy and in aiding the one who was defeated. The Greeks were interested in their own personal happiness. The Greeks showed little love for their fatherland. Their cities had been at constant war with each other. The Jewish religion was always directed at the happiness of the whole community. The Greek religion honored strength and wealth. The Jewish religion honored kindliness and charity.

The Greeks, therefore, in spite of all their wealth and wisdom appeared to the pious Jews as something glittering which was not real gold. In Greece there might be philosophers and scientists, men of wisdom, but the Greeks in Syria were only coarse soldiers and vain pleasure seekers.

Let us not imagine either that our ancestors of that time were all a sad and severe people. Many Jews, faithful to their religion, looked with disfavor upon the Nazarites who denied themselves God-given pleasures. Such Jews believed that "wine delighteth the heart of men." They loved music and dance, and enjoyed their banquets and public celebrations. They traded freely with the Greeks, and may have admired many of their ways. But they had neither the zeal of the Hasidim nor the slavishness of the Hellenists.

Judea too Becomes Hellenized

The wealthy Jewish families who wished to be exclusive and different from their fellow Jews were rapidly becoming Hellenized. They sought to provide instructors to teach their children all the arts of Greece, Greek manners, athletics, and Greek music. These Jews were men of affairs, and they were determined to be in style.

The whole world, it seemed, had turned Greek. The king and governors were Greek. Why should they alone remain members of a little obscure tribe which insisted on being separate?

The older generation among the men of wealth was familiar at least with the Jewish religion and its famous books. They knew that their people had much to be proud of, that they had possessed great prophets who predicted a glorious future for them. They believed in their prophets, though they would also have liked to be Greeks. But their children grew up knowing little of the greatness of the Jewish people. They were more Greek than Jewish. Jewishness was only interfering with their pleasures. Jews might not eat the flesh of swine. They were forbidden to do what they liked on the Sabbath. They were not even permitted to ride or play games on the seventh day. The old-fashioned high priest refused to build a gymnasium in Jerusalem. The young men were certain that if only they had one, they would be champion wrestlers and boxers.

Another Result of Greek Interference—Emigration

The unsettled conditions which came upon Palestine led many Jews to seek a new life in foreign lands. East and west, throughout Mesopotamia, and along the coast cities of Asia and Egypt, new Jewish colonies were forming. Some followed the Greek trade, others went as captives, later succeeding in purchasing their freedom. Emigration was continuing on so large a scale that the rabbis sought measures to check it. A Jew away from Palestine was declared to be under religious disabilities. The lands of the gentiles were declared unclean by the rabbis. These ordinances did not stop emigration, as we shall see later.

SUMMARY

We were seeking to answer the question—How did the Greeks interfere in Jewish Life? We have now an additional answer to those previously given. It was in the example of their lives that the Greeks interfered most seriously. Their presence in Palestine showed the people a new way to live. As a result, the nation became divided into factions which were drawing further apart from one another. The rule of the Greeks also brought about an emigration of the Jews from Judea to other Greek settlements.

WHY WAS THE FESTIVAL OF CHANUKAH INSTITUTED?

We return again to our main question, why the festival of Chanukah was instituted. We saw that it was in some way bound with Greek interference in Jewish life, and we considered how the Greeks interfered in the life of our ancestors.

The Chanukah war did not result from the oppression of the Greek rulers. Let it be said, in fairness to the later Greek governors, that they were not unkind to the Jews. After peace was finally established, Palestine continued undisturbed as a province of Egypt for a century. The disturbances which led to the Chanukah war, you may be surprised to learn, were perhaps due

more to civil strife than to a foreign king. We shall
see how the ill feeling between the Hasidim and the
Hellenists finally brought about a bloody struggle.

How the Hellenists' Power Grew

As long as there were few rich people in Judea, they
caused the nation little concern. Not all of them desired to become Hellenized, nor did they occupy any
position of public prominence. Soon something happened which brought
some of the Hellenists
into power. Joseph, the
son of Tobias, related to
the family of the high
priest, was chosen the
royal tax-collector for
Syria which, as we saw,
included Judea. At that
time taxes were not paid
directly to the govern-
ment office, nor did each

EGYPTIAN TAX-COLLECTORS
The use of the rod was evidently
not spared.

person pay in proportion to his wealth, as we do today.
The tax-farmer paid the king a large sum of money,
for which he received the right to collect as much as he
could. Whatever he exorted above the amount due to
the king, he kept for himself. The king's soldiers were
placed at his command to enforce payment.

Joseph thus became an important officer of the
Royal Egyptian Court. In his office he proved to be
as cruel as all other tax-farmers, and possibly more so

because he had offered to pay the king a larger amount than had been previously paid for that district. Joseph naturally needed many assistants, and he drew these from his own tribesmen and householders. Each assistant tax-farmer had to provide Joseph with a definite amount and kept what remained for himself. Thus, all tax-farmers became wealthy. Since Joseph was the cause of the prosperity of so many Judeans, he became a very important person in Jerusalem. His power as tax-collector, too, made him generally feared, and he was given honors equal to or greater than those which were bestowed upon the high priest.

Joseph and his followers, suddenly grown very wealthy and powerful, dared publicly to violate some of the Hasidic restrictions. Joseph had frequent business at the court of Egypt. In the company of the king and his courtiers, he ate forbidden foods and spent many hours at drinking feasts with singing-women. Joseph's sons, too, considered themselves Greek officers, and tried to live accordingly.

As the party of Joseph increased in numbers and in strength, it grew more bold in its disrespect for the law. It soon began to look with envy upon the office of the high priest, which was like that of the king in other lands.

The members of this party felt themselves much superior to their poorer and simpler fellow citizens. The Jewish Hellenists, however, did not as yet dare to tamper with the high priesthood, either because of reverence or perhaps because they feared that they were not yet strong enough.

Palestine Gets New Masters and Hellenists Rise to Power

A new war had broken out between Egypt and Syria. At the same time there was civil strife within Egypt, due to the fact that the king of Egypt had died and the throne had fallen to a boy of ten. The leading generals were more interested in seizing the internal government than in attending to their foreign war. The misrule within Egypt spread to its dependencies, among which was Palestine. The Jews became impatient with Egypt, and the leaders of Jerusalem, including the sons of Joseph, favored surrendering to the Seleucid ruler of Syria. After the death of Joseph, his sons and their followers turned anti-Egyptian because the office of tax-collector was awarded to the son of Joseph's second wife.

The disorder in Egypt made it easy to invite the Eastern King, Antiochus III, into Jerusalem. Antiochus had defeated a large Egyptian army, and there was no danger of a new Egyptian attack. Still, Antiochus was grateful to the Jews for surrendering Jerusalem without a struggle, and, in recognition bestowed many privileges upon them and upon the Temple.[1]

Judea celebrated its new freedom from Egypt in 198 B.C.E., after somewhat more than one hundred years of Egyptian domination. But the Jews were soon to learn that little was gained in the change of over-

---

[1] Someone might read an account of the decree of Antiochus as given in Josephus, "Antiquities of the Jews" Book XII Chapter v §4, and tell it to the children.

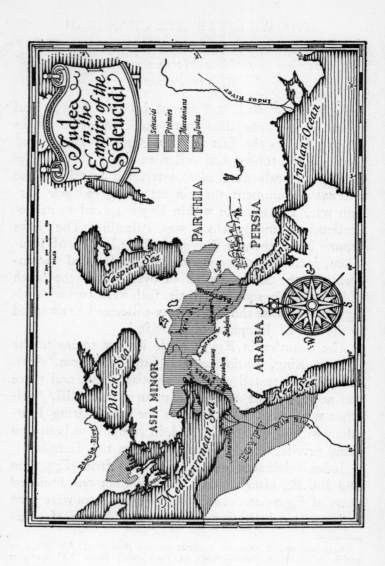

Judea in the Empire of the Seleucidi

lords. As long as monarchs ruled absolutely, the Jews were always at the mercy of possible tyrants. The best kings were too often followed by worthless sons.

The change in foreign rule did not bring peace to Judea. On the contrary, it helped to strengthen the internal division. The party of the Hellenists in Jerusalem was growing stronger. There was strife within the very family of the high priest. No one suspected how serious matters were until the first break occurred.

ANTIOCHUS IV

Antiochus III, called the Great, died, and after a brief reign of eight years by one of his sons, he was

ANTIOCHUS III
From a coin.

ANTIOCHUS IV
From a coin.

followed by his second son, Antiochus IV. This monarch had been brought up at Rome where he was kept a hostage. Hostages were princes of subject nations, or children of noble families, demanded by Rome as security that their nation would remain obedient to Rome. Rome was conquering nations far and wide, and was already the strongest nation of the world.

Antiochus may have dreamed his own dreams of military glory, he may have hoped to establish a great Eastern Empire, for his father had left him a large army and many conquests.

Toward the close of his reign, Antiochus was becoming pressed for money. Armies of great conquerors did not enlist for patriotism's sake. They were usually hired from foreign lands, and were made up of men who had no other occupation than fighting. Even in modern times we have illustrations of such men as the Hessians who were sent to suppress the American Revolution; or more recently the Americans who enlisted in the armies of France or Spain to fight African natives. The soldiers of Antiochus demanded high pay, and were prepared to desert to the opposite side if they could hope for a better offer. If they were victorious, they were permitted to loot the enemy cities. After unsuccessful wars, the soldiers had to be paid out of the king's treasury. Kings were thus often sorely pressed to secure money for their armies.

THE BARTER OF THE HIGH PRIESTHOOD—JASON

Antiochus IV was known for his need and greed, and the Hellenist party decided to use him to their own advantage. The Hellenists had grown so powerful that they were now bent on capturing the office of the high priest. A brother of the ruling high priest Onias, was the head of the Hellenist party. His Jewish name had been Joshua, but he preferred to call himself by the Greek name Jason. Jason sent a secret

embassy to King Antiochus in which he accused his
brother of favoring Egypt. Jason also offered the king
a large sum of money to have himself made high
priest in place of his brother Onias. Unexpectedly,
Onias was commanded to proceed to Antioch to answer charges of treachery, and Jason was appointed
high priest in his place.

This was the first of the revolutions which were to
take place in Judea. The rightful head of the Temple

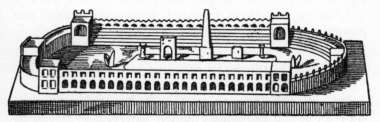

MODEL OF A GREEK STADIUM

was overthrown by a heathen government. The Hellenists who had begun by imitating Greek customs,
finally turned complete traitors to their religion.

The people of Judea murmured, but they were
powerless. They prayed that a visitation of God might
come upon the guilty—instead, new and worse troubles fell to their own lot.

The Hellenists who now controlled Jerusalem
planned to turn it into a Greek city. A gymnasium
was built near the Temple, and many young priests
preferred gymnastics to priestly duties. The Greek
costumes—particularly, Greek hats became fashionable

in the streets of Jerusalem. Pious Jews saw young men exercising naked. The new high priest begged the privilege of the king that he and his party might be called Antiochians instead of Jews. The high priest even sent money as a gift toward the games of Hercules, which were to be held at Tyre. The Jewish high priest was thus publicly contributing toward idol worship, because the games were a form of Greek religion. The Jewish nation was so offended by this last act that the messengers did not dare carry out the instruction of Jason. Instead they asked that the money be used for the royal navy.

MENELAUS OUTBIDS JASON

Jason did not long enjoy the fruits of his treason. As soon as the Hellenists gained power, they began to quarrel among themselves. Jason had shown how easy was the road to power; the one who paid the highest price might become the ruler of the Jews. Barely four years after Jason had seized the high priesthood, Menelaus, another Hellenist leader, made an attempt for the post. Menelaus represented the more extreme Hellenists, those who cared for their nation's ideals even less than the party of Jason. Menelaus offered the king a much larger sum than Jason was paying. Antiochus needed money, and since it mattered little to him who headed the Jews, Menelaus was appointed to replace Jason.

If the nation was angered by the appointment of Jason, it was now outraged by the choice of Menelaus.

Menelaus did not belong to a priestly family at all. According to the Jewish law, a non-priest might not even enter the Temple. But Menelaus had no thought for the holiness of the Temple; he had little concern for the Jewish religion altogether. He was merely interested in ruling the Jews as kings elsewhere ruled other countries. When the time came to pay the large sums which he had promised, Menelaus was driven to an act which Jews and Greeks alike considered a grave crime. He robbed the sacred Temple treasury. Fearing a popular uprising, Menelaus proceeded to a more heinous crime. He was afraid that the nation would restore to the high priesthood the aged Onias who was hiding for safety at a Greek temple from which, in accordance with heathen as well as with Jewish

THE HIGH PRIEST IN HIS ROBES

THE BREAST PLATE OF THE TWELVE STONES

custom, a man might not be taken for punishment. But

Menelaus hired assassins who lured Onias from his place of safety and treacherously murdered him. Even the Greeks were so aroused that they put the murderers of Onias to death. Menelaus, however, escaped unpunished. Two embassies went to Antiochus. One consisted of citizens of Jerusalem bearing complaints against their criminal high priest; the other represented the high priest, bearing costly gifts of Temple gold to the King. Antiochus accepted the gold and pardoned Menelaus. The members of the other embassy were put to death.

Civil War Begins and Hellenists Abandon Judaism

The patience of the Jews was now at an end. Everyone felt that a storm would soon break over the land. A rumor that Antiochus had been killed in a war with Egypt served as a signal for revolt. Jason suddenly returned from his hiding and ordered a massacre of the extreme Hellenists of the party of Menelaus. Thus civil war began.

Antiochus had not been killed. His army was not defeated, but its advance had been thwarted by Rome. Antiochus was within an easy victory over Egypt when the Romans ordered him to stop the war. While he was in this mood, word was brought him of the happenings in Jerusalem. Antiochus determined to vent his anger upon the Jews for rebelling against his appointed ruler and for rejoicing over the thought of his death. The angered king unexpectedly fell upon Jerusalem and ordered a massacre of the inhabitants. Thousands were thus killed in the city, and as many as could, among them the high priest, Jason, fled to the mountains. Antiochus entered the treasure rooms of the Temple and carried away much gold and silver.

Menelaus must have advised the king that it was their religion which made the Jews contrary. Let the king order the Jewish religion abolished, and the troubles would end; the Jewish Temple should be turned into a Temple of Zeus; the king must forbid the observance of the Sabbath and of the dietary laws. The Jews would then be subdued quickly. If they worshipped like all other nations, they would be obedient as the others. At the advice of the Jewish high priest, the Temple of God was turned into a heathen shrine, and the practice of the Jewish religion was forbidden throughout the land. The Hellenists

© Bloch's Bible Pictures

THE INTERIOR OF THE TEMPLE
Artist's Conception.

now broke away from Judaism completely. They became heathen in the midst of the great body of heathens within the Greek Empires. And thus ended another chapter in the story of the struggle of the returned exiles and of Ezra and Nehemiah. The Temple of God for which the early exiles sacrificed life and fortune, was turned by their own descendants into a house of idols.

SUMMARY

We are now almost ready for the reason of the observance of Chanukah. A group of Jews, the Hellenists, representing largely the wealthy classes, felt that their old religion did not suit them any longer. They were men who were anxious to be like their rulers, and who feared to be different from other peoples. They were ready to sacrifice their nation to their desires. They gave up their God and all the achievements of their famous ancestors for the privilege of a Greek wrestling match and a Greek hat.

Does not the struggle between the Hellenists and the Hasidim still persist in a fashion today? Have you not met Jews whose greatest desire is to be like the non-Jew, and to escape from his people? We have Jews who change their Jewish sounding names, who imitate non-Jews even in the religious customs, with Christmas baskets and Easter parties. These are our Hellenists who ask what the Hebrew language is good for, or what concern we have with our brothers in other lands; these are Jews who ask to be called Hebrews or Israelites, or by any other name but Jews.

Why are these Jews so anxious to hide their origin? Their reason is the same as that of the Hellenists of our story: because we Jews are so few, and the others are so many. Some persons can be only what everyone else is. They must speak as everyone else speaks, and believe as everyone else believes. The brave man dares to be different. Our people stood out alone in the world for over a thousand years. They did not yield to the Greeks. Instead, the Greek world finally accepted a form of the religion of the Jews, as we shall see later in our story.

Judaism has accepted the many truths discovered by other peoples. Jews the world over make use of all that has been discovered by science. We enjoy the music, the pictures, and sculpture of the entire world. We play the games of all the nations. But, withal, the true Jew knows that his people have done their share in the world and may freely take of what others have to offer. The wise Jew knows also that it is much better for the world to live in friendly partnership, each people living according to its own ideals, rather than that all should accept the ideals or the habits of any one group.

How Did the Jews Defend Their Religion?

Let us return again to our story. The Hellenist high priest and his party had forbidden the practice of the Jewish religion, upon the pain of death. Jews might no longer observe their Sabbath, the dietary laws, nor worship their God at His Temple.

The Jews refused to obey Antiochus and his hireling high priest. They chose to die for their faith rather than to surrender, and that was something new in the history of the world. Men had died for money, for home and family, or for glory. Men had not yet died for the right of keeping their faith. The world did not yet know that terrible bravery which men display when fighting for religion. The Jewish people itself did not know how mighty it could be until it was robbed of its freedom to worship God.

Menelaus and his party were in control of what Jews there remained at Jerusalem. All citizens who succeeded in escaping death at Jerusalem fled to the villages. The soldiers of the king, under orders from Menelaus, hunted out all the Hasidim and put to death those who were found observing any of the commandments. Many stories are told of the numberless martyrs who died during these persecutions. There is the story of several thousand families, trapped in an underground cavern while at prayer on the Sabbath day. The imprisoned Jews refused to defend themselves on the Sabbath, and were put to death mercilessly. You probably know the legend of the mother, Hannah, and her seven sons, and of the aged Eliezer who preferred to die rather than to mislead his brother Jews.

The Hellenists' crusade against their former religion met with no opposition. The Hasidim were mighty with their pen but quite unready with the sword. For how could their feeble numbers avail against the Syrian king? The only weapons left to them were to die the death of martyrs and to encourage their weaker brothers to follow their examples.

The Book of Daniel

The most famous appeal to the Jews to stand steadfast during the years of terror was the book of Daniel. The book tells the story of a pious Judean named Daniel, who was taken captive by King Nebuchadnezzar. Nebuchadnezzar, according to the story, had issued an order that no person in his kingdom might worship any God save an image of himself. Daniel, who refused to obey the king, was arrested in the very act of praying to his own God. When brought before the king, Daniel denied nothing. The king, in anger, ordered him thrown into a den of lions. Daniel's faithfulness, however, won him the protection of God. The lions refused to do Daniel any harm, and the king was obliged to set him free.

Another legend, too, is told about three companions of Daniel, who in like manner were saved from the fiery furnace.[1] The book then continues to tell how one wicked kingdom after another had tried to destroy the Jews, but had itself disappeared. In the end, the world empires would all crumble, and the son of man, God's chosen ruler, would reign over the entire world. The Book of Daniel thus inspired the Hasidim to be true to their faith.

---

[1] The stories of Daniel and the three youths are very interesting and you should read them in the Book of Daniel.

How Armed Rebellion Began

Companies of soldiers proceeded from village to village setting up altars and demanding that swine be offered as a sacrifice to the Greek god Zeus. One of these parties came to the village of Modin in the mountains of Judea. At that village there lived a family of priests, an aged father and his five sons.[1]

All the inhabitants of Modin were assembled in the market place where the king's herald ordered some leading citizen to offer the sacrifice to Zeus. Mattathias boldly stepped forth and announced that regardless of what other villages might do, the village of Modin would remain steadfast to the God of Israel. The assemblage hesitated between the threat of the soldiers and the fear of Mattathias. Finally, one bold Hellenist went up to the altar and was preparing to sacrifice. The aged Mattathias who was past his eightieth year, rushed up against the offender, and struck him down. "Mi ladonoy elai, whoever is ready to battle for the Lord, follow me!" cried Mattathias. The men of Modin responded readily, and fell upon the detachment of soldiers. The village of Modin began the rebellion in the year 167 B.C.E.

Mattathias and his followers withdrew to a hiding place in the mountains, where other loyal Judeans joined them. The band increased and was able to issue forth at night to attack small parties of Syrian soldiers.

---

[1] We might well remember the names of these sons, because everyone of them becomes distinguished in the service of their people. They were in the order of their age: John, Simon, Judas, Eliezer, and Jonathan.

For several months, Mattathias waged a guerrilla warfare against the Syrians; then his old age could no
longer bear the strain of war. Before his death, Mattathias called his five sons to his bedside, and advised
them as to the future. He counselled them to choose
Judas, called the Maccabee, as their military leader,
although he was third in age. Simon was to act as their
councillor, while the other brothers, John, Eliezer,
and Jonathan, were to follow as soldiers in the ranks.

The Revolt Breaks Out into the Open

A new spirit was felt immediately upon the taking
over of command by Judas. His bravery must have
been well known, for his brothers did not question his
leadership. The very first few months found hundreds of Hasidim flocking to his camp. Judas' little
army now counted several thousands. He was able to
make bolder sallies, appearing in the villages and chas-
tising the faithless Hellenites who, consequently, were
now in terror. They sent urgent pleas to King Antiochus, telling him that an armed insurrection had
broken out in Judea.

A rebellion in Judea gave slight concern to King
Antiochus, as you can readily see by comparing the
size of Judea with the Empire of Antiochus. Imagine
Cuba making war against the United States. Moreover, only a small portion of the Judeans were
involved in the rebellion. The population of Judea at
the time must have numbered close to two million.
We shall soon notice what large armies the Jews were

able to muster within twenty-five years of the first uprising. Judas Maccabeus led only the Hasidim. The Hellenists were ranged against him, like the Tories during the American Revolution. The large mass of peasants were satisfied to be left alone. In their hearts they wished Judas success, but his adventure appeared too foolhardy for them to risk their necks. Antiochus believed that the local forces could well handle the situation.

TWO SYRIAN ARMIES DEFEATED

Appolonius, the governor of the district, who had collected a large army to subdue the rebels, was preparing to drive Judas out of his hiding in the mountains, but before he was quite ready, Judas suddenly fell upon him and routed him. Appolonius himself was slain, and his sword was worn by Judas during the rest of the war. Large quantities of stores and supplies fell into the Jews' hands, so that for the first time Judas' soldiers were properly equipped. This enabled them to fall upon another Syrian army at Beth-horon, near Jerusalem, where the Syrians were again routed.

The rebellion proved to be much more serious than either Jews or Syrians had believed. The two victories inspired such courage in the downhearted people that new recruits were coming into Judas' camp from every corner of the land. Reports began to spread about Judas' great valor, his superhuman strength, and his piety. The Hasidim saw in him the messenger of God, for Judas' army was indeed a pious army. It went into

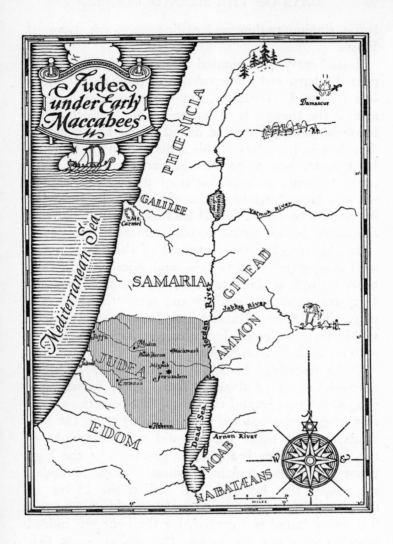

battle singing psalms and calling upon the Lord of Hosts.

Judas' army now counted almost 6,000 men. It appeared a large army compared with the handful which had followed Mattathias, but it was only a handful against the thousands of Syrians. King Antiochus was becoming uneasy over the defeat of his two generals. The loss in the glory to his arms and in the gold to his treasury was more than he cared to incur. Antiochus not only ordered his chief marshal, Lysias, to secure a large force to subdue the rebellious Jews, but in order to be repaid for all his losses, he ordered that the entire Jewish nation be sold into slavery.

Lysias entrusted the command of the army to two well known generals, Gorgias and Nicanor. He gave them enough soldiers to leave no doubt of victory: forty thousand foot soldiers and seven thousand cavalry. The army advanced into Judea and encamped within three miles of Jerusalem, at Emmaus. It met with no opposition on its way.

Judas assembled his small hosts at Mizpah. Many memories clustered about Mizpah. There Samuel had judged the people, and there Saul had been chosen the first king. Judas ordered the people to bring the first fruits and the tithes which could not be brought to the Temple. They brought the garments of the high priest which had remained unused. Judas reminded the people that heathens had defiled the House of God, and implored them to seek the aid of Heaven. The army fasted and prayed, for the hour was indeed a most critical one for Israel. The soldiers knew that

scores of merchants with their bags of gold were following the army to buy them and their families as
slaves.

JUDAS' GREAT VICTORY AT EMMAUS

Judas had his spies in the Syrian camp, and through
them he learned that one of the generals was planning
a night surprise against him. Part of the Syrian army
was intending to leave its camp at midnight and to
fall upon the Jews from the rear. Judas was encamped
on a mountain, and the enemy on two hills opposite.
Upon receiving the information Judas decided to surprise the enemy instead. He left his camp at the hour
when the Syrians were setting out against him. Marching westward, in the direction opposite to the Syrians,
Judas came to the rear of the Syrian camp, and suddenly fell upon the half of the Syrian army which
had remained. The Syrians were completely surprised.
Before the soldiers were quite awake, their camp was
in flames. The bewildered hired soldiers fled in confusion. They left their arms and their stores. The
slave merchants left their money bags. Judas pursued
the fleeing army and made certain that their rout was
complete. Thousands of Syrians died on the field.

Judas now prepared to meet the other half of the
Syrian army. Those soldiers had marched stealthily
the greater part of the night, only to arrive at the deserted Jewish camp. They found tents pitched and fires
burning, but not a Judean in sight. The general, believing that Judas had discovered his coming and fled

into the forest behind his camp, ordered his soldiers
to pursue the Jews in the forest. The army finally
tired of the useless chase, was returning disheartened,
since they could find no trace of Judas or his army.

Courtesy A. M. Burd, Germantown, Pa.

A CHANUKAH MENORAH

Designed and executed by Reuben Leaf, New York City.

Carelessly and in disorder they were straggling back
to their own camp, where Judas was awaiting them.
The disorganized mob was not prepared to offer any
resistance. It took to flight. Thousands of them fell
on the field of battle, and Judas' victory was complete.

The Feast of Chanukah

The third army, too, was a complete loss to King Antiochus, and he was in no position to put another army in the field immediately. Nothing now preventing Judas from marching against Jerusalem, he entered the capital amidst great rejoicing. His first thought was for the Temple. The soldiers of Judas set to work at once to purify it. The Greek idols were demolished, and the stones of the holy altar, which had been defiled, were carried away and hidden. New furniture and new vessels of gold were made; for the greedy Antiochus had stolen the golden table and the other costly furnishings. At last the work of purification was completed. The everlasting Menorah was rekindled. The Temple was dedicated anew with songs, praise and with processions. The celebration continued for eight days. The Feast of the Dedication is called in Hebrew "Chanukat Habayit," or "Chanukah" for short. The rededication of the Temple occurred on the 25th day of Kislev, in the year 165 B.C.E.

Some of the old Chronicles tell that together with the Chanukah celebration, the Jews also celebrated the "Feast of Booths" which they had been unable to observe properly during the war. The people brought palm branches, and encircled the altar every day of the Feast. Many new psalms were written in honor of the celebration, some of which we recite to this day on festive occasions.

Temples had been dedicated before, and each dedication was a great occasion to the Jewish people. The

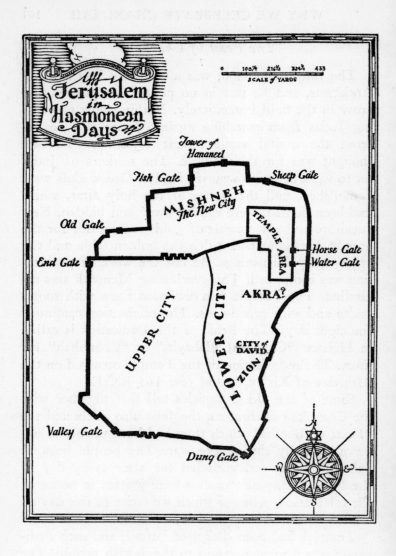

Jerusalem in Hasmonean Days

SCALE of YARDS
0   108¾   216½   324¾   433

Tower of
Hananeel

Fish Gate

Sheep Gate

MISHNEH
The New City

Old Gate

TEMPLE
AREA

Horse Gate
Water Gate

End Gate

AKRA?

UPPER CITY

LOWER CITY

CITY of
DAVID

Mt. ZION

Valley Gate

Dung Gate

rebuilding of the Second Temple by the returned exiles had meant a hard struggle. Yet how small was their sacrifice when compared with that of Judas and his handful of Hasidim. A great power was set against them. Even worse, their own brethren, the wealthiest and most influential were leagued with the enemy. The masses remained indifferent. The few faithful Jews who cared, saved their people. It was as our prophets had foretold—"the small remnant shall return to the living God."

IN CONCLUSION

We are now prepared to understand the meaning of the Chanukah prayer. The victory of the small band of Judeans over the mighty Syrian Empire seemed indeed a miracle. We have recalled the occasion faithfully every season, and as long as we appreciate religious freedom for all men, we shall remember the first war for religious freedom waged by our ancestors against Syria.

2

WHAT WAS THE OUTCOME OF THE VICTORY OF JUDAS?

WE have already answered our main question, "Why we celebrate Chanukah." We saw how Mattathias began the revolt against the interference of Syria in Jewish religious affairs. The war was carried on successfully by Judas who succeeded in defeating several Syrian armies and was finally able to gain possession of the Temple.

Chanukah celebrates the rededication of the Temple, but not the end of the war. The Syrians were expected to return with an even larger army. Judea was still officially a Syrian province. Part of Jerusalem itself was held by a garrison of Hellenists and Syrian soldiers. Jerusalem was a city built on three hills. The southwestern hill was the highest and was known as the Upper City. The Temple mount which Judas held, was on the northeast. There was a third hill on the southeast, the lowest of the three, called the Lower City. On it there was the ancient fortification of Zion, called the Acra by the Greeks who had their garrison stationed there. Thus even Jerusalem itself was not completely under Jewish control.

Internal Troubles Delay Syrian Invasion

Fortunately for Judas, the Syrians were not in a position to send a new army against him immediately. King Antiochus had suffered a severe defeat in the East, and died shortly thereafter.

The death of the king of the motley empire, particularly in the midst of unsuccessful wars, was bound to result in great confusion. The Syrian Empire consisted of many different conquered nations who were held together by force. At the death of the king, the various powerful nobles or generals attempted to set up their own candidates as kings. They paid soldiers out of their own funds, expecting a generous return later if their king was successful. After the death of a defeated king, the soldiers usually remained unpaid, and it was not difficult to tempt them with offers of gold. The election of a king at such a time, therefore, frequently meant civil war.

After the death of Antiochus, the choice of a Syrian king was attended with constantly growing confusion and bloodshed. Let us remember this fact because it will be important for the coming part of our story. King Antiochus left the kingship to an infant son, and appointed his general, Lysias, viceroy,[1] to assist his son in the government. Two years passed before Lysias subdued all his rivals and established a government.

These two years were very busy and important years for Judas who made use of the time to protect his fellow Jews who were scattered in many parts of Palestine. Greeks and Syrians in the surrounding cities were taking the liberty of attacking the Jews, since they knew that the government would approve of their action. Judas punished Edom, Moab and the Philistines. He sent expeditions to Galilee and Gilead to rescue the Jews who lived among the gentiles. The Jewish population of those districts was not very large, and it was thought best to bring them all to Judea.

Another Syrian War and Truce

Throughout this time, the Hellenists imprisoned in the Acra were sending urgent calls for Syrian help.

---

[1] Officer second to the king in power

Their pleas finally brought the new king with an enormous army of infantry, cavalry, and elephants. Lysias was determined to crush the uprising so that he could turn all his forces against other enemies.

Judas had tried to prepare for the war, by building fortifications on the narrow road leading northward to Jerusalem, but he succeeded in holding the Syrians back for only a short time. The Jewish detachment fought desperately, and one of the Maccabean brothers Eliezer lost his life in a great feat of heroism. Noticing an elaborately decorated elephant which he mistook for the king's, Eliezer crawled under it and drove his spear into it. The elephant fell upon him and crushed him by its weight. The Syrians were glad to grant the Jews a truce and permitted them to retire with their arms to Jerusalem.

But now the road to Jerusalem lay open, and Lysias encamped around the walls of the city. That year was a Sabbatical year and food was scarce. The population of Jerusalem, fearing for the outcome of the war, turned to the Hellenists. To Judas, faced by enemies within and without, the situation appeared hopeless.

Suddenly word came that Lysias was ready to declare a truce, for news had reached him of a new uprising at his capital. The Syrian kingship was more important than Jerusalem to Lysias, so that, anxious to hurry back, he was prepared to offer Judas liberal terms of peace. A treaty was drawn up, by which Judas remained the head of his people. All the laws forbidding the practice of the Jewish religion were repealed. The Syrian government promised not to interfere any more in the religious affairs of the Jews. Judas, on his part, agreed to remain loyal to Syria. The walls of Jerusalem were broken down to insure the fidelity of the people.

Lysias was tired of the wars in Judea. He realized that the whole conflict resulted from internal disputes, and he decided to punish the chief trouble maker, Menelaus. On the return to Syria, Lysias ordered Menelaus to be thrown under "a mountain of ashes."

It seemed that Judas had won all that he had hoped to win. His pious followers who saw divine assistance in the saving of Jerusalem were quite satisfied with the outcome of the war and were happy to return to peaceful pursuits. Judas, however, did not have great faith in the results of the victory. He feared that the word of a Syrian king might not always be trusted. Nor was the throne of the king so secure that one could be certain of his remaining in power. A new king might annul all the promises, so Judas felt that the Jews could be safe only if they were freed from foreign yoke completely. For over 350 years the Jews had been under strange masters. Perhaps now they might win their freedom. Hereafter the wars of the Maccabean brothers were fought to achieve the complete freedom of Judea.

Syrians Again Appoint High Priest—Another Civil War

Judas' fears appeared well founded. Within the year the son of Antiochus was killed and a new king reigned in Syria. One of the leaders of a middle Hellenist party, Alcimus, of an ancient family of high priests, applied to the new king to be appointed high priest. Upon the payment of a large gift, the king readily consented. Alcimus appeared in Jerusalem with Syrian soldiers, and one of his first acts in office was to order a massacre of his opponents, the Hasidim.

A new civil war began. A Syrian army once more appeared on the scene, commanded by Nicanor. Nicanor, still bitter over his former defeat at Emmaus, threatened to burn the Temple unless Judas was delivered to him. But Nicanor did not live to fulfil his threat. In a great battle Judas defeated the Syrian army, and Nicanor himself lost his life. For many years thereafter, on the 13th of Adar the Jews observed Nicanor Day, in remembrance of the death of the tyrant and blasphemer.

Judas now hoped to secure the complete independence of his people. He drove out the high priest, Alcimus, and established himself at Jerusalem. He sought to make alliances which would secure him against Syria. A Judean embassy set out for Rome, the new power, which was already ruler of the greatest World Empire. The Roman senate proved friendly and agreed to accept the Judeans as allies.

But the Syrians did not give Judas the opportunity to follow up his successes. Within a month a new Syrian army appeared in Palestine. Judas' forces had scattered. The peasant militia had probably returned to the farms, and many may have deserted at the news that the king's main forces were advancing against

them. The zealous Hasidim saw little further cause
for fighting. It made slight difference to them whether
Judas or Alcimus ruled in Jerusalem, so long as there
was freedom within their Synagogue.

DEATH OF JUDAS

With a handful of men, Judas, nevertheless, risked
battle with the Syrians. His little army estimated at
between 800 and 3,000, was opposed by 22,000 Syrians.
The outcome could readily be foreseen. Judas fell on
the field of battle. Many of his bravest followers fell
with him. A small band, under the leadership of the
remaining Maccabean brothers, fled in hiding to the
Judean deserts. Judas, the lion of the Maccabees, was
dead. The Maccabean followers, no greater in number now than those who first rallied about Mattathias,
were again outlaws. Had all of Judas' victories been
in vain? The end of our story will tell.

Judas was our greatest general during the period of
the Second Temple. Judas was among the first of the
world's heroes to take up the sword for the freedom
of worship. Like Ezra and Nehemiah in their day,
Judas is one of the saviours of the Jewish people.
Strangely, though, very little is said about Judas in
any of the Hebrew writings. Hebrew writers of history gave very little space to men of war. They did
not care to record military victories. There is hardly
a legend, therefore, about Judas himself. The festival
of Chanukah was remembered only for the rekindling
of the Menorah, rather than for the heroic acts which

made it possible. Whatever we know of Judas has come down to us in Greek translations. Other nations which were more interested in soldiery and generalship have pointed out to us what an unusual military genius our Judas was, who with a small band of untrained farmhands had defeated one of the mighty powers of his day. In spite of their overwhelming victory, the Syrians no longer risked to forbid the practice of the Jewish religion. Judas' death won his people religious freedom.

THE HASMONEAN BROTHERS CONTINUE—JONATHAN HEADS NATION

The great Jewish defeat did not put an end to Judas' dream of an independent Judea. Two Maccabean brothers had fallen on the field of battle. Three brothers still remained, and with them was a band of followers which clung faithfully to the Maccabean standard. Jonathan was chosen captain in place of Judas. The small band under his command lived in the desert like nomads, exposed to danger from the Syrians, as well as from desert tribes. In a skirmish with one such tribe, a third Maccabean brother, John, lost his life. Jonathan and Simon alone remained. The Syrian army pursued them, but they constantly succeeded in escaping them.

A few years later the high priest, Alcimus, died. Before his death he had greatly angered the pious Judeans. Within the Temple there had been a partition separating the court of the gentiles from an inner

court reserved only for Israelites. Alcimus broke the
partition down and permitted the Syrians to enter the
court of the Israelites. His death was considered a punishment from heaven, and the people were not eager
to fill the office with any of his descendants. The
Temple thus remained without a high priest, and the
Jews without a leader.

The Syrian general left Judea at this time, and that
afforded Jonathan an opportunity to entrench himself.
His forces began to increase, and he was able to punish
some of his Hellenist enemies. When a Syrian army

© U. and U.

A BEDOUIN ENCAMPMENT IN THE WILDERNESS
In this fashion Jonathan and his followers lived while fugitives
from Syria.

reappeared against him, Jonathan was strong enough to take the field in the open. He held his own so well that he was able to obtain an honorable truce. The Syrians agreed to leave Jonathan in peace on condition that he recognize the sovereignty of Syria and that he stay away from Jerusalem.

Encamped a short journey from Jerusalem, Jonathan soon became the real head of Judea. He assumed the responsibility of enforcing the religious law, and the Hellenists no longer had anyone to whom to appeal. The Syrian kings were tired of their cause. Besides, there were new disturbances at the Syrian capital.

Jonathan Sought as Ally by Syrian Kings— Appointed High Priest

Again the Syrian kingship was being fought over. Neither of the royal contestants felt strong, and each was anxious to enlist as many allies as possible. Jonathan, the rebel leader of Judea, now seemed a very desirable ally. The Syrian king sent a flattering letter to Jonathan, he called him his friend, and appointed him high priest of the Jews, with authority to levy soldiers in Judea. The rival king also sought Jonathan's friendship, and offered him still greater privileges. Jonathan accepted the high priestly dignity, but chose to side with the latter.

The nation which had been without a high priest was happy to have a member of the popular Hasmonean family at the head. Besides, Jonathan's choice of allegiance turned out to be a wise one. His candidate succeeded in becoming king, and the Jews thus had occasion to rejoice again; for in addition to the office of high priest, Jonathan was chosen one of the leading governors of the Empire. His brother Simon was made military commander of a large portion of Syria.

Jonathan and Simon now felt that the time would soon be ripe for the complete independence of Judea. With a powerful army under their command, they even began to dream of a larger Jewish kingdom which would include the more fertile districts around Judea. The Hasmonean brothers wanted to restore the ancient glories of David, to possess the cities on the seacoast from which hundreds of merchant ships sailed for distant ports. They wished their nation to share some of the rich trade of the Greeks.

Jonathan and Simon were becoming more powerful than the king of Syria. Once, when a revolt broke out against the king in Antioch, the capital of Syria, the Syrian king appealed to Jonathan to come to his aid. A Jewish army marched to Antioch to save the king against his own subjects. But instead of being grateful the king of Syria was growing uneasy over the military enterprises of Simon and Jonathan. He undertook a campaign against them, but now Jonathan could muster an army greater than that of the Syrians, and the king was defeated. The king's hirelings were no match for the citizen army of Judea.

Jonathan was now openly an enemy of the crown. He joined the party which opposed the king and which was led by a general named Trypho. Trypho, however, was as jealous of Jonathan's growing power as he was of the ruling monarch. Jonathan was now reigning over a large country extending from Judea through Galilee and Tyre, as you may see on your map. Trypho therefore conspired to kill Jonathan. He invited him for a friendly visit to one of his castles, and treacherously slew him there.

Simon, the Last Maccabee—Judea Independent

Simon was now the only remaining son of Mattathias. Like his brothers, he too was brave in war and clever in statecraft. Naturally anxious to avenge the death of his brother, Simon was prepared to make a league with the reigning king. The king of Syria was, in truth, powerless to control Simon, and was therefore glad to secure Simon's assistance against the usurper at any conditions that Simon might set. For the payment of a large sum of money, Simon received from the king a grant of complete independence for Judea.

The dream of the Maccabean brothers was at last accomplished. The weak revolt of Mattathias, the victories of Judas, the statesmanship of Jonathan, and the final diplomacy of Simon, raised Judea from a small subject province to a position of independence and power. A new era began for Judea, which started to count time from the year of its newly won freedom. It showed its independence by striking its own coins some of which we still have today as shown in the pictures. Had the Hellenists forseen what their movement would lead to, they might have been willing and

proud to remain with their people. But now there was
no more Hellenist party. Those Hellenists who survived the Hasmonean attacks were happy to seek positions in the new royal household.

CHANUKAH, THEN AND NOW

We are now at the end of the Chanukah story and
we ask ourselves again—"Why do we today observe
the holiday?"

Ask your father what he was told about Chanukah
when he was a boy at Hebrew or Sunday School. The
teachers used to explain the Chanukah holiday with a
little legend as fol-
lows: At one time
while the wicked
Greeks were mas-
ters of Palestine,
they took posses-
sion of the Tem-
ple and defiled
it by erecting an
image in it. In
the Temple there
was the everlasting

SILVER COIN OF SIMON

On the side with the cup is inscribed
"Shekel Yisroel" and Year III, meaning
the third year of Hebrew independence.
On the opposite side is "Yerusholaim
Hakedosha," Jerusalem the Holy. The
picture represents the rod of Aaron
which budded—a priestly symbol.

Menorah which was kindled with very pure
oil prepared under the care of the high priest
and sealed with his seal. When the Judeans recaptured the Temple, they wished to relight the holy
lamp, but no pure oil could be found, nor could any
be prepared before eight days. Finally, one small jug

of oil was discovered bearing the seal of the high priest. The small jug, however, might suffice for only one day. But a miracle occurred, and the oil lasted for the full eight days. In remembrance of the miracle, the Chanukah celebration was established.

Is it not strange that so little mention is made of all the great victories and deeds of heroism of the Maccabean brothers? In spite of the importance of their exploits all the great records of our nation, almost to our own day, barely make mention of them. The struggle for independence is forgotten. The success over the Syrians is overlooked. It is pointed out by Christian scholars that had it not been for Greek translators of the Jewish books dealing with the Maccabean heroes, preserved by Christian monks in their monasteries, we should have no Jewish records of them at all.

THE VICTORY IS THE LORD'S

It is not out of carelessness or for lack of gratitude that our ancestors told only of the oil miracle of Chanukah and little of the part played by man. Our sages believed in giving all glory to God and very little credit to the work of man. " 'Not by might, nor by power, but by My Spirit,' saith the Lord of hosts."

We today do not believe in miracles in the same manner. We believe in the help of God, but we feel that it comes through the work of brave and earnest men. God's miracles are not the strange and unusual occurrences, but the regular, wise, well-planned, and bravely executed, work of great leaders. In ages past, God was honored for the happenings which occurred contrary to nature. Today we honor Him for the daily wonders of life, for plants that grow, for the sun that shines, and for wisdom in the mind of men to understand His world.

While our ancestors, therefore, celebrated Chanukah for the miracles that could be related about it, we rather choose to remember it for the part which real men played in it; for real battles fought, for real defeats, and real victories.

As Jews in America, we have further reason to remember Chanukah. American history is filled with its great struggle for freedom. Everything in the nation points to it. The leaders of the revolutionary period are called the fathers of the country. As we read of Washington, Franklin, and Jefferson, we like to recall that our ancestors, too, fought their revolution before there was an England—fought a great power near its own door, and won.

IN CLOSING

What of the mass of people in the days of our story? They were very much as we would have been in their place. They loved their newly won freedom. They died willingly for their fatherland. Yet, beneath their soldiery, their hearts drew them after the teachers of their religion. Frequently they were obliged to choose between one and the other.

How these difficulties arose and how the people

solved them will be, in part, the subject of our next section.

Our main interest, of course, is to find out what happened to the new Jewish state. How long did our forefathers maintain themselves in Palestine? How successful a nation were they, and what brought their independence to a close? We shall turn to answer this question in our next section.

© *From "Ancient Times" by James Henry Breasted; Courtesy Ginn and Co.*

THE ACROPOLIS AT PERGAMUM (RECONSTRUCTED)
Examples of beautiful Greek architecture.

SUPPLEMENTARY WORK

MAP EXERCISES

1. On an outline map of Palestine locate the following places: Modin, Jerusalem, Emmaus, Jaffa, Samaria, Shechem, Hebron.
2. Judging from your map on page 82 how large was Judea in comparison with the rest of the Syrian Empire?
3. Locate Judea, Galilee, Samaria, Phoenicia, Moab, Ammon, Edom, Gilead.

QUESTIONS FOR DISCUSSION AND DEBATE

1. What party would you have honestly joined had you lived at the time of Menelaus and Judas? Why?
2. Compare the parties among the Jews to-day with those of Maccabean days.
3. Resolved that military heroes are less important than heroes of peace.
4. Resolved that it was treacherous of Jonathan to change masters for personal benefit.
5. How would the non-Jews of the surrounding countries view the Maccabean uprising?
6. Is there any similarity between the desire to Americanize our immigrants and the Hellenization of the Judeans?

ADDITIONAL PROJECTS

1. Imagine that you are a war correspondent with the armies of Judas. Send short news items to Jerusalem on the progress of the war.

2. Sketch costumes for a Chanukah masquerade. Include a costume for the high priest, for an Hellenist young man and for a male and female citizen of Jerusalem.
3. Dramatize a meeting of Hellenists over which Jason is chairman. The meeting is plotting to seize the high priesthood.
4. Make a set of posters to announce the coming of Chanukah.
5. Plan a Chanukah party program.
6. Write epitaphs over the graves of Judas, Jonathan and Simon.
7. Prepare a note-book for the study of this topic. Make a suitable design for the cover and head pieces for the inside pages.
8. Prepare a slide talk on Chanukah.

ADDITIONAL READINGS
FOR TEACHERS

Smith, *op. cit.,* chaps. xviii–xix.
Schürer, E., *History of the Jewish People in the Time of Jesus Christ,* Part I, vol. I, pp. 186–233, Part II, vol. I, pp. 1–72.
Margolis and Marx, *op. cit.,* pp. 126–151.
Graetz, *op. cit.,* I, pp. 411–502, 519–531.
Josephus, *op. cit.,* Bk. XII, chaps. i, iv–xi, Bk. XIII, i, ii, iv–vii.
Bevan, *op. cit.,* pp. 16–111.
Radin, *op. cit.,* chaps. vi, ix, x.
Riggs, J. S., *History of the Jewish People,* pp. 14–71, 87–96.
Bailey and Kent, *op. cit.,* pp. 295–321.

FOR PUPILS

Harris, *Thousand Years,* pp. 26–51.
Meyers, J., *Story of the Jewish People,* I, pp. 1–28.
Dubnow, *op. cit.,* II, *pp.* 9–49, 53–55.
Magnus, *op. cit.,* pp. 14–25.

SECTION III

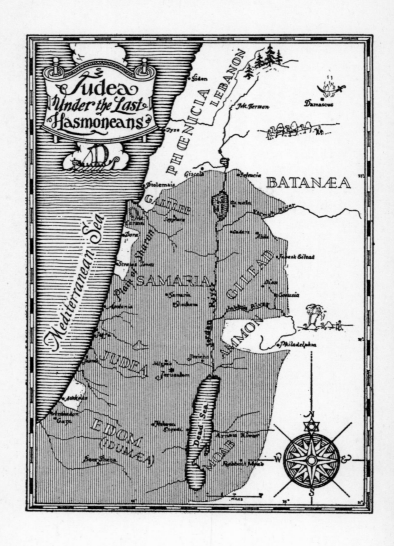

Judea
Under the Last
Hasmoneans

Mediterranean Sea

PHŒNICIA

LEBANON

Sidon

Mt. Hermon

Damascus

Tyre

Giscala

Seleucia

BATANÆA

Ptolemais

GALILEE

Sepphoris

Dora

Plain of Sharon

Strato's Tower

SAMARIA

Samaria
Sychem

GILEAD

Jabesh Gilead

Gerasia

AMMON

Philadelphia

JUDEA

Joppa

Bethel
Jericho
Jerusalem

Ashkelon

Gaza

Bethlehem
Hebron

Dead Sea

Arnon River

MOAB

EDOM
(IDUMÆA)

Beer Sheba

Rabbath-Moab

N
W E
S

MILES

HOW SUCCESSFUL WAS THE SECOND
INDEPENDENT JEWISH STATE?

INTRODUCTORY

THE period which we are going to study in this section lasted 78 years. It began in the year 143 B.C.E. and ended in 65 B.C.E. The first date marks the declaration of the independence of the Jewish state under Simon. The second date records the subordination of Judea to Rome.

Simon:	143–135	B.C.E.
John Hyrcanus:	135–104 " "
Aristobulus I:	104–103 " "
Alexander Janneus:	103– 76 " "
Alexandra Salome:	76– 67 " "
Aristobulus and Hyrcanus:	67– 65 " "
Pompey arrives at Palestine:	65 " "

Here is a chart of the Hasmonean kings who ruled the independent Jewish state, showing how long each one ruled. The important names are underlined and these you had best remember. You need not memorize anything now, though, for by the end of this section the important dates and names will have been sufficiently repeated.

123

WHAT IS THE STORY IN BRIEF?

After the treacherous capture of Jonathan, Simon was chosen ruler of Judea. The rightful king of Syria, anxious to secure Simon's help against the usurper [1]

© U. and U.

SEA-GOING SHIPS IN HASMONEAN DAYS

Trypho granted the Jews complete independence. Later, after the king had been victorious over his opponent, he wished to reconquer Judea, but Simon was powerful enough to defeat him. In the course of these wars Simon's son John proved himself a very able

---

[1] one who seizes power wrongfully

leader. We shall read more of him presently. One of the most important acts of Simon was the conquest of the seacoast cities, of which we shall soon tell more fully.

The last years of Simon's reign were the most prosperous and peaceful in the entire century. Under him the Jewish people found rest after its many years of war. In recognition of the achievements of Simon and his brothers for their people, the nation declared Simon hereditary [1] high priest and ruler of Judea.

Simon had been more fortunate than his brothers, in escaping the risks of war. But his own son-in-law, jealous of his powers, invited him to a feast and treacherously murdered him. The nation was too grateful, however, to the memory of Simon to yield the kingship to his assassin. Simon's son, John (Johanan) Hyrcanus, was chosen king.

The Hasmonean Princes

The early days of John's reign were threatened by an invasion of a new Syrian ruler who besieged Jerusalem and almost reduced the city by famine. The victory was not decisive, however. The Jews lost the war, but the treaty was not severe. It merely called for the payment of a sum of money, and for an alliance between John and the king of Syria.

The Syrian king was shortly killed in war, and thereafter John had no further fear of the Syrians. John Hyrcanus now set out upon a career of conquest,

---

[1] passes from father to son

and extended the bounds of Judea north and south. His sons, too, were able generals, and upon his death he left his country strong and well protected.

John was followed by his son, Aristobulus I, who reigned but one year. Alexander Janneus (Yannai), a brother of Aristobulus, succeeded to the throne. He, too, was a warrior king. During his rather long reign Alexander Janneus fought many wars, in most of which he was successful. He added large tracts of Transjordania—(the land east of the Jordan) to his empire. His reign, however, was marked by a period of internal strife.

At the death of Alexander, his wife, Alexandra Salome, ascended the throne. She proved a very able ruler, and the nine years of her reign were an era of peace and prosperity. But troubles were gathering about the land. Alexandra was a very old lady and was unable to provide for the government after her death. She left two sons, the older of whom, Hyrcanus, should have inherited the kingship. Unfortunately, Hyrcanus was not fitted for a position of leadership. His younger brother, Aristobulus II, was a forceful person who would have made an able king, but he had not the right of succession. Each of the sons claimed the throne, the nation was divided, and a civil war broke out.

At that time, 65 B.C.E., the Roman general, Pompey, was conquering the countries of Asia Minor. The two brothers decided to put their claims before him. Rome was known as the greatest power in the world, and the Jews were confident that a Roman general would decide justly. Little did they foresee that the Romans would use the occasion to make themselves masters of Palestine.

What Interests Us in Ancient Palestine?

We might thus pass over the story in a few short pages. We know now that one king ruled after the other—that a civil war gave the country over to Rome. A period of 78 years, more than two thousand years ago, would hardly hold great interest for us.

Yet the story of the kings and their fortunes tells us very little of what we should really love to know. For this story is of our own people in their days of independence before the present. What sort of people were our ancestors of that time? Were they a civilized nation in their day? Did they use the knowledge which was possessed by the advanced nations? What part did they play in the life of the world? Did they have any dealings with other nations? Were they poor or rich, were they educated or ignorant, were they capable of self-government, or did their state fall because they could not rule themselves? Did their neighbors respect them; did they fear them or were they among the weak and helpless peoples?

Not only are we interested in the past of Palestine, we are also very much concerned in its present. The new State of Israel has the eyes of the entire world fixed upon it. Most of the civilized nations of the world regard the creation of the State of Israel as the only happy outcome of an otherwise most destructive war.

Israel was carved out of a divided Palestine, and consists of the land shown on the map on page 133. In the last ten years nearly a million Jews have come to Israel to begin a new life there. Will this million and the hundreds of thousands more who are planning to settle there find room in this little land? Israel is relatively a small country. It is about 260 miles long, but it is very narrow——at the narrowest point a mere twelve miles and at its widest no more than sixty-eight. For the past 2,000 years the land has been very thinly settled, and its inhabitants were known for their poverty and their ill health. Part of the land is said to be barren and to possess insufficient water. Must we not wonder whether a country that has been so backward for the past 2,000 years, whose soil has not afforded a livelihood for about one-half million, can ever support a large Jewish settlement in modern times?

There are two possible answers which we can give to this question. One answer might be obtained from studying the accomplishments of those Palestinian settlers who have been established there for a long time. The result of the colonization of Israel might be an interesting subject for some members of the class to report on.

Another answer may be found by studying the situation at this particular period, when our ancestors enjoyed their independence in Palestine. How many Jews lived in ancient Palestine, and how well did they live there? Whatever knowledge we may gather about the second Jewish independent state will help us toward understanding the Israel of today.

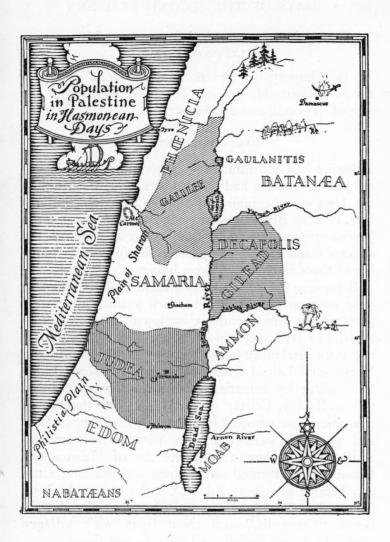

Population
in Palestine
in Hasmonean
Days

Damascus

PHŒNICIA

GAULANITIS

BATANÆA

GALILEE

Tyre

Mt. Carmel

DECAPOLIS

Plain of Sharon

SAMARIA

GILEAD

Shechem

Jabbok River

AMMON

Mediterranean Sea

Jordan River

JUDEA

Jerusalem

Yarmuk River

Hebron

Dead Sea

Arnon River

Philistia Plain

EDOM

MOAB

NABATÆANS

MILES

Comparison between Ancient and Modern Palestine (Israel)

In two important respects modern Israel compares favorably with Hasmonean Palestine, namely, in the size of its population and in its cities.

LARGE POPULATION

Palestine had an immensely larger population in ancient times than it had thirty years ago. At that time the Jews were beginning to come in considerable numbers, and the British government was trying to stop the Jewish stream of immigration on the excuse that the country could not afford opportunities for a large number of these arrivals to make a living.

Returning for a moment to ancient Palestine, look at your map on page 129. The dark shading represents parts settled almost entirely by Jews. The Jewish districts, you will see, consist of three sections—Judea, the main settlement about Jerusalem; Galilee in the North; and Gilead across the Jordan. Between Judea and Galilee lay Samaria, which was an important district in its day. On the western coast were the Philistine cities, now turned Hellenistic. In these cities Jews and heathens were found in very large numbers. South of Jerusalem, around the city of Hebron, the Edomites had formed settlements, and the land actually became known as Edom. On the eastern bank of the Jordan there was a group of ten cities called in Greek "Decapolis," and about them were villages settled by native Syrians or by immigrant Greeks.

Thus there must have been at least two million Jews and a million heathens living in ancient Palestine. If therefore there are at present in Israel a million and a half Jews and several hundred thousand Arabs, we are certainly not worried how they will earn their living there, since Palestine supported almost twice as many people in antiquity.

CITIES IN ANCIENT AND MODERN PALESTINE (ISRAEL)

The second important comparison between ancient Palestine and modern Israel is in the number of cities which existed then and now. Palestine 2,100 years ago possessed many cities of which only memories have remained. The seacoast was dotted with cities, and there were many inland cities as well. Most of the cities which have survived to the present are smaller and less important than they were in olden times. Look at the map on page 132 and find such names as Shechem, Jericho, Hebron, Ashkelon, and Dora, which were considerably larger 2,100 years ago. True, in olden times cities were largely overgrown villages. Jerusalem may have had a population of 100,000, but outside of that the other cities were small. Today there are fewer cities in Israel than in Hasmonean times, but those that do exist are large and contain the greater part of the population. Thus Tel Aviv-Jaffa has about 400,000 people, and Haifa has approximately 200,000 inhabitants.

The Jewish cities have all grown up during the past thirty-five years. The early settlers of modern Pales-

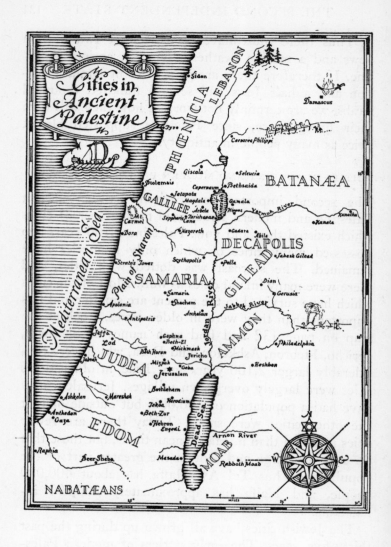

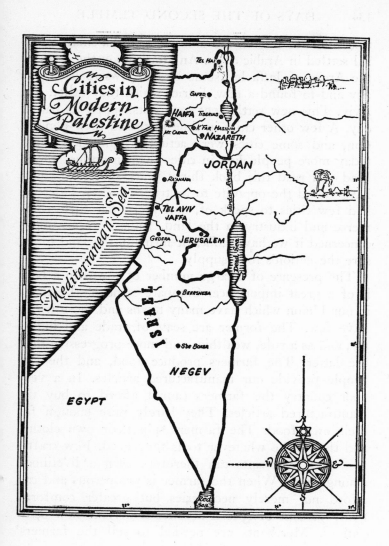

Cities in Modern Palestine

TEL HAI

SAFED

HAIFA   TIBERIAS

Mt. CARMEL   K'FAR HASIDIM

NAZARETH

JORDAN

RA'ANANA

TEL AVIV
JAFFA

GEDERA   JERUSALEM

BEERSHEBA

ISRAEL

SDE BOKER

NEGEV

EGYPT

Mediterranean Sea

Jordan River

Dead Sea

Red Sea

N
W   E
S

tine aimed to live on the land, and only a small handful settled in Arabic cities. An attack upon the Jews by
the Arabs of Jaffa led some of the Jews to leave the
city and to found a new district which they called Tel
Aviv. This new settlement soon outstripped its parent
city. A few other cities in time increased their population, and some cities were actually planned, so that
today more people live in cities than in ancient times.
Had you read this book thirty years ago, you would
have found the opposite to be true. Modern Palestine
had few cities to speak of, and there was little commerce and industry in the land. Indeed we are more
concerned if we have sufficient farms in the land to insure the nation's food supply.

The presence of a large number of towns in a land
is of a great importance. Compare some of the states
in our Union which have many towns and those which
have few. The former are seats of trade and industry, and as a rule, wealthier and more progressive than
the latter. The farmers produce food, and the city
people provide our manufactured articles. In a very
poor country the farmers cannot afford to buy the
manufactured articles. They barely raise enough for
their own food. The farmers spin their own clothes
and they make whatever tools they need. Few craftsmen and merchants can therefore earn a livelihood
among them. When the farmer is prosperous and can
afford not merely necessaries but greater comforts,
many persons of special abilities undertake new occupations. Merchants are needed to sell the farmers'

crops to other cities or even to foreign countries. In exchange they import foreign goods. These merchants and craftsmen gather in cities. Shops are needed to supply them with food; builders, to build homes for them; carriers, to transport their merchandise. In olden times, especially, and even today in most countries of the world, the prosperity of the cities depends upon the prosperity of the farmer.

The fact, therefore, that Palestine had a large population and that many of its inhabitants lived in cities, must suggest to us that the land was prosperous and, particularly, that the farmers enjoyed plenty. Palestine did support a large population at one time. Let us turn to see what were the occupations of the Jews during the period of their last independence.

Types of Crops Raised

The vast majority of Jews were farmers. The common people and even the more educated, looked with suspicion upon the merchants. One of the famous books of the time, known as "The Wisdom of Ben Sira," says, "A merchant shall hardly keep himself from doing wrong; and a huckster shall not be freed from sin." Chap. XXVI, 29. "As a nail sticketh fast between the joinings of the stones, so does sin stick close between buying and selling." Chap. XXVII, 2. That there were merchants in large numbers, we shall soon see. The majority of the nation, however, gained its livelihood from the soil.

City dwellers have the impression that farming is a
very simple occupation. If you have ever attempted
to plant ordinary garden vegetables you may have

© U. and U.

AN OLIVE GROVE IN MODERN PALESTINE

found out that it calls for a good deal of knowledge. There are more precious plants than the common garden varieties which require a great deal of care and skill. California is an agricultural state, and so is Carolina, yet the first is among the wealthiest, the second among the poorest of the country.

WINES AND OILS

Palestine at the time of our study was more a California than a Carolina. The small land, less than one-tenth the size of California, was raising a large variety of costly agricultural products, many of which, together with their manufactured products, found their way to foreign lands. The most famous of these were wines, oils and olives, dates, figs, incense, pomegranates, citrons and almonds. The wines of Palestine were of many sorts, and were as famed in their day as French or Spanish wines are today. There were black wines, white wines, reddish wines, Sharon wines, Carmel wines, and spiced wines. Our early ancestors, as we can see, cultivated many different varieties of grapes with great success. Besides grape wines, there were raisin wines, date wines, apple wines, and other vinous [1] preparations. Judea, particularly was famed for its vineyards, though grapes also grew plentifully at Sharon and on Carmel.

Oils were abundant in Galilee as well as in Judea. Most of the oils were of the olive, but there were other kinds, such as nut oil, and poppy seed oil. Oil

---

[1] made of wine

was in great demand at that time. In a warm climate, long before the use of ice was known, and other fats could not be preserved, oil was used extensively for cooking. Oil was also generally used for anointing the body after bathing, and it was in large demand for medicinal purposes. Palestinian oils were famed not only at home but in the surrounding lands.

DATES AND BALSAM

Palestine dates were a delicacy enjoyed by the Roman Emperor Augustus. There was a famous palm forest

© U. and U.

WINE MAKING IN THE ORIENT
Treading the grapes as in ancient days.

Courtesy Dr. Nelson Glueck

PALM TREES ON THE BEACH BETWEEN HAIFA AND ACCO

at Jericho, extending for almost twelve miles, and the Jericho dates were known far and wide. At a later period, the famous Cleopatra received from Marc Anthony a gift of Jericho and its palm district. Dates were used in a variety of ways. They were pressed and eaten, as today. There was a date wine, as mentioned before, and date honey. There were also date cakes, like our fig newtons.

It would make too long a story to dwell upon all the products in detail. We shall only mention the famous incense and balsam which grew at En-gedi and about the Dead Sea. So costly were these plants that a pound of incense was valued at two or more pounds of gold.

Gilead, too, was a rich spice country as you may recall from what your Bible tells of the caravan which bought Joseph.

There were many other products raised, wheat, barley, and garden vegetables. Fruit grew in great plenty. Nor were the farmers slow to introduce foreign plants. Rice was brought in, probably at the time of Alexander. Egyptian beans, and Persian fruits, and nuts, were cultivated.

We thus see that the Jewish state during its last period of independence had a flourishing agriculture highly developed. Our ancestors knew how to apply the knowledge of their day to the earning of their livelihood. In later centuries we find them spreading some of their agricultural experience to distant Mediterranean lands, as far as Spain.

Occupations Other Than Farming

Many persons were already earning their livelihood through trade and handicrafts. The many cities made necessary the common occupations of butchers, bakers, tailors, and shoemakers. There were builders in stone and wood. There were workers in metal, in gold, silver, iron, and brass; weapon makers, carvers in ivory, weavers in wool, flax, and silk; potters and glass-ware makers, perfumers, druggists, and many others. This list shows us how widely the skilled trades were practiced by the Jews.

Besides the artisans, there were the merchants of many classes. The Jews had taken to trade and manufacture largely through the example of the Greeks. Although Palestine had much wool and flax, and may

After Doré

"AND THEY CUT DOWN A BRANCH
WITH ONE CLUSTER OF GRAPES AND
THEY BORE IT UPON A POLE—"
Numbers xi, 23.

have even exported them, the costly textiles were still brought from abroad as were also the better shoes, furniture, and household utensils. Palestine exported agricultural products and the manufactures of them, such as wine, oil, honey, and dates. It imported textiles, wearing apparel, and hardware. The more common articles were soon produced at home. The rarer and more costly ones continued to be imported. There were, therefore, the wholesale importers and exporters, the large inland merchants and the small store-keepers.

SEAFARING

Trade in Palestine was only in its beginning, but it was to grow more and more important. The thousand years which followed were to see Jewish merchants carrying the trade of the civilized world from China to Spain. The Maccabean conquest of the leading trade cities gave Jewish commerce a strong impetus. At this time was laid the foundation of the Jewish sea trade. Palestine became an important maritime centre. The Hasmonean princes since the days of Jonathan were eager to possess the seacoast. One of the first acts of Simon was to become master of Jaffa, the leading harbor. Other cities, too, were important as seaports. These were Jamnia (or Jabneh), Dora, Strato's Tower (later renamed Caesarea), Haifa, and Acco. Besides these, there were other seacoast cities of lesser importance. Though the coast of Palestine is too regular for safe harbors, we find eleven cities engaged in sea trade.

The Mediterranean commerce had formerly been in the hands of Phoenicians. During the last three centuries B.C.E., the Phoenicians were giving way to the Greeks who became the leading merchants of the world. The Jews, however, were not slow to learn. The Palestine sea trade was gradually taken over by Jews. Marine transportation became a large and important Jewish occupation. The Maccabean rulers proudly erected a ship's mast on their monuments. In later years, Roman conquerors boasted in their triumph that they had vanquished "Judea Navalis"—Judea the sea-power.

Palestine has its large inland lakes, and, these, too, were used in shipping, for transportation, and for fisheries. A considerable fish industry was going on at Lake Chinnereth. Hundreds of fishing vessels were plying its waters. The Palestinian fisheries supplied fresh fish for domestic use and exported salted fish and other preparations. Palestinian caviar was a well known delicacy at Rome.

RESUME

Thus we have one picture of our ancestors during the closing days of Hasmonean rule in Palestine. They were reaching out rapidly in all fields of industry and commerce. They used the gifts of their land to the best advantage. The soil was made to yield rich plants, and these were skillfully manufactured into costly products. Hundreds of foreign articles were imported and hundreds of domestic articles found their way in export trade. We are confident the same will be true of Israel today. Judea was a small nation, but apparently a significant one.

Of course, not all the Jews were wealthy. There were poor men, tenant farmers, unskilled day-laborers, even Jewish slaves. There are poor people even in the richest countries. The United States is now the wealthiest nation in the world, yet it has its poor in large numbers. Rome had its slums and its beggars. There were poor people in Palestine, of course, but, judging from our present knowledge of the subject, the average citizen lived in fair comfort.

Were Our Ancestors of Any Importance as a Military Power?

Military prowess [1] holds a very important place in our judgment of nations. There was a time when the greater part of history books told only of wars and generals. Today we like to think more of the heroes of

---

[1] strength

peace. Yet, nations are still called powers; great powers and small powers, powers of the first rank and of the second rank. Whether or not we care to believe that military power determines the worth of a nation we are interested to know how our ancestors were regarded by their neighbor nations during the last Hasmonean period.

The Jews Never Great Conquerors

The Jewish people was never a great military nation comparable with ancient Egypt, Babylon, Assyria, or Rome; nor did it ever aspire to become the military mistress of the entire world. If it dreamt of world empire at all it was rather of a spiritual empire. Jerusalem would be the religious capital, and all nations would come to Zion to worship the God of Israel.

There were thousands of nations and tribes in ancient times as today, but only a few rose to the position of great conquerors. Our histories tell the story only of the few mighty nations and their wars. We almost imagine that they were the only peoples in their world.

There were long periods, often lasting one or more centuries, when the large empires were inactive. The great empires frequently became too difficult to govern, consisting, as they did of hundreds of conquered peoples, each waiting to rebel at the weakening of the conqueror. At such times the smaller nations had their inning. The stronger among them conquered the

Courtesy Dr. Nelson Glueck

AMPHITHEATRE AT AMMAN

Remains from Graeco-Roman days showing the high civilization
which trans-Jordania enjoyed during Hasmonean days.

weaker ones, and little empires were established on a
smaller scale. Such had been the empires of David and
Solomon, and the more recent Syrian empire of
Antiochus. Such an empire, too, was built up by the
Hasmonean princes.

The Hasmonean Conquest

The king of Syria in the period of his distress, had
permitted Jonathan, the Hasmonean, to raise an army.
Simon, at the time, was the commander of the king's
forces over the whole of Syria from Tyre to Gaza.
When the Hasmoneans saw how weak the Syrian kings
were, they began to dream of extending their own
land.

There were many reasons found for going to war.

On the seacoast there were flourishing cities with a large sea trade, wherein many Jews were already settled. The native population was jealous of their successful competition, and scornful of their religion. Armed clashes between Jews and Syrians, which were not infrequent, had shown the anti-Jewish feeling of the Greeks. Simon felt justified in invading them, and added practically the entire coast to small Judea. The large revenues from import and export duties proved a rich source for the hiring of mercenaries [1] with whom to make further conquests.

CONQUEST OF SAMARIA AND EDOM

John Hyrcanus found cause for attacking Samaria and Edom. The former province lay between two Jewish districts, Judea and Galilee. Jewish festival pilgrims from Galilee, on their way to Jerusalem [2] complained that they were mistreated on their way through Samaria. The rival temple at Mount Gerizim claimed by the Samaritans to be the only rightful place of Jewish worship, must have angered the fighting king-high priest. Samaria was invaded, and the entire district was conquered and annexed. Samaria and the temple on Mount Gerizim was razed to the ground.

Edom, too, was overrun. The Edomites had been old enemies of the Jews. They had occupied Jewish

---

[1] hired soldiers

[2] All male Jews were commanded to make a pilgrimage to Jerusalem three times a year, on Passover, Shabuoth and Succoth. We call these holidays the three festivals.

land, the ancient city of Hebron and the district around it. Many Jews were living among them and were probably suffering oppressions. Edom, accordingly, was also brought under Jewish rule. John Hyrcanus, anxious to make his conquests secure, thought that he could accomplish his aims by forcing the conquered peoples to accept the Jewish religion. The Samaritans and Edomites were thus compelled to become Jews.

INVADE EAST OF JORDAN

The followers of John Hyrcanus—particularly Alexander Janneus—continued the conquests beyond the Jordan. The cities of the Decapolis were brought under Jewish rule. There was now a Jewish empire larger than David's. On the south it reached the borders of Egypt, on the east it was limited by the desert, and on the west by the sea. What the north might have held out is difficult to say. The Romans appeared there first. That ended the dreams of a Jewish empire. That, too, ended Jewish independence.

The Hasmonean princes were not always successful in war. You may recall from the beginning of this chapter that the empire of Syria rallied for a while and almost conquered Jerusalem. At another occasion an army from Cyprus placed the country in great danger. It was saved only by an Egyptian army which was commanded by Egyptian-Jewish generals. But in the main, the Hasmonean kingdom was a mighty power in its corner of the world.

At a time when the whole world was in arms, and nations existed mainly by the sword, our ancestors held their own successfully. Although unused to war for hundreds of years, they took the field, and under the leadership of a family of priests became successful conquerors and empire builders.

Was Our Nation in Palestine Outstanding in any Way?

We saw that our people in Palestine was an active, enterprising nation. It learned rapidly from its neighbors, and was finding its way into the many new and interesting occupations of the world. We saw, too, that among its neighboring nations it was a rather strong military power. When Palestine was conquered by

© U. and U.

BRIDGE BUILT BY HASMONEANS

Rome about one hundred years later, Rome celebrated the victory as a great triumph. It built arches in honor of Titus the Conqueror, and showed on its coins and medals how proud it was of its conquest of Judea.

But were our ancestors anything more than good farmers, merchants and fighters? Were they distinguished for anything else than industry and war?

Religion the Main Distinction of Our People

Persons, like nations, become distinguished if they do something greater or better than their fellow men or nations. The Jewish nation became distinguished because it developed a religion greater and finer than that of any other nation of its time. The larger part of the world has accepted and is now following some form of Judaism. Our ancient sacred books are the holy writings for most of humanity.

Since religion was that which marked the Jews from other peoples, let us note some of the outstanding differences between the religion of the Jews and that of their neighbors.

GOD INVISIBLE

The Jews worshipped an invisible God, a notion which was strange to their neighbors. Other peoples could not understand how men could worship an imaginary God. The gods of the non-Jews were either figures of men or figures of animals. The Jews could certainly not represent their God in the form of a beast. But they would not picture their God as a person, either. God, to them, was much greater than man. He is man's maker and man's guide. The mightiest king is but clay in God's hand. It was enough for the pious Jew to think of what God did. God was the provider for the world, its life giver, who governed His world with mercy, and His creatures with loving kindness.

Man could never make a picture of Him, because God was more than any small image which even the cleverest artist could devise.

Heathen wise men scoffed [1] at the Jews. Vicious men invented lies about the Jewish religion. Some said that in the Holy of Holies of the most sacred Temple stood the head of an ass, which was Israel's supreme idol. Others, confused because the Jews spoke of God as in heaven, or simply as heaven, said that the Jews worshipped the skies.

But there were many who understood and were drawn to the religion of Israel. The simple but great Temple of Jerusalem, famed more for its sacredness than for its architecture, drew constant throngs of visitors other than Jews. Daily, among the sacrifices offered, were the gifts of heathens. Thousands of *Gerim*, converts of all shades, could be found in Judea as well as in other places where Jews dwelt. Some merely abstained from work on the Sabbath, others observed the dietary laws, too, while there were some converts who fully accepted the Jewish religion with all its laws and customs.

---

[1] made fun of

MONOTHEISM

The second outstanding fact about the Jewish religion was monotheism, or the belief in one God. Other nations believed in many gods. Each god had his own tasks to perform. One brought rain, another ruled the winds, a third presided over wars, and still another blessed wine and its drinkers. There were scores of gods and half-gods, all of whom could protect men or destroy them. You might choose whichever god you pleased as your special protector. He might be a good god or an evil one. The one could be of use as much as the other. When we read of the cruelties of Rome, of the savagery of its generals and rulers, we understand how the worship of the war-god influenced people.

The Jews of this period declared that one God rules the entire universe, and that it is He Who is the cause of good as well as of evil. A man cannot hope to be a favorite of God except through proper conduct, for a pure and upright life is the only means of pleasing God.

GOD THE FATHER OF HIS PEOPLE

Let us now consider another very important idea in the Jewish religion. Other peoples spoke of their gods as kings and rulers. Men fear their rulers. They must obey them, on pain of punishment. Only the chiefs and kings considered themselves the chosen of God. The heathen religions taught that God was more in-terested in the nobility than in the common people because the nobles were direct descendants of the gods. The common people were only subjects and slaves. The ruler of Egypt called himself the son of God, or even God.

The Jews called their God "Our Father—Our King." Not only is God king over His people as over the rest of the world, He is also the Father of His people. All Jews alike are children of God. God loves them all and is eager that every Jew, even the most humble, come before Him in prayer.

Possessing one Father made all Jews brothers. It is the religion of our people which laid the foundation for the statement in the Declaration of Independence that all men are created free and equal.

THE JEWISH RELIGION, A REVEALED RELIGION

The Jewish religion had one more very important distinction. Other religions were considered mysteries. No one knew how to satisfy God except the priests. There were certain magic ways of reaching God. One had to speak only in a given manner and go through some fixed motions. Only the priest knew the right magic words and the proper movements. The magic formulas were kept secret by the priests. Father priests passed the magic secrets to their priestly sons. The priests usually practiced their arts for pay. Whenever a person or a tribe was to sow the field, make war, or prepare for the hunt, the priest was called to chant his magic. Man could only speak to God or pray to Him through the aid of a priest.

The Jewish religion asserted the very opposite. The Jews are children of their God, and a father does not keep his ways and desires secret from his children. Judaism did not permit its laws and commandments to become a mystery, the possession of priests. Each man might read God's Law for himself. There must be no magicians, sorcerers [1] or diviners in God's nation. "Would that all of God's nation were prophets," says Moses. The Bible calls all Israel a nation of priests and a holy people. Ours was to be not a religion of fear and trickery. It was to be a religion of intelligence and understanding.

We can scarcely imagine how important this fact was in the history of our people. It made our people far different from any nation of its day, and brought to it benefits and ideals which the rest of the world has obtained only recently, or in many places has not yet obtained. Let us see what some of these benefits and ideals were.

RELIGION A HABIT OF LIFE

Since every Jew knew what his God wanted of him, he was expected to live in accordance with God's wishes. The pious Jew is commanded to keep God's words always before him. He must be mindful of his God every minute of the day, and in every act of his life.

The pious Jew of Hasmonean times tried to obey the Law to the very letter. He directed all his acts to-

---

[1] magicians

ward the service of God. When he arose in the morning he was thankful that God had restored his life to him. When he ate his meal he thanked God for His bounty. He nailed part of God's Law over his door post. He began his day's work with prayer and with the wearing of phylacteries (Tefillin).[1] Three times daily he recited his prayers. The pious Jew could no more forget his prayers than his breakfast.

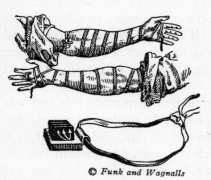

© *Funk and Wagnalls*

PHYLACTERIES (TEFILLIN) FOR HAND AND HEAD

The phylacteries are small leather boxes containing portions of the Holy Scriptures. They are worn on the left hand and on the head. The illustration shows how both sides of the same hand look.

The result of this religious life showed itself in greater devotion to those interests which make for human welfare, charity, and acts of kindness. We saw the beginning of this type of life already in the century following Ezra and Nehemiah. There was justice at Jewish law courts two thousand years ago. There were taxes imposed for the benefit of the poor, and special care for the orphans even to the extent of providing for their schooling. Our ancestors visioned the dream of the Messiah, of an era of peace on earth

---

[1] These are small boxes containing parts of the Law.

and good will among men, which is now the hope of all mankind.

The Spread of Education

The Sh'ma prayer with which you are undoubtedly familiar contains the command that the laws of God must be taught diligently to the children. Like all other laws of God, this was obeyed strictly. It was of the highest importance that every person receive an education. An ignorant man cannot be fearful of sin, says one of the rabbis. Today, too, we feel that there can be no true democracy unless every citizen has the opportunity for an education. Not only must every child have the opportunity, but, as we believe today, every child must be compelled to use his opportunity. Two thousand years ago, our ancestors made compulsory education the foundation of their state. This is one of the outstanding achievements of which our people can boast. The Hasmonean state in Palestine set about to abolish ignorance. The reform was heartily received by the people. After their state was destroyed, the school was never dispensed with, even in lands where Jews were reduced to beggary. Indeed, children were sent to school at the earliest age possible.

The educational reforms centre about two persons. The first reformer is Simeon b.[1] Shetah who lived in the period which we are studying. The other is Joshua b. Gamla who lived some years later (66 C.E.).

---

[1] The letter b. stands for *ben* which means son of.

Simeon b. Shetah was the brother of Queen Alexandra Salome, and one of the leading rabbis of his time. When Alexandra Salome ascended the throne, she was eager for his advice and service. Simeon b. Shetah thus became one of the important ministers of state, and exercised his authority to spread the Torah among the people.

The first provisions for general education, which are believed to be the work of Simeon b. Shetah, appear to have been made for orphans. Later Joshua b. Gamla, a high priest, extended the law to all other children. The laws provided that every town and village consisting of as few as ten families were obliged to secure a teacher for every twenty-five children, and two teachers for every fifty.

THE COURSE OF STUDIES

A collection of sayings of the early rabbis, called "Ethics of the Fathers," written several hundred years after our period, tells us at what age children entered school and what they studied. A child began his schooling at the age of five with the study of the Bible and continued his elementary studies till thirteen. Many children then received a higher education in the schools of the rabbis and wise men.

Children in those days studied very much the same subjects as we do today. They learned to read, to write and to cipher. They devoted most of their time to the study of the Bible which was for them a combination of several of our studies. It was history, civics, literature, religion, music, and training in manners. It even contained many interesting facts of nature study and of the geography of surrounding lands. We today possess many new branches of knowledge, mainly the sciences, which were not known twenty centuries ago. But when we consider how few children today receive any education higher than that of an elementary school, we need not imagine that people the world over really are much more highly educated than were the majority of our ancestors.

There were higher schools for men who wished to study the Law more thoroughly. There were also opportunities, particularly in the surrounding Hellenistic cities, for the study of other languages—chiefly Greek —and for the study of medicine.

Our people could proudly assert not only that it possessed the world's greatest book, but that it did all in its power to bring education to every home, rich or poor. So great was the honor awarded to learning that the leading teachers became the heads of the nation.

Religion in Politics—Scholars Party Leaders

As you study history you must undoubtedly notice how much of its story deals with rulers and with government. The government of a people is a very important fact to study. It tells us whether the people was troubled with wars, or whether it enjoyed peace. Under a good government which is truly patriotic and has the interest of its subjects at heart, a nation can progress. Under a selfish government which merely aims for power and wealth of the ruler and his court, a nation is often driven to ruin.

How was our Jewish state governed during its past independence? Was it an absolute monarchy, was it a republic, or a constitutional monarchy? How did the

COINS OF THE LATER HASMONEANS

In addition to the old Hebrew which gives the name of the king, "Yehonatan Hamelek," the other side gives the same in Greek. Notice the anchor crossed by two bars on one coin. The other has a flower reminding us somewhat of the budding rod on the coins of Simon.

rulers behave toward the people? How did the people act toward the rulers?

And let us pause at one more question. How does the heading "Religion in Politics, etc." fit what is to follow?

THE JEWISH STATE A MONARCHY

Let us answer these questions in order. We already know that the Jewish state was a monarchy. It was obliged to be a monarchy because of the constant dangers of war to which the country was exposed. In your study of American history you must have noticed that during the Civil War or the World War our republic behaved like a monarchy in many ways. The president was given the right to punish persons without jury trial, and the post-office was authorized to forbid the mailing of harmful literature. Some people think it is not proper for a republic to behave in this manner during a war. You might debate the question at some time. But you see that in time of danger, even now, all powers are entrusted to a commander-in-chief.

Kings of old were commanders-in-chief of their armies. Simon the Maccabee was chosen ruler because of his victorious generalship. Simon and his son, John Hyrcanus, did not use the title of king, but they enjoyed kingly power. The successors of John, however, openly began to call themselves kings.

Kingly government did not seem to be successful in the countries surrounding Judea. Few kings could claim the loyalty of their subjects. Many rulers were adventurers who seized the throne, with the aid of a hired army of mercenaries. The breaking up of the Syrian empire was caused by the numerous pretenders who constantly kept the country in a state of civil strife.

When a nation is obliged to organize a new government it usually models it after the existing ones about it. The new Jewish state had the example of usurping kings in all its neighboring countries. But it must be said, to the credit of the Hasmonean rulers, that they were devoted, patriotic princes, and that their aim was to increase the prosperity of their citizens. They made war on the cities on the Mediterranean coast to make sea trading more profitable for their subjects. They taxed commerce on the west, as well as in the Transjordanian cities to enable them to reduce taxes at home.

The Hasmonean rulers were not perfect. In all courts there are jealousies and slanders. Many persons who seek their own advancement are always found at royal courts, stirring up the king against his relatives. There were several court quarrels in Jerusalem. Some kings imprisoned their brothers. Later there was open strife between two brothers. In comparison with surrounding states, however, the Judean rulers might almost be called exemplary.

THE PARLIAMENT

The Jewish king did not rule alone nor altogether absolutely. The king's authority was limited by a parliament called in Hebrew *"Hever Hayehudim,"* or in Greek "Sanhedrin." The last became the accepted Hebrew word, so we speak of this parliament as the Sanhedrin. It consisted of seventy members, and was the chief legislative as well as the chief judicial body.

The Sanhedrin was not an elected parliament like our Congress. Its representatives were not chosen by the people directly. We might therefore conclude that the people had no voice at all in their government. Yet we should not decide until we have completed our entire story.

The Sanhedrin was in the nature of a House of Lords. The important priests were members of it. So were, undoubtedly, the leading generals and the heads of the most important families. The high priest was its president.

JEWISH LAW, RELIGIOUS LAW

LET us ask again—What voice did the common people have in the government? This will bring us back to the main question which we have considered in this section, the peculiar character of the Jewish religion.

Today we distinguish between certain duties which the government enforces and certain others which the Synagogue or Church asks people to observe. For example, the government may demand honesty, while religion may ask for more than honesty; it may command kindness and charity.

Our ancestors had only one law, the religious law. They considered every business transaction as done in the sight of God. All justice is God's, and therefore all law is God's. The law, which we call civil today, was as much a part of religion as were general problems of character.

God's law needed no police force, or king, or parliament to enforce it. The word of the holy teacher was of far greater weight with the people than all official decrees. The king and his councillors might pass their ordinances, but the people followed their religious leaders.

There was thus a formal and an informal government, the aristocratic government, and the people's government. It was to be expected that the two would clash. The story of the struggle of the people for power in the last Jewish independent state, the first real democratic movement of an entire people, is one which should be dear to every Jew. Let us analyze the story and see how it came about and how the battle was fought.

THE Jewish state could never be an absolute monarchy because it had a constitution. The Torah, the Law of Moses and the prophets, was binding upon king as well as upon commoner.

The difficulty with a constitution is that it has to be explained or interpreted. New cases arise which are not covered by the constitution—which the framers of the constitution could never have thought of. Let us take an example from the constitution of the United States. Our constitution says that Congress shall pass no laws depriving people of the freedom of speech or of the press. Suppose that Congress should pass a law forbidding certain types of speeches on the radio. One group might claim that the constitution should be interpreted broadly, and that freedom of speech must be afforded in all its forms. Others would insist that the constitution says nothing about radio and that therefore Congress can act as it pleases in regard to it.

You might recall from your early American history the long struggle between the strict constructionists and the broad constructionists. The same struggle was taking place in Judea. There was a party of strict constructionists called the Sadducees and a party of broad constructionists called the Pharisees. Each party contained only several thousand members, but the parties were important for their influence on the mass of the nation. The Sadducees were the party of the nobility, while the Pharisees had the sympathy of the common people.

There was another point of dispute between the Pharisees and Sadducees. The question was not only how to interpret, but who was to do the interpreting. The constitution of the United States provides for a judicial branch which is to interpret the laws. The Torah is not at all clear on the matter. The Sadducees claimed that they alone were empowered to interpret the Torah, while the Pharisees insisted that the right was theirs. The struggle within the Jewish state thus centered about these two parties, the Sadducees and the Pharisees.

Why were these two parties taking sides against each other? What principles held these parties together? What interests did each group have which separated it from the other?

The Sadducees

We shall consider the Sadducees first. This party as we saw was composed of the nobility and the aristocracy. It included the highest ranking priests, the generals, and the wealthy men of Jerusalem.[1] The interests of this class of persons was naturally different from that of the rank and file of the people.

---

[1] Do you recall whether there was any such party at the beginning of the United States government? What was it called and what did it advocate?

CLAIM RIGHT TO MAKE AND INTERPRET LAW

The Sadducean party held the ruling power, and was anxious to claim all rights and priviliges for the priesthood. It denied the right of any one else to exercise any authority or to make any laws—religious or otherwise. The Sadducees claimed the sole right to interpret the Torah and to make new laws for the priesthood. The Torah, they insisted, expressly gave them that right.

Many rabbis since the days of Ezra had introduced changes into the Jewish religion. The observance of the Sabbath had grown much more severe through such enactments.[1] Many new prohibitions had been decreed in regard to food and drink. Very many new regulations had been introduced concerning purity and cleanliness. A Jew was always expected to be in a state of purity for worship. Not only was a Jew commanded to be generally clean—to wash at rising, before prayer, and for meals—he was also prohibited from touching certain things which made a person impure and unfit for worship. Such objects might include reptiles, beasts, or corpses. Most important of all, touching a person who touched something unclean, or even entering a house where there was a corpse, rendered a person impure. If a person thus became unclean he had to go through certain rites of purification. Non-Jews who naturally did not observe these laws of purity were all considered unclean.

The Sadducees were men of large business enter-

---

[1] laws

prises, and of necessity they had to deal frequently with non-Jews. Governmental affairs, too, brought them in contact with gentile Greeks. They could not very well avoid non-Jews, or refrain from entering their homes. On the contrary, they desired to be on close and friendly terms with the non-Jewish population.

The Sadducees, therefore, naturally objected to the decrees of the rabbis which made it difficult for them to mingle with non-Jews. The rabbis of the Synagogue were anxious to keep Jews and heathens separate. They forbade eating with non-Jews, or drinking their wine. They even declared unclean the lands of the heathen. The Sadducees and the Pharisaic rabbis were clearly at odds.

We may now be prepared to understand why the Sadducees were strict constructionists of the Bible. The Sadducees said—"We shall be guided by the Bible only where the law is clearly stated. We shall observe the Sabbath day as commanded. We shall keep the feasts and the sacrifices. But on all questions where the Bible is silent, we shall use our own judgment."

DISBELIEVED IN LIFE AFTER DEATH

Another belief which separated the parties was the Pharisaic teaching of a life after death. The party of the Sadducees included the leading men of war for whom conquest meant glory and wealth. It contained men of wealth for whom conquest meant lower taxes. War was the noble occupation of brave men.

Prosperity was the dream of the large merchants and landowners. A nation victorious in war, politically independent, and commercially prosperous, was all that the Sadducees desired. Their golden age was at hand in this world. They looked forward to no other future. They laughed at the Pharisees who were concerned with another life, after death.

WERE SEVERE IN ENFORCEMENT OF CRIMINAL LAW

The Sadducees had reason to be satisfied with their present lot, and therefore did not desire any change. They were what we call conservatives, men who are anxious that everything remain as it is. In their anxiety to preserve the old order of life, the Sadducees were very severe in the enforcement of the criminal law. The Bible states, "An eye for an eye, a tooth for a tooth." The rabbis had long recognized that this method of punishment of an older age was too brutal to be continued. They had decreed that the punishment be changed to a money fine. The Sadducees insisted on keeping strictly to the words of the Bible, even in such a harsh case as this. They also inflicted the death penalty on much weaker grounds than the Pharisees.

SUMMARY

Let us now summarize briefly what has been said of the Sadducees. They were the party in power, and wished to preserve their hold on the government by

insisting that the priests were the only rightful inter-
preters of the constitution. As men of affairs, the Sadducees were anxious to mingle freely with other
peoples in foreign cities, limiting their acts only by the
actual commands of the Bible. They refused to be
bound by the restrictions of the synagogue rabbis. Being men of war, they rejoiced in the successful military operations of their land. They were conservative,
and feared that the rise of the common people to
power would bring the government to ruin. Finally,
as soldiers and officials, they tended to be very severe
in the enforcement of their laws.

The Pharisees

The Pharisees were the religious opponents of the
Sadducees. They were a religious fraternity, a society
of friends, bound together to observe the word of
God. This society was not very large, but among its
members were the teachers, and doctors of the law,
the heads of the colleges, and learned men of the
Synagogue.

CLAIM ONLY LEARNED MEN CAN INTERPRET THE LAW

The Pharisees were the men who spread learning and
devoted themselves to the study of the holy law. It
was but natural that they should believe themselves
the true authority for interpreting the law. Only
learned men, they insisted, might explain and teach
the Torah.   True, the priests constituted the executive

A MODERN PHARISEE—Studying the Holy Books

branch to carry out the teachings of the Torah; but the priests as well as the rest of the people must act in accordance with the true meaning of the Torah, which only the learned understood. For example, the Torah merely forbade work on the Sabbath, but students of the Torah must list every case where Sabbath peace would be disturbed. The Pharisees argued that every possible case can be solved through reference to the Torah. "Turn it and turn it for everything is in it," taught the rabbis. The great rabbis of old, insisted the Pharisees, were not making new laws; they were simply finding them in the Torah. The Pharisaic teachers of their own generation were not inventing any new laws either. They, too, were only discovering and declaring them.

The rabbis thus claimed to be the real governors of the people. The priests and Sadducees might fill the Sanhedrin. The Pharisaic rabbis claimed the right to declare the acts of the Sanhedrin unconstitutional—not in accordance with the Torah. The Pharisaic teachers were private persons. Their opinion about the constitutionality of the acts of the Sanhedrin might have been no more important than the opinion of any private person today about the acts of Congress. The Pharisaic rabbis held no office. They were officials neither of the city nor even of the Synagogue. The word rabbi merely meant head master or doctor. But the Pharisees were the recognized heads of the Synagogue.

The true social life of the people was centred about their synagogue. There they gathered for worship. There was their house of study, and the centre for all thought and discussion. The people honored the Temple. They visited it on festivals, and sent gifts upon occasions of exceptional good fortune. But their true, everyday religion and everyday patriotism was nourished by the Synagogue. The priests were rulers of the Temple, but the Pharisees ruled the Synagogue, and the Synagogue ruled the people. The Sadducean Sanhedrin might pass laws, but they had to be Pharisaic laws if they were to receive public obedience.

DISSATISFIED WITH PRESENT-HOPE FOR IDEAL FUTURE

We saw that the Sadducees believed they were living in their golden age. The Pharisees, as men of the schoolroom and the synagogue, were far from the field of battle and from thoughts of military glory. They were little impressed with the blood which the house of the Hasmoneans was shedding. They saw in it no golden age, for their dream was of an era of peace when spears would be beaten into plowshares, as the prophets had foretold.

When the king, fresh from battle, attired himself in the garments of the high priest, and stood before the people as the official head of their religion, the leading Pharisees regarded it as profanity. They pictured the first high priest of their nation a man of peace, pursuing peace, and bringing men nearer to God. Their warrior high priests were far from such an ideal. The king of peace was yet to come.

The Pharisees sharing more closely the struggles of the poor, tried to bring them consolation.[1] They taught the poor people to bear their lot in this life in the hope of a better state after death. There would be another life after the earthly existence is passed. The wicked would be punished, and the righteous would enjoy eternal bliss. In the end of days, the dead would come to life again when the king, the Messiah, ruled the world.

SUMMARY

We shall now summarize briefly the position of the Pharisees, recalling also what we told about them in connection with the Sadducees. As the educated men of

---

[1] comfort, cheer

the nation and its teachers, they considered themselves best fitted to interpret the Torah. In opposition to the Sadducean priests, they were a peace-loving party, and opposed a high priest who was also a soldier. They were anti-Hellenistic and anti-foreign. They were ready to change the law in the interest of the common people, and were milder than the Sadducees in the administration of justice. Finally they taught the belief of a life after death, when the righteous would live in eternal happiness.

Clashes Between Sadducees and Pharisees

The struggle between the Sadducees and Pharisees was not one of words alone. On several occasions bloody fighting took place. The first outbreak occurred during the rule of John Hyrcanus, the successor of Simon the Maccabee. Simon, like his brothers, was a man of the people and did not assume princely airs. During the greater part of his reign, John Hyrcanus followed the example of his father.

But almost fifty years passed. New generations of Jews yearly celebrated the victory of the Maccabees. Children grew accustomed to Maccabean princes; they knew of no others. The Hasmonean priests probably intermarried with the family of Zadok, the ancient family of high priests, thus joining themselves to the former aristocracy. Together they formed the party of the Sadducees, which in Hebrew is pronounced *"Zedukim"* and is believed to mean the descendants of the House of Zadok.

JOHN HYRCANUS BECOMES SADDUCEE

The aristocratic party was naturally anxious to win the king over to its side. To the very last years of his life king John Hyrcanus must have struggled between retaining the love of his common subjects and joining the court party. In the end the Sadducees won the king over.

The story is told that once at a banquet an insolent [1] Pharisee insulted the king. The king appealed to the Pharisees to punish the offender. The Pharisaic court, which tended to be mild in its sentences, ordered the penalty of flogging. According to their views it was no worse offense to slander the king than to slander a private citizen. The king, instigated by his courtiers, accused the Pharisees of siding with the offender. He declared himself a Sadducee, and ordered a persecution of all leading Pharisees. It seems that for a number of years the great Pharisaic teachers were in hiding, and the study of the Torah was seriously interrupted.

CIVIL WAR

The next two kings, Aristobulus I and Alexander Yannai, were Sadducees. Had it not been for their foreign mercenaries, it would have been doubtful whether they could have retained their power. Aristobulus reigned but one year. Alexander had several clashes with his subjects who were mostly followers of the Pharisees. It is told that once during the Succoth fes-

---

[1] insulting, fresh

A PROCESSION WITH CITRONS IN THE SYNAGOGUE   © *Funk and Wagnalls*

Still observed in Orthodox synagogues on the first seven days of Succoth except the Sabbath.

tivities, while the king was officiating as high priest in the Temple, the people threw their *esrogim* (citrons) at him. The king, on his side, ordered his soldiers to make reprisals.[1] A short time thereafter, the king waged a campaign against Arabia, but was unsuccessful. Upon his return he found his own capital barred against him and his subjects in revolt. The king's bitter opponents demanded his death as the sole condition of surrender. They even invited the king of Syria, the ancient foe of their people, to assist them against the Hasmonean ruler. For almost six years the city held out against its king, but this last act of inviting the Syrians robbed the rebels of the sympathy of their own people. A large part of the city defenders deserted to the king, whereupon Alexander Yannia entered the city and ordered a general massacre of all Pharisee leaders.

PHARISEES IN POWER

For a number of years the Pharisees were outlawed again. But the king knew that his own reign was not successful, nor would any reign be, unless it had the support of the common people. Legend tells that he advised his queen before his death, to make peace with the Pharisees. The queen, Alexandra Salome, heeded his advice most earnestly.

Queen Alexandra Salome was a staunch Pharisee. Upon her ascension to the throne, the Sadducee officials were replaced by Pharisees, and Sadducean law was

---

[1] to get even with the people

replaced by Pharisaic law. The leading Sadducean generals were sent to garrison distant fortresses, away from the active management of affairs. A Pharisee became head of the Sanhedrin. Already we mentioned the educational reforms of Simeon b. Shetah, famous Pharisee, and brother of the queen.

The reign of Queen Alexandra was the turning point in the struggle between the Sadducees and Pharisees. The Sadducean generals later returned to power. A Sadducean high priest headed the Sanhedrin. But thereafter, there were always some leading scholars to be found among the Sanhedrin, whose opinions were greatly respected. Thereafter, too, in important matters, the Sanhedrin followed the Pharisaic opinion in spite of their own opposite inclinations.

The Essenes

After having read the story of the Sadducees and the Pharisees, it might be well to glance at a third group in the Jewish state of our period. We could not include this group in the former discussion because this party did not care to control the government. It did not desire to rule, nor did it trouble itself as to who did. This party, instead, wished to flee the strife and confusion of practical affairs. It preferred to go off to a quiet corner where it might live in peace, and serve its God without giving a thought to the state and its politics.

This party was called the Essenes. What the name means is unknown. The Essenes were a secret society with its own creed and ritual [1] which its members were sworn not to reveal to the outside world. The aims of the society were to enable its members to escape the struggles of the world by giving up those things over which men usually fight. The Essenes owned no personal goods. They were a communistic group. This means that whatever property they had, was turned into the common treasury, and they received from it what they needed for their livelihood.

THEIR IDEAL OF A PURE LIFE

The Essenes generally took no wives and reared no families. Thus they avoided the jealousies over women and anxiety for wealth, which heads of families are apt to feel. They forbade all luxuries, for the same reason. Their meals were frugal, and they had but two meals a day; their garments were of coarse material, and they were worn threadbare. The Essenes did not permit themselves the use of oils for anointing their bodies. They owned no slaves, every man being expected to do his own share of honest labor toward the support of the community.

In their concern for purity the Essenes far outstripped the Pharisees. At the least suspicion of impurity, at the touch of any person who was not an Essene, they bathed their entire bodies. The Essenes were up with the sun to say their prayers, and bathed in the cold morning waters. Their garments were

---

[1] a method of performing ceremonies

white, the symbol of purity. The food they ate was prepared by priests, for they considered their meals a sacred religious duty. Needless to mention, they prayed before and after their meals, and they observed the Sabbath much more strictly than did the Pharisees.

The Essenes avoided certain occupations because they considered them in conflict with their principles. They refrained from trading, which they believed dishonest. They refused to engage in the manufacture of weapons or of other harmful substances. The majority of the Essenes lived together as farmers in their main settlements around En-gedi. Some of them were also craftsmen who offered their services in village and city. Their honest workmanship was generally recognized and greatly desired.

The Essene could live poorly but freely, for he had none of the fears which hound the poor man. In case of illness or old age his community provided for him. If he travelled to another city, the Essene elders arranged for his comfort. He might even give charity from the public fund except that in the case of his own relatives, he had to ask the permission of the elders.

THEIR RELATION TO OTHER PARTIES

We can see, of course, that the Essenes were interested only in the righteousness of their own members, and shared little in the life of the nation. The Pharisees laughed at their constant baths. The Sadducees excluded them from the Temple because the Essenes were against all animal sacrifice, except those directly commanded in the Torah.

Since the Essenes did not raise families they could not transmit their beliefs to future generations. The Essenes will continue for a while in our story, and little by little they will disappear.

SUPPLEMENTARY WORK

MAP EXERCISES

1. On an outline map of Palestine locate Judea, Samaria, Galilee, Gilead and Edom. In each section, write the name of one important agricultural product which was raised there in Hasmonean days.
2. On an outline map show with colored crayons how the Maccabean state grew from the days of Jonathan to the time of Alexandra Salome.
3. On an outline map of Israel name important seacoast cities.

QUESTIONS FOR DISCUSSION AND DEBATE

1. Because several million persons lived in Palestine two thousand years ago, can we be certain that as many could live comfortably there to-day?
2. To-day we believe in the separation of church and state. How may the experience of our ancestors as discussed in this section help us toward this question?
3. Do you or do you not admire the Essenes? Why?
4. Do you believe it wise to "make a fence around the Torah," as the Pharisees advised?
5. If you had lived in Hasmonean times, would you have joined any of the three parties? If you would have joined one of the parties, which would it have been? If you would not have joined any, what are your reasons?
6. How much of Jewish education do you think every American Jewish boy or girl should have?
7. Which of our acts to-day would we call religious habits of life? Have we enough such habits, too few or too many?

8. What is the history of the Negev? What promise does it hold out for Israel's future? What lessons can Israel learn from the Hasmonean state?
9. To-day, when so few people really believe in idols, is there still any distinction in Jewish monotheism?

ADDITIONAL PROJECTS

1. Dramatize a council of war in the camp of John Hyrcanus. The question for consideration is whether or not the king should force the Samaritans to accept the Jewish religion.
2. Let your class be a village of farmers who have just heard that a compulsory education law is being considered by the government. The farmers will express themselves in favor and against the proposed law.
3. Make a products map of modern Palestine.
4. Draw up a list of agricultural products that you would advise modern Palestinian settlers to cultivate. In drawing up the list consider the question of possible markets for the products.
5. Imagine that you have been asked to prepare seals for the three Jewish parties, the Sadducees, the Pharisees and the Essenes. Draw designs which you think would be appropriate symbols for each party.

ADDITIONAL READINGS
FOR TEACHERS

Schürer, *op. cit.*, Part I, vol. I, pp. 234–312, Part II, vol. I, pp. 149–206, Part II, vol. II, pp. 10–52, 53–88, 190–218.

Margolis and Marx, *op. cit.*, pp. 151–161.

Josephus, *op. cit.*, Bk. XIII, chaps. viii–xvi, Bk. XVIII, chap. 1.

Bevan, *op. cit.*, pp. 111–131.

Riggs, *op. cit.*, pp. 97–131.

Graetz, *op. cit.*, II, pp. 1–56.

Bailey and Kent, *op. cit.*, pp. 321–326.

FOR PUPILS

Meyers, *op. cit.,* I, pp. 28–30, 37–93.
Harris, *Thousand Years,* pp. 77–89.
Dubnow, *op. cit.,* II, pp. 55–72.
Magnus, *op. cit.,* pp. 25–33.

SECTION IV

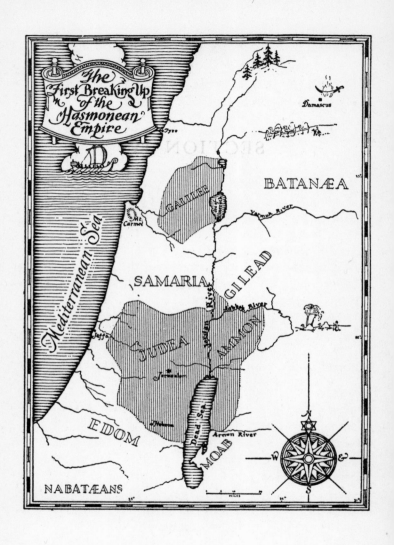

The First Breaking Up of the Hasmonean Empire

Mediterranean Sea

Damascus

BATANÆA

Tyre

GALILEE

Mt. Carmel

Yarmuk River

SAMARIA

GILEAD

Jabbok River

Jaffa

Jordan River

JUDEA

AMMON

Jerusalem

Dead Sea

Hebron

Arnon River

EDOM

MOAB

NABATÆANS

MILES

WHY THE JEWISH STATE DID NOT LAST

1

THE PROBLEM

BARELY seventy years passed before the preciously gained freedom of the Hasmonean state was lost. Seventy years is a long time in the life of a person, but it is a very brief existence for a state. The second independent Jewish state was very short lived.

We wonder why our ancestors could not keep their independence. Were they incapable of governing themselves? Were they so unpatriotic, had they so little love of country, that within less than a hundred years they surrendered their freedom?

TROUBLES AT COURT CAUSED DOWNFALL OF STATE

We turn to the story of the period. We read that after Queen Alexandra Salome died, she left the government to her older son, Hyrcanus II. During her life, Hyrcanus had acted as high priest. The office of high priest was generally held by the kings, but the queen, a woman, could not hold such an office. After her death, it was expected that the high priest would become king. Hyrcanus had the support of the Pharisees and the majority of the people.

Hyrcanus unfortunately did not possess the qualities necessary for a ruler. His younger brother, Aristobulus II, did possess them very strongly. The Sadducean nobles, the generals, and a large part of the army, preferred the younger brother, Aristobulus, for his superior ability as well as for the fact that he was member of their party. A civil war broke out which proved fatal to the nation.

Judea a Sufferer in World Calamity

We should answer our question, then, that possibly the Jews did not know how to govern themselves, if after the death of one ruler a civil war was needed to settle who was to be the next king. Yet we do not understand our history if we do not first pause to consider all the other happenings in the surrounding world. Events were taking place at that time which are strange to us living in a peaceful country under orderly conditions.

You have noticed that persons who are usually pleasant and well-mannered often act quite rudely and disagreeably under influence of rage or excitement. In like manner, there are times when the whole world, or a large part of it, is excited, and behaves strangely.

A large part of Europe and Asia is living through such a period now (1955). The fear of Communist Russia hangs like a pall over Europe, and the fear of Communist China paralyzes the nations of Asia. Everywhere men are unhappy and preparing for war. Indeed a large part of the world has long been engaged in what is called "the cold war" and fearing a "hot war."

During World War II Russia seized all the small nations within her reach. Communist China aims to follow suit. The small nations all over the world live in fear.

The world during the last century of the common era was living under such conditions. There had been endless wars, and people were forever changing masters. It mattered little who ruled. There were no nations. There was little patriotism or love of country.

Rome Upsets Peace of World

Rome was the mistress of Europe. The entire basin of the Mediterranean, and northward as far as Rome could force its way, was part of the Roman Empire. But Rome itself, that great state which had begun as a republic, was at this period the plaything of its generals. Elections were still held at Rome, and there was a senate which supposedly ruled. But a successful general with his legions could frighten the senate and the elected tribunes and consuls into doing his desire. Rome, capital of the world, was ruled by its army.

The common people were kept satisfied by the distribution of free bread and free shows; the soldiers were satisfied by high pay—and the entire world had to pay the bill. All the wealth which was squandered at Rome came from the provinces. The government of the provinces was generally awarded as a gift to retired generals or ex-consuls who held office for but a brief time, giving way in a few years to new favorites. The only interest of these officials in their posts was to extort large sums in taxes from their subjects. Most of the tax money they kept for themselves, after paying their soldiers and sending a share to Rome. The poor peasant in Iberia (Spain), or in Gaul (France), had to support Rome, her armies, and her generals.

PEASANTS JOIN MERCENARIES

It hardly repaid the ordinary peasant to till the soil. Wars and raids multiplied the number of slaves endlessly. Peasants could neither afford the high taxes, nor did they care to compete with slaves. Small farms were given up, and large landowners cultivated them with slave labor. For the average man there was a much more attractive occupation—fighting in the army.

The army was not usually a national army, such as we have today. Each general raised his army. Private persons raised armies by contracting to provide a certain number of soldiers. They had armies for rent.

The armies had to be rented out, otherwise they were too expensive to keep, and they might start mischief. A man who, today, has a shoe factory, must use it to make shoes; if the factory is idle, he loses money. Likewise, a person who had an army for rent had to use it, or he lost money. If no one wanted his men, they became highwaymen, waylaying travellers or caravans on the road. In time of war they stole food from the surrounding lands, whether friendly or hostile.

Rome itself maintained a tremendous army. The barbarians from all conquered lands were drafted into it. Each general was anxious to increase his force, often for fear of attack by a fellow general.

Hasmonean State Born in This War-Torn World

In such a world of soldiers, our ancestors tried to maintain a separate, independent government. We should have liked to think of our forefathers as being better than the rest of their world. We must bear in mind, however, that it is too difficult for any one nation to be reasonable in an upset world. A large part of our people was indeed different. The educated classes of our nation would have been satisfied with more peace and with less conquest. But its rulers wished to be like other rulers, and the common people could always be aroused for a war.

Let us repeat again what we noticed before. New nations have the example of existing governments before them. They fashion their government after those of the peoples about them. The Judean state had bad examples to follow. Around it there were constant civil wars. Royal brothers, sons, cousins, or merely generals, were raising armies to establish themselves in power. It was customary to invite foreign armies to settle internal disputes. You may recall from a previous section how Jonathan with a Jewish army suppressed a rebellion in Antioch.

Besides foreign armies there was an additional source of civil war in another class of hirelings, Greek councillors, courtiers, flatterers, military advisers; all to be had for money. These adventurers floated about, seeking employment. They often joined a weak and timid prince. They frightened him with imaginary plots. They induced him to wage war and thus gain power which they were planning to exercise for him.

In the midst of such a world, the Pharisaic teachers and their followers dreamed of a Kingdom of God, of a holy people which would bring peace to the world.

SMALL STATES COULD NOT LAST

The age was not one in which small nations could flourish. There were practically no nations at all. Few peoples of any consequence retained independence. On one side of the world was Rome, corrupt,[1] and divided in factions, but too large to be overcome. In the east, lay the great domain of the Parthians. All other nations within their reach were soon to become part of one of these empires.

The independent state of our ancestors did not last, because no other state lasted. The quarrel over the throne was merely the immediate cause which made the nation an easy prey for foreign conquerors. What remains for us to see is what a struggle our ancestors made to retain their freedom. We shall return to the fateful civil wars between the Hasmonean brothers, and shall follow what happened as a result.

THE CIVIL WAR

During the last days of Queen Alexandra Salome, her son, Aristobulus, and the leading Sadducees were already plotting for the throne. The queen, who was a

---

[1] very bad

Pharisee, had tried to prevent the revolt. She had sent the leading Sadducean generals to garrison small fortresses far from the capital. But the queen was old and was unable to suppress the plots. Immediately at her death, the Sadducees set out to crown Aristobulus by force.

In a very brief time Aristobulus II defeated his brother and was master of the land. An agreement was reached between the two brothers on oath, in the Temple, that Aristobulus was to have the crown, and Hyrcanus was to remain high priest.

Had there been no outside interference, Hyrcanus would have remained happy in his priestly office, and Aristobulus on the field of battle. The nation, too, would have preferred that the two offices be separated. But here enter the courtiers, the ambitious buzzers, the carpet-baggers of the period. A man, called Antipater, from Edom, of a family of Jewish converts, saw an opportunity of rising to power at the cost of national independence. Antipater was a man of great governing ability. He knew that he could have little influence with Aristobulus, and therefore decided to become a friend of the high priest, Hyrcanus, whose confidence he won by flattery. Antipater persuaded Hyrcanus that his brother, Aristobulus, had robbed him of a throne which was rightly his. He assured him that he was a much abler ruler than his brother. Finally Antipater began to arouse fear in Hyrcanus. He hinted that Aristobulus was planning to murder him, and influenced the household of Hyrcanus to believe him. Soon Hyrcanus was so terrified that he agreed to flee the country for safety to the king of Arabia. The common people, who did not know what was happening within the royal palace, believed that the king had broken his pledge. The nation was again divided into two camps, and another civil war was in the air.

Now enters the next evil—foreign armies. Antipater secured a large Arabian army. The Arabs had many old scores to settle with the Hasmonean kings. In addition, the Arabs felt that placing a ruler on the throne of Judea would surely be a profitable enterprise. The Arabians were joined by a large section of the Jews, partisans of Hyrcanus. Jerusalem was besieged and fell into the hands of Antipater and Hyrcanus. Aristobulus fortified himself on the Temple mount, and the victorious army besieged him.

ROME BECOMES MISTRESS OF PALESTINE

The siege lasted a long time, and the followers of Aristobulus were beginning to suffer from hunger. Then happened the final misfortune. New forces appeared on the scene which settled matters in their own interests. Rome invaded Syria.

In olden days, when news travelled slowly, and the journey between Jerusalem and Rome was made across a dangerous sea, the Jews had vague notions of the Romans. They had heard of Rome as the Imperial City, the mistress of the world. Their ancestors in time of war, in the fight for their independence, had sent ambassadors to Rome. The Roman senate had received them kindly, had called them friends of the Roman people, and warned the surrounding kings not to make war on the "Friend of Rome."

The Roman armies were now marching eastward to the Euphrates. The famous general, Pompey, was conquering Asia Minor. His advance guard had reached Syria. Both brothers believed it would be to their advantage to present their case before Rome.

Jews Appeal to Rome

Accordingly, Aristobulus and Hyrcanus, prepared with rich gifts, set out to the Roman camp. The Roman general heard their stories and was impressed with Aristobulus, who proved the more eloquent. The Roman general decreed in Aristobulus' favor till the following year when Pompey himself should arrive.

POMPEY

The decision did not bring peace. Each party prepared to present its case before the great general himself, who was master of Rome at the time. Pompey arrived at last, and both brothers hastened before him. Each one brought a treasure of gold to help him decide fairly. Pompey accepted the gifts and asked the brothers to return later. He saw that Aristobulus was the more able, but for that reason the more dangerous to Rome.

A third embassy came before Pompey, representing the people, the Pharisees of the synagogue. The learned and peace-loving Jews were tired of this strife. They did not wish either brother to be chosen king. They did not want a king at all. They complained that the Hasmoneans, who were chosen to be merely heads of the Sanhedrin, had seized royal power and were ruling as monarchs. This party asked that the Jews be ruled by a high priest and a council of elders, as in days of old, under Persia.

The Jews being honorable, peace-loving scholars, imagined that the Romans, too, were as noble as themselves. They were soon to learn that Roman rule was far different from Persian. They had innocently walked into the den of lions.

Rome Takes Advantage of Jews' Dissension

Aristobulus was shrewd, and understood that Pompey was planning to seize Judea. Pompey was supposedly marching eastward, and Aristobulus hurried back home to gather a national army to oppose the Romans. Pompey, too, was watching Aristobulus. As soon as Pompey saw what Aristobulus was planning to do, he had him taken prisoner and demanded that he turn over the Judean fortresses to the Romans. Aristobulus at first refused, but when he saw that the meagre Judean armies were in no way prepared for the enormous forces of Pompey, Aristobulus was forced to agree.

The Romans sent a force to occupy Jerusalem. The

THE ROMAN STAN-
DARD BEARER

followers of Aristobulus decided to resist in spite of their king's surrender. But the Romans, with the aid of the Hyrcanians, easily entered the city. Then followed a massacre in which the Sadducean priests displayed superhuman bravery. They continued the Temple service in the midst of the carnage,[1] and when one priest was struck down, another peacefully resumed his duties.

Antipater had the greatest difficulty in persuading his new allies to put an end to their bloodshed.

Judea Loses Independence

When the Romans satisfied themselves with enough booty and prisoners of war, they withdrew from Jerusalem. Aristobulus and his sons were taken prisoners to Rome, to be displayed in Pompey's triumphal march. Hyrcanus was to be head of the Jews. But Pompey was ready to satisfy the Pharisaic delegation. Hyrcanus was not made king. He was merely appointed high priest and head of the Sanhedrin. But the Sanhedrin itself was stripped of much of its power. The land was no longer an independent kingdom; it might not coin

[1] slaughter, killing

its own money nor make war. It was subject to the will of Rome. The real ruler was now Antipater, the friend of Rome.

Nor was this all that the land suffered. Pompey decided to weaken Judea. It was too large a kingdom to trust to remain friendly. Accordingly he detached from Judea the portions shown on the map (page 184), the Decapolis (the ten Greek cities east of the Jordan), and the seaport cities which were so important in the newly developing commerce. Samaria, too, was taken away from Jewish dominion in order to separate Judea from Galilee. In addition, he imposed the heavy Roman taxes for the support of the armies of the east.

Thus began the downfall of the Jewish state. The end had not yet come, though it was already in sight.

THE HASMONEANS ATTEMPT TO RETURN
(56–55; 40–37 B.C.E.)

The oppressive Roman taxes and the rule of the Idumean, Antipater, made all classes of Jews feel what a sad choice they had made. The Roman victory over Judea served more to arouse than to subdue the people. Only a leader was needed to begin a rebellion. Such leaders did appear from the family of the deposed Hasmoneans. The first was Alexander, a son of Aristobulus, who fled Rome and was hailed by the patriots of Judea as their savior. The uprising was suppressed with great bloodshed and thousands of Judeans were sent to the Roman slave markets. Hardly had the

Romans celebrated their victory, when Aristobulus himself escaped from Rome and raised the banner of revolt anew. Large numbers joined him, but the Roman forces were too numerous. Aristobulus was recaptured and sent back to Rome. Thousands more died, and thousands of new Jewish slaves were distributed throughout the world.

Before the pain of the last defeat was quite forgotten, a new Roman outrage aroused a fresh rebellion. A Roman general, Crassus, one of the three rulers of Rome, on his way toward the Euphrates, entered Jerusalem and robbed the sacred Temple. Great treasures of gold had been gathered at the Temple; the offerings of Jews from all lands. The greedy Romans had dared to enter the Holy of Holies where the high priest alone came in but once a year. When news arrived, therefore, that Crassus had been killed in war, the Jews took it as a sign from God that He was displeased with the Romans. There was a new war with more losses and added embitterment.

Julius Cæsar Brings Momentary Hope

For a moment a ray of hope was kindled. At Rome, Julius Cæsar was waging war against Pompey. Cæsar was victorious, and was preparing to establish his authority over the whole Empire. Anxious to gain the support of Pompey's enemies, Cæsar empowered Aristobulus and his son to regain their throne. But the enemies of Aristobulus were active even at Rome. Aristobulus was poisoned at Rome, and his son was way-

laid and killed on the journey back to Judea. In the
meantime, Antipater made haste to win the favor of
Cæsar as he had previously ingratiated [1] himself with
Pompey. Cæsar reestablished him in power, and even
gave him an official title, and made him a citizen of
Rome. Cæsar was kindly disposed to the Jews. He restored all the provinces to them which Pompey had
taken away. But the rule of Rome remained, with Antipater to enforce it.

Hope Fades As Antipater Extends Power

Antipater now appointed his sons to the most important offices of the land. His son, Phasael, was made
chief tax collector over Judea, and another son, Herod,
was appointed the military governor of the North
(Galilee). The Jews saw with deep anger how the government was being taken out of their own hands and
given to strangers. They were enslaved in their own
land. They despised Antipater and his sons. They still
hoped that some Hasmonean prince would return to
occupy the throne.

A new happening heightened the fury of the Jews.
In the mountains and caves of Galilee there had collected bands of desperate men who would not submit
to the yoke of Rome. In their mountain fastnesses they
organized guerilla bands to fight the Romans, to way-
lay them, and to drive terror into their midst.

The best known leader of this movement was Hezekiah, the Galilean. He was to the common people a

---

[1] made himself liked

Robin Hood, a man who despised the rulers and loved his fellow folk. Herod sent an expedition against Hezekiah, captured him and his men, and had them executed without even a trial.

HEROD DEFIES SANHEDRIN

There was such a cry of protest raised in the land that king Hyrcanus was forced to call Herod to trial before the Sanhedrin. The people demanded that Herod be sentenced to death, but the king was afraid of the wrath of the Romans. Herod did appear before the high court, but his appearance was most unusual. Accused persons were supposed to come before the Sanhedrin clad in black and without any weapons.

Courtesy Dr. Nelson Glueck

ENTRANCE TO NATURAL CAVES IN WILDERNESS OF JUDEA

One of the many caves in Judea and Galilee which served as dwellings for the poor and hiding places for outlaws.

But Herod came armed and gaily attired, as for a celebration, followed by an armed guard. The members of the Sanhedrin were frightened, and no one dared raise his voice against Herod. Finally an aged rabbi arose and denounced the cowardice of his fellow members. He reminded them that if this day they feared Herod more than God, God would not readily pardon them for their perversion of His Law. He reminded them further that if the prisoner were set free he would return some day to demand their heads.

The Sanhedrin regained courage. It was prepared to pronounce the death sentence. But the king was not. He begged that the sentence be delayed for a day. During the night he helped Herod escape. As the aged rabbi had foretold, Herod did return with an army against Jerusalem, bent on punishing the Sanhedrin. Only the entreaties of his father succeeded in persuading Herod to return to Galilee.

Hasmoneans' Last Stand

You can well understand how a proud people would regard this affront to its government. The time seemed opportune for an uprising. There were revolutions in Rome. Julius Cæsar had been killed, and new generals were fighting to rule the world. The Judeans used this opportunity for another rebellion. Antipater was poisoned. A new Hasmonean had appeared. Antigonus, a second son of Aristobulus, secured the aid of the Parthians, the only powerful enemies of Rome. With their assistance, he invaded Judea and wrested it from the Romans. Antigonus destroyed what he could of the house of Antipater. The armies of Herod were routed. Herod himself escaped, hated and pursued by many of his own soldiers.

Judea was free of Rome, but the Parthians were hardly easier masters. Yet the people endured them more gladly. They thought they had at least succeeded in throwing off the yoke of the Idumean, Antipater.

But Herod had not given up the struggle. He was bent on claiming the authority of his father. If the people hated him and drove him out, he might still rule without their consent. He would force them to accept him as their king. Herod went to Rome. Before the Roman senate he complained of his sufferings at the hands of the Judeans because of his friendship for Rome. Rome naturally did not relish Parthian occupation of one of its provinces. The senate appointed Herod king of the Jews, and the armies were ordered to restore him to power.

Herod returned to Judea with the Roman commission. Wealthy Samaritans advanced him large sums of money with which to hire armies. Herod's hirelings and his Roman auxiliaries made war upon the Jews. It was a desperate war and lasted for almost a year. Every city, every wall, was contested and bitterly defended. At last the Jews lost against Rome. Antigonus was killed. Jerusalem was almost destroyed. Herod triumphed and became king of the Jews. Judea was now considered a friendly kingdom, an ally of Rome. Herod was a king friendly to Rome, but the despised conqueror and oppressor of his own subjects.

THE REIGN OF HEROD (37–4 B.C.E.)

Did the Jewish state come to an end under Herod? The Romans would have said that they left the Jewish state undisturbed. Did they not appoint a Jewish king with full power to rule, practically free of all interference from Rome?

The Jews were too tired to object any longer. The ten years of civil and other wars left the nation exhausted. A foreigner had seized the throne. He had soldiers to back him. There was no use resisting, but they did not recognize his government as lawful. The Essenes and Pharisees refused to take an oath of allegiance; the Sadducees and the common people surrendered for fear.

For Herod could never be a true Jewish king any more than a foreign born citizen might be president of the United States. He was a usurper who, to hide his illegality, pretended to be descended of an ancient family which had returned from Babylon with Ezra. It may have pleased Herod to invent the story. The people knew it was a falsehood. He married a Hasmonean princess, the daughter of Hyrcanus, but his treatment of her did not gain him any added love of his subjects.

Herod's Barbarity—Official Murders

Even if Herod had been a rightful ruler, his first acts upon coming to the throne could not but disgust the nation. More savage barbarity would not have been expected even of a Roman general, or a Gallic chieftain. Herod's first concern was to destroy all possible claimants or opponents to his throne. There began a massacre of the leading nobles, whose property was eagerly confiscated by the king. Herod thus found a way of destroying his enemies and of amassing wealth at the same time. It was dangerous to be rich or influential during Herod's reign.

As might be expected, the remaining Hasmoneans were the first to fall under the suspicion of Herod. The most important Hasmonean survivor was the old king Hyrcanus, who had been taken captive by the Parthians during their occupation of Judea. The Jews of Babylon would not permit a former high priest to be a prisoner. They ransomed the old king and gave him great honor in their midst. Another important Hasmonean was Herod's own wife, Mariamne, whom Herod had married to ally himself with the reigning house. With her there had also remained her mother and her brother. Herod laid plots to remove them, one after another.

The first to be murdered was Mariamne's brother, a lad of seventeen. Herod appointed him high priest, and within the year had him drowned. Next he turned his attention to the aged Hyrcanus in Babylon. He persuaded the old king to return to Judea, promised him royal honors, and in due time had him executed as a plotter. Herod's own wife, whom he dearly loved, yet also feared, was next to mount the scaffold, and a short time thereafter her mother, too, shared her fate. Then followed friends and sympathizers of the murdered queen. Thus Herod inaugurated his kingship over the Jewish people.

Among the very first to feel the vengeance of the new ruler were the members of the Sanhedrin. As the aged sage had foretold at the time of Herod's trial, so it happened. Only a few of the most famous leaders were spared; the others were put to death. Herod hoped to appease [1] the people by favoring the Pharisees in selecting the new Sanhedrin. But he deprived the Sanhedrin of all political power. That body could occupy itself only with strictly religious matters. The people thus did not feel grateful to Herod.

Sale of High-Priesthood

Besides the murders, there were many other acts of Herod which offended the nation. Herod abused the holiest office of the high-priesthood by selecting unknown and undeserving priests for the office. Usually they paid a large sum for the privilege, and the result was that every few years Herod chose a new high priest. The nation had no respect for these servile priests. How much the condition of the priesthood must have reminded them of Jason and Menelaus!

Foreign Advisers and Courtiers

Herod knew that the people hated him. He feared to entrust any important offices to men of his own na-

---

[1] quiet, satisfy

tion. A supposedly Jewish king secured Thracians, Germans, and Gauls, for his army. Foreign, barbarian officers ruled his people. His court was filled with Greek advisers who flattered him and called him the Great Herod.

How strangely the patriotic Jews must have felt! A supposedly Jewish kingdom was ruled by a half Jew, supported by foreign mercenaries, officered with foreign officers, practicing the most un-Jewish practices. Were the king and his court strangers, or were the people strange in their own land?

Outward Prosperity and Building Activity

There was peace and seeming prosperity during the greater part of Herod's reign. Herod had ascended the throne in 37 B.C.E. During the first few years he was busy suppressing rebellions and fighting off his enemies, the Nabatean Arabs. He was having some difficulties with Rome too. Cleopatra, the beautiful Queen of Egypt who was sharing the rule of Mark Antony, disliked Herod and deprived him of many provinces. But after five years, Antony was defeated by Octavian, who became the first Roman emperor under the name of Augustus Caesar. Herod made haste to gain the favor of the new conquerer. Augustus was so won by Herod that he confirmed his throne and added large territories to his kingdom. Augustus saw that Herod would be a faithful slave of Rome, for without Roman aid he would be open to many enemies on all sides. Particularly valuable was the gift of the seacoast cities which, after Julius Caesar's grant, had again been taken away from Judea. Herod could now control the large Palestinian sea trade. He could collect import and export taxes.

REMAINS OF SAMARIAN TEMPLE

HEROD A GREAT BUILDER

Herod was a man of great energy and ability. He was anxious to do great things, to become famous. He would have longed to make wars and extend his territories, to seek glory on the field of battle. But the Romans forbade that. Their dependent kings could not wage war without their consent. The vassal kingdom might become too powerful for the safety of Rome. Herod turned his energies, therefore, to the arts of peace, to building cities, palaces, fortresses, and heathen temples, in all parts of his land. Throughout all corners of the land he built fortifications named after himself, or after members of his family. His most famous work of building was the city of Caesarea in honor of the emperor. Herod wished to make this city the leading seaport. To protect large ships against the stormy sea and the regularity of the coast, he built a breakwater far out into the sea so that large ships could safely discharge their cargoes. In the middle of the city of Caesarea, on a hill, stood a palace for the emperor Augustus Caesar whom the heathen citizens of the Roman Empire worshipped as a god. Herod could not establish the worship of the emperor on Jewish territory. He therefore built temples to the emperor in those cities where many Greeks lived. Caesarea was soon to become the rival of Jerusalem.

BUILDS AMPHITHEATRES AND ARENAS

Jerusalem, too, was adorned with new and beautiful structures. Yet most of them were hardly such as a

pious Jew might find delight in. There was an amphitheatre for races and games which were celebrated in
honor of the emperor. Such games were a form of
heathen worship, which to the pious Jew seemed idola-
try. Herod built a theatre for boxing matches and
gladiatorial combats between men, or between men and
beasts. Either two men fought each other to death, or
a man fought a wild beast till the man or the beast
perished. That was Rome's sport, the enjoyment of the
Roman citizen. We can understand how our ancestors,
a God-fearing people, refusing even to eat blood,
looked upon all this unnecessary shedding of blood.

But Herod continued building. He was anxious to
be considered great among the non-Jews. The Romans
were mocking the Jews. They were calling them super-

© U. and U.

REMAINS OF A STREET OF COLUMNS IN ANCIENT SAMARIA

stitious. The Greeks thought the Jews uncivilized. Herod would prove to them that the Jews were civilized, that they were more Greek than the Greeks. Far and wide Herod's bounty spread. Not only Palestine, but heathen lands as well, shared his generosity. Antioch received rows of columns to beautify its streets. The Island of Rhodes was presented with a temple. Even distant Athens was not overlooked.

Jews Overtaxed

Where did all the money come from for this very great generosity? Perhaps the distant cities which re-

© U. and U.

KING SOLOMON'S STABLES
Really the underground buildings of Herod's temple.

ceived his gifts did not know, nor did Herod wish them to know. But his own subjects knew. Every year, taxes were growing more burdensome. The new harbors did encourage trade, and the enormous imports and exports did yield large revenue, but the income was not enough, and taxes spread to every article of property—to every business transaction in the market place. The poor buyer had to bear the cost of the king's extravagances. A new tax on homes, never before collected in Jerusalem, was introduced, adding to the burdens of the common people. All these taxes were in addition to the priestly gifts, the several tithes, and local taxes for school organization and village needs. Poor Galileans went without bread that Ashkelon might have baths and Damascus might have temples.

Herod Tries to Win Favor of Jewish Subjects

Herod tried hard to win the love of his own subjects. On numerous occasions he tried to show them kindnesses. Several times during his reign there were famines in the land, and Herod spent large sums of his own money helping the poor. He excused a large part of the taxes, and he is even said to have sold some of his own gold and silver vessels to aid the poor.

Herod suppressed banditry and made the roads safe for commerce. Safe roads were a most important condition for prosperity. The region west of the Sea of Chinnereth had been a marshy waste where outlawry flourished. Herod converted the region into a well-settled, fertile, agricultural district. He brought colonists, war-like Jews from Babylon, and Greeks from other countries. These were excused from taxes, and they formed a powerful border guard.

HEROD'S TEMPLE

Herod's best known achievement for his people was his re-building of the Temple. The old Temple was being surrounded with palaces and tall fortifications. The five hundred year old Temple looked small and poor alongside the new buildings. Herod offered to rebuild the Temple on a fitting scale. At first the people objected because they feared that the old structure would be destroyed and no new one would be substi-

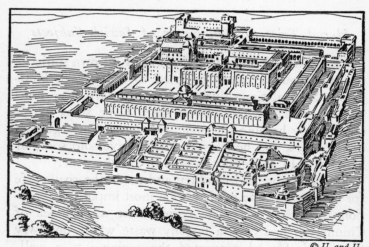

© U. and U.

THE TEMPLE OF HEROD
Reproduction of the famous Shick model at Jerusalem.

tuted. The people did not trust Herod. They also objected to the opening of the holy courts of the Temple to the laity.[1] The king satisfied the people on both of these points. He had a thousand priests trained in the work of building, so that none but priests would be employed at the Temple. The building work was carried on so that the regular activities of the Temple were not interfered with. The old Temple was replaced part by part. The main work of the building lasted eight years, though the adjoining courts, pillars and defense walls occupied several score of years more. The Temple was reputed to be the most beautiful building in Palestine. The rabbis used to say that one who had not seen the Temple of Herod never saw a really beautiful structure.

Oppression Outweighs Favors

But the few favors which the nation received could not atone for all the misery which the Jews suffered under Herod. Taxes outstripped prosperity, and heathen abominations robbed whatever joy there might have been in the new Temple. Even this one greatest act of kindness to his people, his Temple, was spoiled for them by Herod's placing a golden eagle over the front gate. The eagle was the emblem of Rome, but the Jews were very severe against any graven image. An eagle over the Temple was like a slave collar around their necks.

The general result of Herod's reign was deep, gen-

---

[1] those who were not priests

eral dissatisfaction. In a monarchy where the king rules through his army, there is no other way to secure change than through bloodshed and revolution. Herod feared a revolution. He lived in dread of plots against his life. He filled the land with his spies. He forbade any sort of gatherings. Suspects were daily hurried away from their homes to distant dungeons, never to be heard of again.

Herod's Last Days

Herod seemed to live so very long. Everybody was anxious for his death, and Herod knew it. As he grew old, he became more savage and more afraid. His household was full of plots and suspicions. Herod had many wives and many sons. The sons began to accuse one another in the presence of their father. They succeeded in setting Herod against his two sons by his murdered wife, Mariamne, the Hasmonean. Several times Herod imprisoned them, but spared them through the interference of friends. At last the king's suspicions were so inflamed that he ordered both his sons to be executed. Close upon the executions of his sons came the discovery by Herod of new plots against his life by another of his sons. Herod being ill, two rabbis thought the opportunity ripe for vengeance against the golden eagle. With a group of their students they tore the eagle from the Temple gates. This was an occasion for a new massacre. Five days before his death Herod succeeded in ordering another of his sons killed.

Herod is said to have directed in his will that on the

day of his death all the leading Jews were to be gathered at Jericho and executed. He feared that the nation would celebrate at the news of his death, and he wished to make the day a general occasion for mourning. Whether the story is true or not, the execution was not carried out. The nation did rejoice. Herod was dead, and now it expected relief. Herod could not pass his kingship to his children. Rome would have to choose the successor, and the nation thought it might influence Rome to make a just choice.

SUMMARY

We have our answer now to the question why the second Jewish state did not last. Our ancestors had the misfortune to live through a period in the history of the world when small independent nations were at the mercy of organized marauders. It was a world of force, of paid armies, of generals who ruled, of republics which crumbled. Our ancestors did what they could to defend themselves. They were overpowered. We shall yet see how they refused to give up, how they rose again and again till the nation was drenched in blood. But that is a later story.

2

THE GOVERNMENT OF THE RABBIS

WE have seen why the Jewish state could not last. The long period of unrest which swept all of the ancient world wrought its havoc with our ancestors as with all other peoples small and large. The State was to continue for a century, under a form of self-government. We saw, however, how little self-government the Jews really enjoyed under Herod.

But while the Jewish state was passing away, the Jewish nation did not. Other peoples accepted not only the rule of the conquerors, but also their religion and customs. The Jewish people insisted on its own mode of life in spite of its conquerors. We saw in an earlier chapter how the Jews lived largely under the rule of the rabbis and the synagogue. When the Jewish state was completely destroyed, the Jews were prepared to be governed by the rabbinical colleges.

The authority of the rabbis had been exercised since the organization of the Pharisees. We might perhaps say more truly that it continued since the days of Ezra. But the rabbinic government gained new power and importance in the days of Herod. This was due to two reasons. The first we might readily guess. The Jewish nation hated Herod more than it did any other king. Herod oppressed them and denied them any share in the government. The Jews would naturally turn to their more democratic synagogue leaders.

The second reason for the growing importance of the rabbis was the presence of Hillel, a teacher and leader, the greatest since Ezra. Two factors united to make Hillel outstanding. He possessed great learning combined with powers of leadership. But he is even more famed for his unusual character, for his great love of his fellow men, for his kindliness, patience, humility— all the virtues which we picture in a holy man. Herod and Hillel are the two opposites in every element of personality.

Our story would be incomplete if we did not tell of the life of this great man. The life of Hillel is not directly connected with the answer to our question of why the Jewish state did not last. It will help, however, to answer the question of how the Jews were able to continue as a people without their state.

The Story of Hillel

Strangely, we know very little about the life of this famous man. Aside from Hillel's teachings, all other records of his life are mostly legendary. Yet from the legends we can select bits of fact that tell us of his early life. We gather that he was a Babylonian and that he probably began as a teacher of the Torah in Babylon. Hillel's brother, a well-to-do business man, urged Hillel to enter his business. When Hillel refused, his brother supported him while he devoted himself to study.

The schools of Babylon and their teachers were not advanced enough for Hillel, so he decided to go to Palestine to continue his studies there. Hillel arrived at Jerusalem, poor and penniless. He set about earning his livelihood at some unskilled occupation. He became a wood cutter and earned about a half-denar a day (about ten cents). Hillel was obliged to pay half of this sum for tuition, and he lived as well as he could on the remainder. Thus, like so many poor Jewish lads today, Hillel was working his way through school.

Window at Central Jewish Institute, N.Y.C.

HILLEL INSTRUCTING THE
PROSELYTE
"What is hateful unto thee do not
unto thy neighbor."

The legend tells that one day, Hillel had not succeeded in earning the fee for admission into the school. Anxious not to miss the lecture and unable to enter through the door, Hillel climbed to the roof of the schoolhouse and tried to listen as best he could through a roof-window. It was winter and a snow was falling. Hillel, intent upon catching every word, did not notice that he was being snowed under. Someone in the room suddenly saw the figure in the window. They brought Hillel down and restored his frozen limbs with difficulty. Thereafter Hillel was permitted to enter, without payment.

Whether or not the story is true, we can see that Hillel must have loved learning indeed, if such a story could be told of him. We do know, though, that it took many years before Hillel's leadership was recognized. Hillel was a foreigner in Judea and had to make his way against prejudice. We do not know what official post Hillel held. He might have been a member of the Sanhedrin, a chief justice, or perhaps merely the head of his famous college, Beth Hillel (The House of Hillel). In later days, people felt that such a man must surely have been the head of the nation, and they thought of him as Nasi (prince or president). Hillel, however, was the uncrowned prince. He was accepted as the leader of the nation because of his true inner worth.

The Teachings of Hillel

We shall know Hillel best by understanding his sayings and the little stories connected with them. Each of the sayings or groups of them, will show us Hillel's character.

HILLEL AS THE LOVER OF HIS FELLOW MEN

Perhaps the most famous of the teachings of Hillel is the one known as the "Golden Rule." A gentile, it is told, once came before Shammai, another great rabbi always spoken of together with Hillel. The gentile said to Shammai, "I shall accept your religion if I can learn it in as short a time as I can stand on one foot." Shammai, who was severe by nature, drove the would-be convert away, because he believed that the gentile was mocking him. The man then came before Hillel. Hillel was not at all displeased. On the contrary he was quite prepared to do as the heathen wished. "Our entire religion," said Hillel, "consists merely of this one sentence, *'What is hateful unto you, do not unto your neighbor'*—the rest of the Torah is merely an explanation of how one can live such a life." It is said that the mocking heathen actually became converted.

Another of the best known sayings of Hillel, found in the "Ethics of the Fathers," reads—*"Be ye of the disciples of Aaron, lovers of peace, pursuers of peace, loving your fel-low men and bringing them near unto the To-rah"* (to the knowledge of a good life). In a world of armies and conquests, under the rule of a Herod, it was indeed a strange teaching that Hillel was advancing.

© *Funk and Wagnalls*

ENTRANCE TO A TOMB BELIEVED TO BE THAT OF HILLEL

Another evidence of Hillel's great love for his fellow men is shown in this saying, *"Do not trust yourself till the day of your death,"* and *"Do not pass judgment on your neighbor till you have completely placed yourself in his situation."*

Hillel taught unselfishness in the duties that a man owes to all his fellow men. *"Do not separate yourself from your community,"* teaches Hillel. *"If I do not provide for myself,"* says Hillel in another place, *"who will provide for me? But if I care for myself only, then what am I?"* No person can exist by his own efforts alone. The share which each man performs in his daily work enables all other men to live. We are only now recognizing the great importance of our duties to the community.

HILLEL THE LOVER OF THE TORAH

Perhaps the most easily recognized teachings of Hillel are those stressing the great importance of learning. Have you heard the man who says, "I have never been to school and I am none the worse for it?" "It is not true," says Hillel. *"A boorish man can not be fearful of sin nor can an ignorant man be pious."* Some religions teach that if a man believes in God he has fulfilled all his religious obligations. Not so the Jewish religion. A man must study and know the will of God, to live a good life. A person must continue to study all his life. One must never offer the excuse that he is too busy. *"Do not say I shall study when I have free time, because you may never find the free time,"* says Hillel.

Learning must be for pure and holy purposes. A person must not use his learning or his degrees for personal glorification. Hillel himself was known by no title or degree. He was merely Hillel. *"If anyone uses his Torah as a crown,"* says Hillel, *"he will pass away."*

Beth Hillel and Beth Shammai

This is the story of Hillel, the kind, the wise, the student, and teacher. We have already mentioned that he was the head of a school which continued for a long time after his death as the House of Hillel. The story would not be complete if a word were not said about the other great rabbi, head of an opposing school, whose name was Shammai, and who is always thought of together with Hillel.

Shammai was a severe, irritable man, easy to take offense, and not to be trifled with. He was a great teacher, also, and many students clung to him. His motto was *"Say little and do much."* He was a very just man and was anxious to enforce the law strictly, whereas Hillel was lenient. Though the House of Shammai and the House of Hillel usually disagreed, the decision accepted by other rabbis was generally that of Beth Hillel.

The government of the House of Herod lasted another brief period. The government of the followers of Hillel replaced it. The Jews had lived for more than a thousand years in their own land. The government of the rabbis was to endure twice as long in strange lands.

SUPPLEMENTARY WORK

MAP EXERCISES

1. On an outline map fill in the main political divisions of Herod's kingdom, at its height of power.
2. On an outline map, color the Roman Empire at the time of Augustus, and make a circle around Judea.
3. Color the districts taken away from Judea by Pompey.

QUESTIONS FOR DISCUSSION AND DEBATE

1. Was it wiser for the Jews to choose a ruler who had the rightful claim to the office or the one who had the greater ability?
2. Would you have preferred peace under Herod to war under the Hasmoneans?
3. Were the Jews unreasonable in objecting to the golden eagle over the Temple?
4. Many persons claim that the rule of one able man is preferable to that of a republic, the officials of which are often inefficient. Would the experience of our ancestors under Herod offer any help in answering this question?

ADDITIONAL PROJECTS

1. Imagine that you are an orator and that your class is a street crowd shortly before the ascension of Herod to the throne. You have just heard of the escape of Aristobulus and you are urging your fellow Judeans to rally about him. You will recite all the troubles which have overtaken Judea since the rise of Antipater and you will re-

223

count the glories of Hasmonean days.

2. You are an Athenian writer and the news has reached you that King Herod of Judea has presented a Temple to your city. Write a short article about it which is to be read to the Assembly of Athens.

3. Draw a poster announcing a performance in Herod's theater at Jerusalem.

4. Select one or several mottoes for your home or class from the sayings of Hillel. Engrave them properly on posters.

ADDITIONAL READINGS
FOR TEACHERS

Schürer, *op. cit.,* Part I, vol. I, pp. 313–325, 371–399, 416–467.

Graetz, *op. cit.,* II, pp. 57–117.

Margolis and Marx, *op. cit.,* pp. 161–176.

Josephus, *op. cit.,* Bk. XIV, chaps. i–ix, xi–xvi, **Bk. XV, i–xi,** Bk. XVI, i, iii–v, vii–xi, Bk. XVII, i–viii.

Bevan, *op. cit.,* pp. 132–162.

Bailey and Kent, *op. cit.,* pp. 327–344.

Riggs, *op. cit.,* pp. 131–139, 154–214.

FOR PUPILS

Harris, *Thousand Years,* pp. 91–115.

Meyers, *op. cit.,* I, pp. 30–36.

Dubnow, *op. cit.,* II, pp. 73–94, 97–103.

Magnus, *op. cit.,* pp. 33–47.

SECTION V

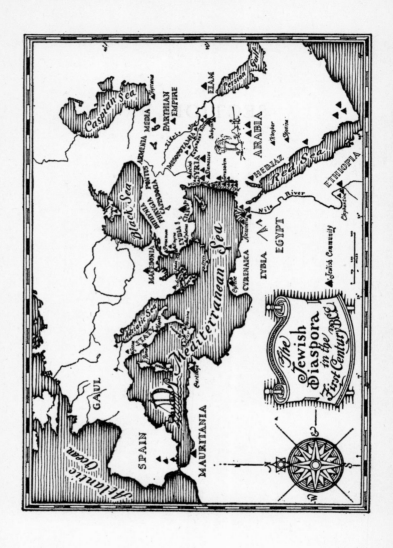

HOW DID THE JEWISH DIASPORA OR
SCATTERING COME ABOUT?

THE PROBLEM

HAVE you ever read a story of which you knew the end? Were you not then interested in finding out what made the story end as it did?

You know the end of the story which this book tells. You are the end. Your family, living in this land, your friends and their families living today in all countries of the world, are the end of this story. But how did the end happen? How did it come about that you were born in the United States—that your father or some earlier ancestor was born in Germany, or Russia, or Poland, or Austria, or some other European country? If we could trace our ancestors back far enough we should find them in Palestine. Why are we not living in Palestine? When did our ancestors first leave Palestine?

It would take too long to tell the entire story. You recall from an earlier section that in the century following the death of Alexander, the Jews were already leaving Palestine to settle in new lands. These migrations continued for over two thousand years, to our own day. It will require perhaps another whole book to tell of the last two thousand years.

But the period of the Second Temple marked the first wide spread of Jews over the world, particularly in Europe. The Jews were becoming a migrant people. Large numbers of them were settling among strange nations, under strange laws, and amidst new languages. If we are at all curious to follow the story of the two thousand years' journey from Palestine to America, it might be well for us to pause for a while at the early stopping places. We may wonder how the Jews found life with other nations. Were conditions then in any way what an immigrant finds today? Were the Jews accepted as citizens in their new homes? Did they fit into the business and agricultural life of the community? Did they experience anti-Semitism as the Jews do today in many countries? Was their freedom of worship interfered with? In general, were they regarded as what we would call "desirable immigrants" or undesirable ones? Let us answer these and like questions.

It may surprise you to learn that toward the close of Herod's reign, there were more Jews outside of Palestine than in it. We have no exact figures of how many Jews there were in the world at the time, but it is estimated that over 2,000,000 Jews lived in Palestine, and about 3,000,000 Jews lived in the Diaspora (the dispersion-lands outside of Palestine). Jews were to be found in all countries of importance.

WHERE DID THE JEWS OF THE DIASPORA LIVE?

Study this map and you will see how widely the Jewish people was already spread at this time. From

Persia in the east, going westward, one could find Jews in all lands, as remote [1] as Spain and even Gaul (modern France). It was already said at that time that there was no civilized land where Jews did not live. The small triangles on the map indicate great numbers gathered in one place. Outside of Judea proper, many Jews were found in Egypt, Babylon, Syria, Cyrenaica, Rome, and the Greek Islands. Egypt alone possessed half as many Jews as the mother land Judea. Over one million Jews found their homes in the land of the Nile. Alexandria, the capital of commerce as well as of learning, counted more than two fifths of its population Jewish. It is told that the main synagogue at Alexandria was so enormous that directions to the worshippers had to be signaled with a cloth.

Babylon, too, was the home of as many Jews as Egypt. There were whole sections settled almost entirely by Jews. Notice the town of Nahardea, which was probably the centre of settlement of the Babylonian Jews. Another such central district was the town of Nezivin.

Egypt

Some of the settlements had a long history and some were very new. The oldest of these was that of Egypt where many Jews had settled even before the destruction of the first Temple. During the entire period of the first Jewish kingdom, there was always a large Jewish party friendly to Egypt. When Nebuchadnezzar

---

[1] distant

captured Jerusalem, (586 B.C.E.) many Jews fled to Egypt to escape Babylonian exile. The prophet Jeremiah is said to have been among that number.

The Jewish settlers spread southward along the Nile as far as Elephantine (see it on the map). This is a distance of about 700 or 800 miles from the coast. They built a temple there, and looked upon Egypt as their home. The Egyptian government found the Jews very valuable in defending the land.

The Jewish Egyptian settlement grew very considerably in the days of Alexander the Great, who brought Jews to Alexandria. His successors in Egypt, too, largely increased the number of Jews. They brought many Jewish captives from their Judean wars, who were later freed, and thus increased the Jewish population. The period of the Maccabean wars brought another large stream of Jews to Egypt. Among the last immigrants were many distinguished priests who built a new Temple in Egypt. Thereafter a steady stream of migration to Egypt continued.

Babylon

You undoubtedly know how there happened to be Jews in Babylon. First, the ten tribes of Israel had been taken captive to Assyria. Later, Judah was led in two captivities to Babylon. We recall from our first section that conditions in Babylon made it possible for the Jews to prosper there. The later conquerors of Babylon carried their national capital eastward. Many Jews were attracted there, to Susa and to Seleucia, by the promise of special privileges. Later, in Greek times, the provinces of the west, in Asia Minor, became the most important. Antioch and Damascus became the large centres of population, and Babylonian Jews were drawn toward them.

The Babylonian Jews especially, were given lands in new and dangerous places, because of their military fame. They were assigned the guarding of the frontiers in return for which they received land and freedom from taxation.

INSCRIPTIONS FROM ROMAN-JEWISH TOMBSTONES

The tombs are of a somewhat later period. Notice the Jewish symbols used —the shofar, Menorah, palm, the word Shalom, also the lions, possibly the ark and oil jugs.

Rome

We do not know when or how the Jews came to Rome. The Jews probably began their relations with Rome during the days of Judas the Maccabee, when they had sent an embassy to seek a Roman alliance. The later Hasmoneans renewed their friend-

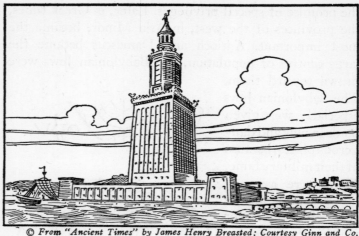

© *From "Ancient Times" by James Henry Breasted; Courtesy Ginn and Co.*

THE LIGHTHOUSE AT PHAROS, THE PORT OF ALEXANDRIA
Rising over thirty stories in height. An example of the skill and prosperity of Alexandria.

ship with Rome. It is possible that many Jews began to settle in Rome since the first Judean embassy. Their numbers were greatly increased by the Jewish captives brought to Rome by Pompey. Many were undoubtedly ransomed by their fellow Jews of Rome, and others purchased their own liberty. As freed slaves they were entitled to the citizenship of Rome.

Greek Cities

Colonies of Jews could be found in all the Greek cities along the Mediterranean, and on all the important islands. The Jews settled there mostly for trading purposes. We recall that in the days of the Hasmoneans, Jews were turning to trade and to the sea. The long troubled periods of war led many to seek new homes along the sea paths toward Greek cities and islands.

Northern Coast of Africa

Jewish settlements followed the trade routes westward along the African shores of the Mediterranean as on the European coast. Cyrenaica, west of Egypt, already had a large Jewish population. A small but steady stream was gradually pushing westward. In the next few centuries very important Jewish communities dotted the entire North African coast.

WHAT SORT OF IMMIGRANTS WERE THE JEWS?

In general, our ancestors were successful settlers in all their new homes. They accustomed themselves rapidly to the new lands. They entered all the occupations which the land afforded. In Alexandria we find Jews among the leading merchants, skilled artisans, and able farmers. They rose to important government posts and to high military command. In the armies of Egypt, at one time, Jewish generals were the commanders-in-chief. We mentioned already that in Babylon Jewish soldiers were numerous and very powerful. A story is told of two Jewish brothers, weavers, who gathered about themselves a band of followers and established themselves as an independent tribe. For twenty-five years they held the Parthian armies in check, till a

quarrel within the tribe broke their power. The Jews
on the Greek islands left us little record of their life.
We can gather, however, that they must have been quite
prosperous, because of the large gifts which they sent
to the Temple, and which so frequently aroused the
greed of the Roman officials. At Rome, too, the Jews
soon became an important part of the city. We find
them established about the Campus Martius, which
was Rome's leading business section. Like all other citizens of Rome they received their public share of grain
and oil. Whenever grain was distributed on Saturday
the government saw to it that the Jews received their
share on Sunday. The Roman government went to the
extent of providing the Jews with kosher oil. From
one of the speeches of Cicero, the famous Roman orator, we gather, that the Jews were influential even in
Roman law courts.

ACTIVE CITIZENS IN NEW LANDS

We saw that our ancestors were successful immigrants in the lands where they settled. We shall now
ask another question which is of importance to us today. As American Jews, we wonder how far we should
act together with our American fellow citizens, and to
what extent we should engage in activities which are
separately Jewish. Shall we have Jewish schools at all,
shall we maintain Jewish charitable societies, Jewish
social centres, etc.?

While the experience of our ancestors will not answer
all our questions it will at least help us to see how our

people acted in times past, for they too, faced the problem. How far were they to be one with the citizens of their adopted country? How far were they to remain apart?

The Jews of the first century B.C.E. were an intimate part of the lands in which they lived. Almost everywhere they had rights of citizenship, which they used fully. In western lands, mostly in the Greek countries, the city corresponded to our state. It was the unit of a great empire which might be compared with our federal government. Most of the city states were governed by a local council. Jews voted, and held memberships in the city councils, and were chosen for public offices. They took part in the wars of the land, and provided their full share of soldiers and officers.

In places where there was no city assembly, the Jews had their own organization which contributed its share in taxes and in public management. Thus in Alexandria, where there was no city representative body, the Jews were organized under their own head, called the Ethnarch. In Babylon, where the Jews formed a very old settlement, they were organized under their own Exilarch.[1]

Participate in Culture

The Jews participated not only in the government, but also in the social and cultural life of their cities. Not alone did the Jews speak the language of the

---

[1] ruler of the Jews in captivity

land, they also studied its literature and mastered its
education. The Jews familiarized themselves with all
of Greek knowledge which they believed valuable.

So completely did the Jews adapt themselves to
their new lands that they modified some very important habits of their own because of their new
surroundings. They became so accustomed to their new
languages that they began to use them in their worship and in the education of their children. They even
went as far as to translate their sacred writings into
Greek. The translation of the Bible into a foreign
tongue was an event of great importance in the history of our people and possibly in the history of the
entire world.

STORY OF THE BIBLE TRANSLATION

We might perhaps turn from our subject for a moment to tell the story of the first Bible Translation.
Today, when the Bible has been translated into over
eight hundred dialects,[1] we take it for granted that
the Bible belongs to all peoples and tongues. At that
time, however, many Jews seriously debated whether
the Holy Writings might be written in any other than
the holy tongue. So important was the occasion that
a legend grew up about it. The legend tells that
Ptolemy Philopator, one of the rulers of Egypt, was
collecting the famous Alexandrian library. When he
had gathered all the Greek writings he was told by
his librarian that here was yet one great book which

---

[1] forms of language

should be secured for his library, the Jewish Bible. Since the Bible was written in Hebrew, Ptolemy became anxious to possess a Greek translation of it. Accordingly, he sent a delegation to the Jewish high priest, with gifts, and asked that seventy wise men be sent him to translate the Jewish writings. Upon their arrival in Egypt, the seventy wise men were set on a quiet island, each man by himself. The scholars worked seventy days, during which time each man

Courtesy Dr. David Philipson

AMERICAN BIBLE TRANSLATORS

The American translation of the Bible is known as the Holy Scriptures. It was prepared by the above scholars and issued by the Jewish Publication Society of America. It was copyrighted 1917.

translated the entire Bible. When the copies were compared, all the seventy translations agreed word for word.

The entire Bible could hardly have been translated in seventy days, nor could seventy different translations agree in all details. But it may well be that the translation was made by seventy people, on which account it is called the Septuagint, from the Greek word for seventy. In Hebrew it is called the "Translation of the Seventy." The completion of the translation was the occasion of a great celebration for the Jews of Egypt. Now they would be able to read their religious books in a language that was familiar to them.

The Temple of Onias

The Jews of Egypt felt so much at home in that country that they even built a Temple, after the model of the Temple at Jerusalem. It happened that a group of important priests came to Egypt. Onias IV, a son of the high priest, Onias III, who was deposed by Jason, was hoping that the victories of Judas would return him to office. When, finally, Alcimus was appointed to the high priesthood, Onias saw that there was no more hope for him, and he left for Egypt. The king of Egypt, Ptolemy Philometor, was impressed with Onias and gave him permission to build a Temple at Leontopolis.[1] All the taxes of the district were given over toward the maintenance of the Temple. The new

---

[1] About 200 miles south of Alexandria

Temple was thus an official part of the government of Egypt.

The rabbis at Jerusalem, disturbed by the translation of the Bible into Greek, felt uneasy over this new step which might interfere with the Egyptian Jews' loyalty to the Temple at Jerusalem. The Jews of Egypt, however, rejoiced greatly in that they were establishing themselves more firmly in the new land.

What Were the Jewish Activities of Diaspora Jews?

We have used the example of the Jews of Egypt, but the same attempt to become part of their new home was true of all the Jewish colonies.

The Jews did not, however, forget that they had many duties to perform as Jews, and that there were many activities which they could not share with their Greek fellow citizens. The Jews could not participate in Greek religious observances, which often were connected with the affairs of government.[1] They did not take part in the sacrifices or in the public festivals, just as we Jews do not celebrate holidays like Christmas or Easter. Even entering as contestants in public athletic meets was looked upon with disfavor. Only Jews who were not strictly observant participated in the chariot races, boxing matches, and even in gladiatorial combats. Pious Jews did not favor these practices.

---

[1] To this day religion is connected with government in most European lands. The United States and France are quite exceptional in that church and state are separate.

Religious Worship

Everywhere, the Jews maintained their own worship in their own synagogues. Then, as now, the Synagogue Centre was the place for all Jewish social life. The children's school, classes for adults, and all festivities were held there. The Jews housed all these undertakings in their house of worship because they wished them all to be carried on in the spirit of their religion. The Jews were anxious that their religion continue pure in their new homes, for they felt that they had a finer faith than their neighbors.

Education and Literature

Because they were so greatly concerned over their religion, the Diaspora Jews educated their children in their own schools. Above any other education, the children were taught the holy writings. Then, as today, most children studied their Bible in the original Hebrew. The few who failed to master Hebrew had to study it in the language of the land.

Although the Jews spoke and wrote in Greek, they did not imitate the subjects of Greek writings, but interested themselves in Jewish questions. We have many books on Jewish themes which were written in Greek, or if written in Hebrew were preserved most popularly in Greek. The best known of such collections are the Apocrypha and the Pseudepigrapha. Most of the Apocrypha was written in Palestine, and carried to foreign lands in translations. In the Apocrypha are the Books of the Maccabees, from which we get our Chanukah story. Perhaps the most famous of the Apocryphal books is the one called Ecclesiasticus, or the Wisdom of Ben Sira. It is a book like the Book of Proverbs in the Bible. But the Apocrypha also contains much that was written outside of Palestine, mainly in Egypt. There are legends which add to some of the Bible stories. Thus there are additional stories of Ezra, Esther, Daniel, and of the three men in the fiery furnace.

The Jews, away from their land, would naturally write their interesting stories in a language which the young could understand.

Many kinds of books and writings have come down to us from the Greek-speaking Jews. They wrote their history, aiming to show the Greeks their distinguished ancestry. They wrote historical poems and even dramas. Their best known writings are those dealing with philosophy. The most famous of the Alexandrian Jewish philosophers whose name we might well remember is Philo. The Jews who studied the work of famous Greek philosophers were anxious to show that their

© *Funk and Wagnalls*

GREEK INSCRIPTION ON ROMAN-JEWISH TOMBS

The early Jews of Rome apparently spoke Greek.

own great men were also interested in all the questions which troubled the Greeks. The Jewish philosophers thus tried to prove that all the wisdom of the Greeks is already found in the Jewish Bible.

The Greek-speaking Jews had another reason for their writings. They were proud of their nation's thoughts and were anxious to spread them among non-Jews. Many and many a successful book was written to explain Judaism to the heathen. Many Greeks in all parts of the world were becoming seriously interested in the Jewish religion.

Self-Government

The Jews had their schools and synagogues, their teachers and writers, as we have today. But the Jews were more strongly organized in the various lands of their dispersion [1] than are the Jews of the United States. Outwardly they were organized as we are now. In the early stages of settlement each synagogue was an independent unit. In lands where the Jews had lived for a longer time, the synagogues were united. Thus, in Egypt there was a national Jewish organization. The same was true of Babylon. In Rome, it seems, each synagogue was an independent organization.[2]

But the Jewish organization interested itself in a wider range of problems than our synagogue organi-

[1] where they were scattered
[2] It might be interesting for you to compare the progress of organization among the various religious bodies in the United States.

zations do. In many respects the Jews in the Diaspora were self-governing. Rabbis tried cases of law, and it was considered highly improper for a Jew to bring his law suit before a heathen court. The official governments recognized and enforced the decisions of Jewish courts. In some cities the Jews had power even to sentence their criminals to death. In sections of the city wholly inhabited by Jews, the Jewish councils appointed all police officers, inspectors, and town criers, as well as synagogue officials.

We have now answered our two questions. We saw how the Jews shared the life of the land of their adoption. They spoke its language, they engaged in its commerce, they helped in its defense, they studied its writings, and, particularly in Egypt, added richly to the literature of the land. But since national and religious life were really inseparable, the Jews lived in their own communities and enjoyed a very large measure of self-government.

What Held the Jews of the Diaspora Together?

And now we should probably ask one more question— Did the scattered Jews in all the corners of the world have any means of keeping together? Was there any bond of brotherhood which helped scattered Israel to feel as one people?

We might ask in like manner whether there is anything today which unites all Jews. There are several bonds which unite us, though not all Jews are held by the same bond. Some Jews are held together by the bond of religion. Others feel even more strongly the need to help our suffering fellow-Jews in all parts of the world. Still others are united by the desire to re-build Palestine. In all cases, the Jews collect money—their voluntary tax toward the greater needs of the Jewish people.

Religion Fatherland

During Second Temple days, the bonds of union were of a somewhat different nature. The state was still existent in Palestine. Regardless of conditions there, it was still the home-land. And it was the thought of the home-land which held the loyalty of the Jews the world over.

But it was not merely the thought of the father-land. It was an unusual fatherland—the holy land, the seat of the sacred Temple, the only place where God could rightfully be worshipped. The Jews of Egypt had built a Temple of their own, yet never for a moment did they place their Temple on an equality with the one at Jerusalem.

TEMPLE TAX AND PILGRIMAGE

There were two main duties which every Jew, wherever he lived, was eager to perform toward the Temple. The first was the payment of the Temple tax which consisted of two shekels of silver. In addition to the regular tax, many sent gifts of money in place of sacrifices which they might otherwise have offered at Jerusalem. So large were the sums thus collected that often an escort of several thousand soldiers guarded the bearers of the money to the Temple.

The second duty toward the Temple was to visit it at the festivals. Each of the three festivals, Passover, Shabuoth, and Succoth, was the occasion of great pilgrimages to Jerusalem. At one time, it is told, there were over one million visitors in Jerusalem for the Passover feast. It was a grand reunion for Jews separated by months of travel over ocean or desert. Israel then felt its vastness and its might. It felt its worldwide brotherhood.

The Torah

There was another bond of union, perhaps even more important than the fatherland or the Temple, though not as evident. It was the bond of the Torah, the one religion by which all the communities lived. They all followed one law, and they all sought it from one source—the famous Pharisaic schools in Jerusalem, which served as the supreme court for Jewish religious law. Jerusalem was also the main university for the study of Jewish law. Eager scholars came from many lands to study the meaning of the Torah.

At this time the two famous schools, Beth Hillel and Beth Shammai, were the centers of learning. Hillel himself had been a Babylonian and had come to study in Palestine.

Social and Political Ties

Thus the Jewish people lived, far flung over the world, united mainly by their God, His law, and His Temple. There were, of course, other bonds, which would arise naturally. The great pilgrimages would also be excellent opportunity for trade, especially for trading with foreign lands. The foundations were already being laid for the Jewish interest in import and export trade. Throughout the early Middle Ages when Europe was steeped in darkness and barbarity, the Jews were the main agents of civilization. They brought to the rude barbarians the skill, the learning, and the refinements of a more civilized East.

Occasionally, the scattered Jewish communities secured benefits through Judea, their fatherland. Herod, who was well liked by the Romans, often pleaded in behalf of the Jews of various settlements, and was frequently successful. Thus Judea looked after its scattered sons, while the sons in their turn looked after the mother country.

WAS THERE ANY ANTI-SEMITISM?

Let us now ask our last question. Did the Jews then suffer from anti-Semitism as do our brothers today, in so many lands? Did they suffer persecutions or pogroms as Jews did even recently in many parts of eastern Europe, or were their lives secure as are ours in this land?

The answer, of course, must be that the condition

of the Jews depended on the country and on the nature of the times. When a land prospers and everyone is comfortable, anti-Semitism is not likely to break out. When, on the contrary, times are very hard, or when a nation suffers disaster, as in war, the nation is irritable and seeks some defenseless persons on whom to vent its anger. Anti-Jewish outbreaks have usually followed wars, general hard times, or revolutions.

Let us take Egypt as an example because we know most about it. For many years the land enjoyed peace and prosperity, and the Jews, too, lived peaceably and happily. There were always disputes between the Jews and the heathens. The Jews ridiculed idol worship, and the Greeks responded by making sport of the Jews. The Egyptian Greeks did not relish at all the stories in the Bible of how God plagued the Egyptians. They therefore invented stories of their own that the Jews were a band of lepers whom the Egyptians set to work in their mines, apart from other persons. The Jews in their turn wrote books to glorify their ancestors and their religion. Thus a struggle of writers went on which did slight actual harm.

Troublous Times Lead to Outbreaks

But as the Roman wars and conquests were bringing ruin to Egypt as to other lands, ill feeling began to grow more and more open. When there was enough work for everyone, there was no cause for quarrel. But when work grew scarce, the Greek merchant and writer saw the Jew taking what they considered their trade. Bitter spirit developed which led later to many serious outbreaks and massacres. With the Roman occupation of Egypt the difficulties of the Jews had begun, and the same was also largely true in other lands.

The Roman government was not at fault. Rome officially permitted the Jewish religion. It forbade interference with Jewish worship or with funds collected for the Temple. We noticed before how the Jews in Rome were treated as citizens, and received their share of corn and oil.

But Rome brought poverty to the provinces, and in lands of misery the Jews could not thrive. In the Syrian cities especially, the Jews were becoming more and more serious competitors of the Greeks. Wars had been going on in Syria ever since the days of Antiochus Epiphanes. There was very little peace and very great unrest. Bloody attacks were therefore quite frequent.

We should bear in mind, however, that the Jews, like all other men of their day, were trained in the use of arms. If there was fighting the Jews were not always on the defensive.

THE EASTERN JEWS

We have spoken chiefly about the Jews around the Mediterranean. We know very little of the Eastern Jews of this time. We might assume that since the Parthian empire was constantly on the defensive against Rome, it could not readily permit any internal dissension which would weaken it.

IN CONCLUSION

We have gathered a few glimpses of our ancestors not only in their home-land but also in their dispersion amongst the nations of the earth. Consciously or unconsciously we have been comparing that period with our life today. Perhaps the world two thousand years ago was not so different after all.

As we prepare to end the chapter a new thought occurs to us. We have heard it said that the Jews gave religion to the world. Did the world come to the Jews, or did the Jews go to the world? May not the Diaspora, the dispersion of Jews throughout the world, have had something to do with the spread of religion? We notice the date of the death of Herod, about 4 B.C.E. Are we not very close to the time when these religious changes happened? How did the Jews give religion to the world? This will be the problem of the following chapter.

SUPPLEMENTARY WORK

SOLVE THE FOLLOWING PROBLEMS

1. A messenger is sent from the school of Shammai in Jerusalem to enlist support for the school from the communities of the Diaspora. On an outline map, draw a line with arrow heads, (like this ⟩→⟩→⟩→⟩→⟩→⟩→⟩→⟩→⟩→) to show the route over which he would travel. Write on your map the names of all the countries which he would visit and the names of the cities where you think he would have to spend more than one day because of their large Jewish population.

2. A similar messenger is sent to-day by the Hebrew University at Jerusalem. Show in like manner the places which he would visit. Fill in the names of about fifteen cities throughout the world which you would advise him to visit. You will find help in solving this problem in the American Jewish Year Book.

3. Draw a bar graph to compare the Jewish population of Palestine during the Second Temple days, with its population to-day.

4. On an outline map of the world color in red the three or four countries which had the largest Jewish population at about the year 1 C.E. Color in blue the three countries which have the largest Jewish population to-day. Write the name of the country in each case, and under the name, in parentheses, write the language which the Jews of that land use or used: for example;

United States

(English)

If you are not certain of the language ask your teacher.

5. Are all Jewish communities prosperous to-day? Which are
   and which are not? Why are some large Jewish communities suffering great need at present?
6. In the days of the Second Temple, when the rights of Jews
   in any part of the Roman Empire were violated, the government of Judea would take up their complaint. To
   whom do persecuted Jews now turn in times of trouble,
   and how are they helped?
7. In what manner, and for what purposes, do Jews tax themselves to-day?
8. What is the main bond which holds us together as Jews
   to-day?
9. Since the Jewish people did not always speak Hebrew, why
   should we insist that every Jewish child study Hebrew?
10. Why did the Jews of America find it necessary to issue a
    special Jewish translation of the Bible in English?
11. Do you know of any books on Jewish themes written in
    English during the last twenty-five years? Name six
    authors and ten titles of books.

ADDITIONAL READINGS
FOR TEACHERS

Schürer, *op. cit.,* Part II, vol. II, pp. 220–327.
Graetz, *op. cit.,* I, pp. 503–519, II, pp. 135–137, 177–190,
   200–221.
Josephus, *op. cit.,* Bk. XII, chaps. ii, iii, Bk. XIII, iii, Bk.
   XIV, x, Bk. XVI, ii, vi, Bk. XVIII, ix.
Radin, *op. cit.,* chaps. vii, viii, xi–xvii, xix.
Riggs, *op. cit.,* pp. 72–79.

FOR PUPILS

Harris, *Thousand Years pp.* 67–71, 136–145.
Meyers, *op. cit.,* I, pp. 102–105.
Dubnow, *op. cit.,* II, pp. 50–52.
Magnus, *op. cit.,* pp. 12–14, 52–53.

SECTION VI

JERUSALEM—A STREET IN THE OLD CITY

HOW DID THE JEWS GIVE RELIGION TO THE WORLD?

The Problem

YOU must have heard it said—Rome gave the world laws, Greece gave it art, and the Jews gave it religion.[1] When did the Jews give religion to the world? We are very close to the year one. The Christian world counts that year as the birth-date of the founder of its religion. Jesus was a Jew. Apparently, therefore, somewhere at this time the Jews must have given religion to the world.

We, as Jews, are naturally curious to know how our small nation gave religion to such a large world. Why are we still such a small people? Why has the world been so unkind to us in return for what we gave it? The answer to these questions is a long and very interesting story which we shall proceed to tell.

Our Main Questions

Before setting out upon a long study, it is always well to think out what our study ought to tell us. We wish to find out how our ancestors gave religion to the world. Let us subdivide this question into several smaller ones. Let us ask—

---

[1] Christianity and Mohammedanism have sprung from Judaism.

255

1. Did the Jews in the Diaspora, who were scattered throughout the nations of the world, have any effect in spreading their religion?
2. Why did Christianity, an offshoot of Judaism, spread, and not the original Jewish religion?
3. Who was Jesus, the Jewish founder of the new religion, and how did he break with his own Jewish religion?
4. How did the new religion spread?

We shall begin with the answer to the first question.

DID THE JEWS IN THE DIASPORA SUCCEED IN SPREADING THEIR RELIGION?

There is no doubt that the Jews of the Diaspora had great influence in spreading their religion among the peoples with whom they lived. In Europe and in Asia, east and west, there are many proofs of the keen interest which the local population took in Judaism.

We know about the influence of the Jews on Rome. Almost all the famous writers, such as Cicero, Horace, and Juvenal, complain of Romans who join the Jews. The Roman writers, of course, regard Roman interest in Judaism as unpatriotic, just as we look down upon persons who desert their Jewish faith. The Roman writers tell mockingly how a man is drawn into the Jewish fold. He begins by frequenting Jewish synagogues to listen to the sermons. Soon you find him observing the Sabbath and the dietary laws. He may be too old to remake his own life, but he wishes his son to be a good Jew, and brings him up accordingly.

The Romans did not quite understand the nature of the Jewish worship. Their own god was Jupiter, and they called the Jewish God Jupiter Sabazios, the Sabbath-Jupiter. This shows us how well known the Sabbath was in Rome. There is much proof that a considerable part of the population of Rome observed the Jewish Sabbath.

Egypt, one of the three largest Jewish settlements in the world, had many converts. We learn that fact from the writings of Philo, the famous Jewish philosopher of Alexandria. The Jews of Egypt wrote many books to persuade gentiles to join them.

Judaism Spreads in the East

In the Greek-Syrian city of Damascus, it is reported that all the women attended the Jewish synagogues, since it was easier for women to accept Judaism than for the men. Many of their children must have been brought up in the Jewish faith.

Jewish merchants converted the entire kingdom of Adiabene in Arabia. First Queen Helena of Adiabene, and later her sons accepted Judaism. In time the whole people of Adiabene followed. The queen and her sons became very devout Jews. Queen Helena built a palace in Jerusalem, and during a year of famine she sent large gifts for the poor of Judea.

The queen also had her tomb built in Jerusalem and was buried there. The tomb is still to be seen today. By mistake it is called the tomb of David. During the Jewish revolt against Rome, King Munzab of

Adiabene fought in the Jewish army in defense of his religious fatherland.

Here is a map showing the journeys of Paul, the Christian Apostle. We shall tell more about him later. Here we need only point out that at all cities where Paul stopped and preached, he found large numbers of gentiles interested in listening to Jewish preachers. The ground was already prepared for Paul by the interest in Judaism, which had been spread by the Jews living in those cities.

But in the end, not Judaism, but a sect which broke from it, Christianity, succeeded in winning the gentile world. Why, we wonder, was Christianity more successful than Judaism?

WHY DID CHRISTIANITY PROVE ATTRACTIVE?

Christianity appealed to the gentiles more than Judaism. The gentiles were offered all the advantages of Judaism without any of its hardships.

Let us first understand why the gentiles were so eager and ready for a new religion. In those early days every man needed to have his own god just as children need parents. If a child has no parents, someone else must look after him. If a person of that period had no god he adopted some other person's. The belief was common at the time, not only among the ignorant, but even among the most educated, that the world was filled with ghosts and evil spirits. All illness and all misfortune were the work of these enemies of man. No person was safe unless he secured the pro-

tection of a spirit stronger and more powerful than the evil demons. Unless he was so protected, his crops would not grow, his ships might sink at sea, his house might burn, or he himself might become sick and die.

Each country was believed to have its own god. A man living in the land of his birth enjoyed the protection of his native god. But the Roman wars had uprooted men from their homes. Peasants from the farms were now in cities, engaged in new occupations, facing new dangers, and needing new protection.

The many conquered peoples could hardly learn to love the Roman gods who had brought all their misfortune upon them. They needed a new god, and they heard much about the powerful, mysterious gods of the east. Many were joining some form of eastern religion. The Egyptian gods drew many followers. The Persian and Chaldean worships attracted many. The Jewish religion, too, as we have seen, was in the field.

Appealed to Poor and Oppressed

The Jewish religion as taught by the Judeo-Christians appealed particularly to the large mass of poor and oppressed. The Jewish-Christian God was kind, loving, and forgiving. Strangely (so the gentiles thought), this God loved only the poor and the meek. He did not like the rich, the bold, and the haughty. One did not need to bring Him costly gifts. All that the Christian teacher asked was a belief in God and in Jesus, His son. God loved these poor peasants so much that he sent His only son to die for them as a

RĀ—THE SUN-GOD

One of the Eastern mysteries.

AMEN—FATHER OF THE GODS

Another of the Egyptian mystery gods.

pardon for their sins. Jesus, God's son, was stronger than all evil spirits. He would protect them from all harm in this life. After death, too, he would care for them. They would be taken into heaven, and would enjoy everlasting happiness.

ADAPTED TREASURES OF JUDAISM

The Christian teachers brought to their converts the treasures of Judaism. These new Christians considered themselves Jews. As such, they became the possessors of the greatest religious book, the Bible. The Bible taught "Thou shalt not steal . . . thou shalt not kill . . . a just weight and a just measure . . . and, thou shalt love thy neighbor as thyself." The Bible granted them rights which they had been denied all their lives. Very eagerly these poor and oppressed folk accepted the words of the Bible. They could readily feel that such a religion was a nobler one than the mysteries and tricks which were practiced by the idolatrous priests of other faiths.

The Christian teachers gained authority by their declarations that they had personally seen Jesus perform miracles and cures. Often, at the meetings of the new sect, some of the worshippers became strangely excited, and began to preach in an unnatural manner, and to "speak with tongues." They addressed gatherings, speaking for hours at a time, about God's coming Kingdom, without being conscious of what they were saying, or even that they were speaking at all. It seemed as though some outside spirit was speaking through their mouths. The worshippers regarded such unusual behavior as prophecy, and were further convinced of the truths of the new religion.

Why Christianity Gained over Judaism

The reasons given thus far explain why Christianity was able to gain so many converts over other eastern religions. Christianity was also able to gain over Judaism because it permitted many practices which Judaism did not.

Judaism was too hard for the average gentile, and Christianity was easy. Judaism was a religion which demanded not merely belief; it required acts which would bind the believer to the Jewish people. It insured the fulfillment of right conduct by enacting it into religious law. A man was not merely advised to cease work on the seventh day, the law punished him if he did work. Charity contributions for the poor were demanded as an official tax.

Judaism Demanded Change of Habits

Many additional difficulties faced the gentile who might desire to become a Jew. He had to be circumcised. He had to change all his food habits. He would have to deprive himself forever of his favorite dishes. It is small wonder, therefore, that many gentiles who may have sincerely tried to accept Judaism, could not make the necessary adjustments in their lives.

There was another demand made by the Jewish religion, which was difficult for gentiles to fulfill. A Jew, by religion, was also a member of the Jewish nation. The Jews believed that God would send them a heavenly ruler who would establish Israel above all other nations. The hopes of the Jew were always for his people, not for himself.

The gentiles were not interested in nations. They were concerned with saving themselves. Rome had destroyed nationality and patriotism, and Greek habits and culture had made little of local traditions. The cities contained men of all races and tribes. What could these care for a small land somewhere in Asia? Would it mean anything more to them than the exchange of one master for another?

Jews Maintained Ideal of a Holy Nation

Perhaps the main difficulty which prevented non-Jews from accepting Judaism was that the Jewish God could not be seen, nor even imagined in a picture. Most heathens could not understand an invisible God, nor could they be absolutely certain that He existed, since no one had seen Him.

The Jews had no objection to the non-Jews visiting their services, or observing some of their laws. They even had a special name for them. They called them *Gere Hashaar*—Strangers of the Gate. But the Jews would not alter their law to make it suit the needs of non-Jews. The Jews believed it their duty to be an example of a holy nation to the world. Any one who wished to join them might do so by rising to their standard. Although the Jews were eager to gain converts to their faith, they permitted no compromise. Christianity did not require circumcision, it did not forbid pork or other heathen foods, nor did it require the observance of any of the Jewish laws. Later we shall see why Christianity excused its members from the Jewish observances.

At this point we have probably been wondering how the Christian religion came about and how it became Christian and anti-Jewish. We all have heard of Jesus. We must be wondering where he fits into the story and what he had to do with the formation of Christianity.

How Did Christianity Arise and Why Did It Break Away from Judaism?

Christianity came about for two reasons. (1) It was the outcome of Jewish hopes for a Messiah. (2) It came about through the life, the teachings, and the death of Jesus of Nazareth who claimed to be the Messiah. Let us explain each reason in turn.

Bad Times Arouse Hope for a Messiah

After the death of Herod, the Jews lived through one of the most unhappy periods of their history. Their land was in the hands of cruel masters, and the nation was too weak to attempt any resistance.

The Jews believed themselves God's chosen and beloved people. They, of all nations, had recognized and worshipped the true God. To them alone did He entrust His sacred law. The Jews firmly believed that at some time in the future the whole world would recognize the truth of their teachings and would worship the God of Zion.

But why did God permit His people to be so mistreated in the meantime?

The answer which the Jews gave to themselves was that all their suffering was temporary. The various nations might enjoy their brief period of power, till Israel was sufficiently purified through suffering. When the measure of Israel's punishment was full, God would avenge His people. God would send them His own chosen ruler, the King-Messiah, a descendant of the house of David. The prophets described the King-Messiah and his rule. He would be the king of justice, the prince of peace. There would be no more evil in the world, no more wars of nation against nation. The whole world would be at peace, and all men would come to worship the God of Israel at Zion. The King-Messiah and the Jewish people would rule the world forever. There would be no more death, no more disease, no worry for worldly goods, no hatreds, and no jealousies. The Kingdom of God would be everlasting happiness.

The rabbis had warned the people that the suffering would have to be extreme, indeed, before the Messiah might be awaited. The whole world would be at war. There would also be civil strife within. "Children would rise against their own parents and servants against their masters."

JEWS BELIEVE DEPTH OF MISERY REACHED

The Jews of this period were certain that they had arrived at a stage where conditions could become no worse. They had passed through many trials and struggles. Thousands had lost their lives in the brief years between the last Hasmoneans and the ascent of Herod. The people had become destitute; farms were abandoned because of too high taxes; business was at a standstill. Persons of wealth feared for their life and property; men with opinions, who still cherished dreams of freedom, were hounded by spies. The Temple itself had not been spared. A supposedly Jewish king had set up an image over its gates, and two rabbis suffered the death of martyrs in the attempt to remove it.

Eagerly the nation had waited for Herod's death. From about 37 to 4 B.C.E., Herod held the power of life and death over the Jews. Finally he died. The nation's hopes rose. A new era would begin. How could they imagine that the new era would be even worse than the preceding one?

NEW POLITICAL UPRISING AFTER DEATH OF HEROD

The nation had been too exhausted with war when Herod ascended the throne. It had offered all the resistance it could in the last Hasmonean uprisings against Rome. But in thirty years a new generation had arisen. New young men were demanding their rights and were prepared to obtain them by force, if necessary, from Herod's successor.

Herod, at his death, divided his kingdom among three sons. The most important section, including Judea, Samaria, and the coast, fell to Archelaus. Herod's choice had to be approved by Rome, and before Archelaus left for Rome the people demanded of him that he grant them reforms. They asked that the taxes be lowered, particularly the sales' taxes that were imposed upon every article that was bought or sold. The cost of living had mounted beyond the means of the poor. The people also demanded that the murderers of the two rabbis be punished.

When the answer of Archelaus was not forthcoming, mobs began to threaten the government. Archelaus thereupon responded by calling out his army, and a massacre followed in Jerusalem. The nation then understood that there was merely another Herod on the throne.

This massacre was the beginning of a new series of oppressions by the Romans. While Archelaus was away in Rome to receive the emperor's approval of his office, riots occurred between visiting festival pilgrims and some Roman soldiers. In the affray, the Romans set fire to the Temple pillars, and in the confusion their general used the opportunity to rob the Temple treasury. At the news of the outrage to their religion the Jews rose in arms. Wherever there was a Roman garrison it was attacked and besieged.

But the Jews were not prepared for war against Rome. A large Roman army from Syria entered the land, relieved their besieged garrisons, and took its usual Roman revenge upon guilty and innocent alike.

RULE OF ARCHELAUS FOLLOWED BY
DIRECT ROMAN RULE

Archelaus returned after there was supposedly peace in the land. His subjects were quiet; now he might rule as he pleased. There began again a period of unbearable taxation. Year after year, complaints reached the Roman emperor. The people were exhausted by kings. They begged that they might have an opportunity to rule themselves through their own Sanhedrin, and be directly responsible to Rome. After ten years of Archelaus' misrule the request of the people was finally granted, and the kingship was abolished. The high priest and the Sanhedrin were now the heads of the Jewish nation. Over them was appointed a procurator, a Roman governor.

Those who clamored for the change could hardly have forseen that under direct Roman rule matters might grow even harder than they had been under the Herodians. Yet so it turned out to be. When an ignorant peasant in Roman uniform undertook to dictate their worship, in addition to wringing their last pennies from the poor farmers, then everyone certainly believed that the end was near, and that the Messiah was soon due.

THE PROCURATOR AND HIS RULE

The Roman procurators were usually retired generals who were rewarded for past service with the position of governor in the provinces. Away from their homes, in a strange and usually hostile land, they repaid themselves by extracting money from the people. It is said that as a rule there were so many complaints against Roman provincial governors that they were called back for trial before the emperor. They therefore made certain to collect enough money to bribe all the imperial [1] judges.

The taxes were collected not directly, but by tax-farmers, or publicans. We remember from a previous chapter how these publicans were sure to leave a sufficient share for themselves. Publicans and thieves were always mentioned together in those days.

In addition to satisfying the greed of the emperor, the procurator, and the publicans, the nation had also to support the Roman army quartered in its midst.

Very frequently, when the procurators were over-greedy, and feared that they might not succeed in escaping punishment at Rome, they sought to stir up a riot or rebellion. After a rebellion the Jewish complaints would not be received at Rome. If the com-

---

[1] belonging to the empire

plaints were listened to and a new procurator was sent, the cycle of oppressive taxation began anew. The exchange usually turned out for the worse.

More irritating even than the oppressive taxation was Roman meddling in Jewish religious affairs. The head of the Jewish political and religious life was the high priest. But the procurator appointed the high priests and removed them at will. Each appointment naturally, was for a large price, and the removal was to make way for a new appointee.

Nor could the high priest perform his duties freely without Roman restriction. For a time, the high-priestly robes were held under the lock of the Roman procurator at Caesarea. The high priest might not have charge of his own sacred vestments.

ROMANS MORE OPPRESSIVE THAN ELSEWHERE

The Romans did not generally interfere in the religion of conquered peoples. In none of the other provinces were native forms of worship suppressed. Even in Palestine the Romans meant to respect the Jewish religion. A Roman soldier who wilfully entered one of the Temple courts forbidden to gentiles, was put to death by the order of the procurator.

Rome could be tolerant of other religions because other religions could tolerate that of Rome. It was as natural for Rome to have its god as for the Germans to have theirs. Besides, Roman and German were united in emperor worship. In empires, there was

GREEK TABLET WARNING NON-JEWS NOT TO ENTER THE
TEMPLE

Photograph of actual tablet recovered from Temple of Herod.

practiced the custom of worshipping the emperor as a
god. His statues were set up in the principal temples,
and the subject nations gave particular honor to
emperor-worship, to win the favor of the ruler.

The Jews were the only people who could neither
pay any honors to any form of Roman worship, nor
even permit the Romans to set up any images for the
use of their legions on Jewish sacred soil. The Jews
would not even permit the Romans to carry their military eagles through Jewish territory. The threat to set
up the emperor's statue at Jerusalem almost caused a
revolt.

The Jewish religion was so completely strange to
the Romans that the Romans acted as do all ignorant

people toward something unfamiliar; they made fun of it. The Romans called the Jews superstitious. They called the Jews lazy for resting on the Sabbath, and for not ploughing their fields every seventh year.

The Jews were forced to protest so frequently against Roman abuses of their religion, that Rome gained the impression that the Jews were a rebellious nation which needed severe treatment. The Roman hatred of the Jews was readily shared and increased by the Syrian Greeks who lived in and about Judea. The Romans, to anger the Jews, granted favors to the Syrian Greeks. They favored them in their business rivalry against the Jews. They tried to make Caesarea the leading city of the country in place of Jerusalem.

The Jews felt Roman oppression all the harder because they could not respect their masters. Persia in its day, and Greece under Alexander, represented civilized countries. The Roman armies collected from the barbarians of all the provinces were merely savage hordes. Could the Jews imagine any worse conditions? Their land was impoverished. God's own Temple was not spared. The Jews had suffered now for several generations. The Kingdom of God must surely be at hand. Might not the Messiah now be expected in earnest?

Attitude of Parties Toward Messianic Hope

Various groups among the Jews gave different answers. The Sadducees, priests and nobles, still retained whatever power the Romans permitted them. The large merchants paid their taxes, and had sufficient money left. The wealthy priests sent armed servants to the threshing floors in order to take the priestly tithes by force. The Sadducees might wish for better times but they were satisfied to leave well enough alone.

The Pharisaic teachers, the leaders of the synagogue, were of the poor people, and felt keenly all the Roman oppression. But they found their joy in the study of the Torah. The Romans had not interfered with that. They believed faithfully that God would send His Messiah in due time, but they felt that the time was not yet ripe. It is of no use, they urged, for human beings to hasten "the end"—the coming of the Messiah —by force. "Submit to Rome, be lovers of peace like Hillel, and pray to the Lord." This was the motto of the leading Pharisees.

A PARTY THAT HELD ALOOF——THE ESSENES

The Essenes wished to have nothing to do with the government and its troubles. They needed little for their sustenance and they worked hard to earn it. In their own colonies, praying, bathing, thinking of God, they led a quiet life which neither the Romans nor the Zealots could disturb.

A NEW PARTY——THE ZEALOTS

The mass of young, spirited Jews, who suffered the brunt of Roman oppression and could not agree to submit willingly to Rome, formed a new party called the Zealots. The Zealots were devoted to their faith, and ready to give their life for the cause if necessary. The Zealots were the most active party at the time. They believed that God would help them only if they helped themselves. They were preparing for military resistance against Rome and her Jewish allies, the Sadducees, the wealthy classes. A constant guerilla warfare against both was waged by the Zealots who were frequently caught and executed by the Romans.

The Zealots had begun as a party in Galilee in the days when Herod was governor there. At that time Herod had put some of them to death. During Herod's long reign the Zealots had slowly grown into a strong underground organization which hoped to raise the banner of rebellion some day.

This party was quite prepared for the Messiah. Their ideal of the Messiah was of a brave general who would lead them against Rome. Several persons did appear who claimed to be Messiahs or prophets. One called upon the people to follow him across the Jordan where God would perform a miracle for them as in the days of Moses and Joshua. A detachment of Roman soldiers ended his life and adventures. Another Messiah gathered about him thirty thousand believers who followed him to the wilderness, where he promised to lead them against Rome. The Roman legions ended his career, too. But the Zealots were by no means discouraged in their belief of the speedy coming of the true Messiah. The others, they felt, were false Messiahs.

© *Funk and Wagnalls*

'THE LAST OF THE FALSE MESSIAHS

Shabbethai Zebi, who lived in the seventeenth century.

There remained a large mass of the common people, too poor to care who ruled, and too weak to do anything about it if they desired a change in rulers. In this group were many peasants, day laborers, and idlers. A prophet or any unusual person could readily gain the ear of this group since, in any event, it had nothing to lose.

The largest part of the Jewish people—the Zealots and the common people—were expecting the Messiah in their own day. Their feeling was strengthened by the fulfillment of half of the prophetic promise. The prophets had foretold that before the Messiah came the Jews would be scattered throughout the world. At the coming of the Messiah, God would gather them all together again to Zion. Never before had the Jews been so scattered. There was not an important city where Jews were not found.

John the Baptist

Everything was thus ready for a Messiah. Any unusual man might be God's messenger. We have already mentioned that several persons thought they were Messiahs, and suffered death at the hands of Rome for their dreams. One of these men, Johanan, or John as he is called in English, is worth remembering. He called himself the herald of the Messiah. He lived apart from men in the wilderness of the Jordan. His food consisted of wild honey and pure locust; his sole garment was a girdle of camels' hair, like the one worn by the prophet Elijah.

© *U. and U.*

BAPTISM IN THE JORDAN TODAY

John became known for his preaching that the Kingdom of God was at hand. Anyone who wished to prepare to enter the kingdom must repent of all his sins, and as a sign of a new birth must bathe or be baptized in the Jordan. For that reason John is known today as John the Baptist. Hundreds of persons, expecting the speedy arrival of the Kingdom of God, repented of their sins, fasted, prayed, and finally were baptized by John in the Jordan. So numerous were John's followers that the king of Galilee, Herod Antipas, feared that John might declare himself a Messiah and lead a rebellion. When John the Baptist reproved King Herod for an unlawful marriage, Herod imprisoned him, and a short time later had him executed. But since John had not claimed to be the Messiah but the forerunner of one, many people were certain that the Messiah would soon appear.[1]

A RESTATEMENT OF THE QUESTION

Many pages have passed since we set out to find an answer to our questions as to how the Jews gave religion to the world. We saw that the many scattered Jewish settlements had great influence in spreading Judaism among the gentiles. Yet we noted that in the end it was not Judaism but Christianity which finally converted the Greek and Roman world. We desired to know (1) the reason for the messianic hopes among

---

[1] You may have heard the legend about the princess Salome who danced at her father's court feast, and asked for her reward the head of John the Baptist. The legend relates to the John of whom we have just told.

the Jews; and (2) who was Jesus of Nazareth, and why is he the founder of a new religion?

THE LIFE AND ACTIVITIES OF JESUS

We have answered the first of these problems. We saw how a large class among the Jews was actually expecting the Messiah. We shall now approach the second problem. We shall tell of the man, Jesus of Nazareth, who claimed to be the Messiah. We shall tell of his life, and his work, and why his name has come to occupy so important a place in the world's history.

Jesus is the Greek for the Jewish name Joshua. Jesus was born of Jewish parents, Joseph and Mary, in the town of Nazareth in Galilee. Christian legends have invented many stories about his birth, but so far as we can tell, Jesus was the son of a poor carpenter, and was educated accordingly. We recall that there were schools in every Jewish village. Jesus, a bright lad, rapidly mastered the Torah and other writings which formed the main subjects of study for young boys. Later he followed his father's trade, making wheels and wooden ploughs. Otherwise, we know very little of the early life of Jesus.

His later life shows that he was a very religious man, and loved God dearly as a father. Boys and girls who love their parents strongly will readily understand how Jesus felt. God, his imaginary father, was more real to him than his parents. Jesus loved to dream of the heavenly court, and particularly of the Kingdom of God which would soon begin on earth.

At about the age of thirty Jesus had heard of the
activities of John the Baptist, and went to be baptized
by him. Legend tells that after his baptism Jesus imagined that he saw the heavens open and the spirit of
God descend upon him like a dove. It seems that the
baptism inspired him to begin publicly as a teacher in
the synagogues.

Jesus Begins Preaching

It was the custom in Palestinian synagogues, as it
is today, to read the weekly portions from the Torah
and from the prophets. After the reading, some learned
man usually volunteered to explain the passages to the
congregation. There were no salaried rabbis then, as
we have today, and any person, regardless of his occupation, might preach in the synagogue. Galilee,
where Jesus lived, was a district of little learning and
even a carpenter with some education could pass for a
learned teacher among the Galileans.

Jesus' preaching soon began to attract attention. He
spoke so simply and clearly, illustrating his remarks
with parables or little stories, that the most unlearned
men could not only understand but even enjoy his
words.

In contrast to the famous rabbis who liked to speak
before assemblies of educated people, Jesus seemed
to prefer lowly audiences. He selected as his listeners
the poor and down-trodden, even the publicans and
sinners. He considered himself a doctor of souls. When
accused of being too often in the society of persons of

bad repute, Jesus answered that the sick are in need of a physician, not the healthy.

Jesus brought a strange message to these common folk. He announced to them that the Kingdom of God was at hand and that only the poor and oppressed could enter it. The wealthy classes would under no circumstances be admitted into God's state. He spoke with such certainty of the coming kingdom that thousands of persons believed him and became his followers.

Acquires Reputation As Healer

Jesus became famed among his fellow Galileans for another reason. Word spread that he could cure the sick with the word of God. It may seem strange to us that people should go to a preacher to be cured, yet the practice is continuing even in our own day. Christian Science believes that one is cured through faith in God. In backward countries—even in the more ignorant sections of our own city—the belief still exists.[1] People at that time believed that certain nervous ailments, particularly hysteria, are caused by the entrance of a devil into the person. Such afflicted persons could be cured only by a great rabbi who was able to cast out the devil. Many persons were really cured because their illness was due to a disorder of their imagination. Strong and cheerful encouragement from a great man gave them new energy, which enabled them to overcome their fears.

---

[1] Examine the religious advertisements in a Saturday's newspaper, and see how many notices there are of "healing" services.

Courtesy Dr. Nelson Glueck

ENTRANCE TO THE SYNAGOGUE AT CAPERNAUM
The remains of what must have been a beautiful building.

Jesus apparently was a commanding personality as well as a lovable leader. When Jesus therefore commanded devils to leave the body, the sick person truly believed that the devil did leave him. Their belief "made them whole", as Jesus is reported to have said.

Of course there were many sick who were not cured. At one time it is told that Jesus visited his home town, Nazareth. He preached in the synagogue and tried to heal the sick, but he could not cure even one, for his townsmen had no faith in him. Only the successful cases were remembered and spoken about. The unsuccessful 'cures' were forgotten.

Even Jesus' enemies believed in his power to cure people, for even the rabbis believed in the power of such cures. Other famous teachers were also reputed to be possessed of healing power. The opponents of

Jesus, however, accused him, saying that he was curing people not through the aid of God but through Beelzebub, king of the devils.

Arouses Suspicion of Government

The large crowds which followed Jesus became a cause of concern to the government. Jesus was living in Capernaum (K'far Nahum) a city in Galilee. The ruler of Galilee, we may remember, was Herod Anti-

Courtesy Dr. Nelson Glueck
FROM THE RUINS OF A SYNAGOGUE AT CAPERNAUM
Dating back to days of Jesus.

pas, the man who had executed John the Baptist for fear of a messianic rebellion. The king was quite superstitious, and he began to imagine that Jesus was John the Baptist come to life again. He must have ordered

his arrest, for Jesus had to flee the land. A small group
of disciples or followers traveled with him throughout
his wanderings. These later became known as the Apostles, or messengers.

The Teachings of Jesus

What were the teachings of Jesus which obtained
so large a following? Jesus was a Jew and his teachings were Jewish. The rabbis taught and preached the
same truths. Only in few instances did Jesus introduce
new elements into his instruction. It was chiefly his
method that distinguished him from other teachers.

We cannot list all the teachings of Jesus. We shall
merely mention the most important ones, and those
which boys and girls can best understand.

Jesus sincerely believed that the Kingdom of God
was at hand. It might come tomorrow, the next day or
next week. He told his followers that most of them
would see it in their own lifetime. But the Kingdom
of God was a very different kingdom from that of
man. There, man needed no wealth. Everyone would
be provided for in all his needs. In God's Kingdom
there is no jealousy, no strife, no families, and no marriage. All will live happily and enjoy the presence of
God.

PREPARATIONS FOR ENTERING THE KINGDOM OF GOD

Not all persons might enter this heavenly kingdom.
Only those who were pure of heart and spirit, who

were of the highest moral character, might enter it. Jesus demanded that those who desired to prepare themselves for the Kingdom be more righteous even than the law demands of them. So kindly must a man be that he will not offer any resistance to one who attacks him. We must learn to love even our enemies. "If a man strikes you on one cheek, turn the other also. If a thief wishes to sieze your cloak, give him also your coat."

Not only must we refrain from hurting another, but we may not even call him names, such as fool or empty-head. One must never be angry with his neighbor, or use harsh words or oaths.

In addition to observing all the moral laws, a person who would enter the kingdom of heaven must give up all worldly possessions. There is the story told of a wealthy young man who came to Jesus and asked what he should do to be ready for the kingdom of heaven. Jesus told him to practice the commandments. "These have I done all my life," said the young man. "Then take all that you have and divide it among the poor," said Jesus. But the young man was unwilling to do that, and went away sadly. At this Jesus said to his disciples: "A camel could sooner pass through the eye of a needle, than a rich man into the Kingdom of Heaven."

Jesus asked his followers to take an example from the birds of the field and from the flowers. The birds do nothing but sing all day, yet the heavenly Father provides for them. The flowers neither sew nor spin, yet King Solomon himself was not dressed as beautifully as the lilies of the field. Will not a God who gives a thought to the birds and the flowers give heed to his most important creature, man?

STRESSES RELIGION OF THE HEART

The religion of the heart, taught Jesus, is more important than the performance of prescribed acts. For example, if a man truly loves God, it does not matter if he fails to wash for meals in accordance with strict law. One may pluck ears of corn on the Sabbath if he is hungry, or one may cure on the Sabbath even if the condition of the patient is not serious. The Sabbath, said Jesus, was made for man, not man for the Sabbath.

Jesus Claims to Be the Messiah

These are some of the more important teachings of Jesus. And why, you may ask, did not the Jews accept them? What objections did the Jews find to Jesus? Let us first continue with the story of his life, and then we may be in a better position to understand the reason.

One day when Jesus was with his disciples, of whom he chose twelve,—one for each of the tribes of Israel —he asked them, "Who do you think I am?" One said he was a prophet, another thought he was Elijah, and still a third called him John the Baptist. Then one of the disciples, by the name of Simon, whom Jesus had surnamed Peter (the rock), said, "I believe you are the King Messiah." The answer pleased Jesus. The disciples were greatly stirred by the announcement.

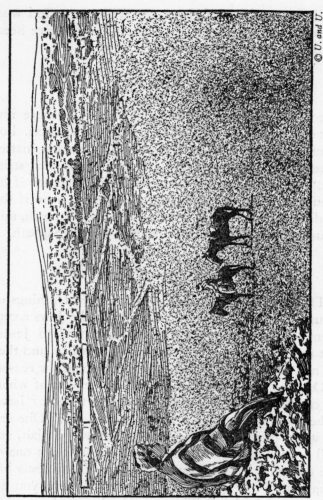

JERUSALEM, THE CAPITAL OF RELIGIONS

They felt that the heavenly kingdom was soon to be ushered in, and they wished to know what positions they would hold in the new government. Jesus promised that each would rule one of the tribes of Israel.

Since Jesus declared himself the Messiah, it was necessary for him to proclaim himself as such in the Temple at Jerusalem. It was the season of the Passover pilgrimage when hundreds of thousands of pilgrims were streaming to Jerusalem. Passover was also the feast of freedom. How fitting it would be for a Messiah to appear at that time!

Although Jesus had asked his disciples to keep his Messiahship secret, the news spread rapidly, and throngs gathered at the entrance of the city to greet Jesus the Messiah and to lead him triumphantly into the Temple.

There was a belief among the Jews that the Messiah would enter as a poor man, riding on a white donkey. Jesus, accordingly, ordered that a white donkey be found on which no man had yet ridden. His followers arranged their garments in place of a saddle. Amidst cheers and cries of 'Hoshana' (Help, I pray), Jesus was led through the streets of Jerusalem. Men threw flowers and palm branches before him.[1]

Jesus in Jerusalem

Jesus proceeded directly to the Temple, and entered it like a victorious commander. There was an official

---

[1] This occurred a week before the Passover, and is the reason for the Christian celebration of palm Sunday.

guard of priests which looked to the proper order of the Temple. Jesus paid no attention to them. He passed through the outer gates and found himself in the Court of the Gentiles.

The people had come to regard the Court of the Gentiles as outside of the sacred enclosure. The Temple area rose in terraces, one above the other. The more sacred courts were above the Court of the Gentiles. In the lowest court many activities were carried on which one would not expect in the Temple proper.

The Temple service consisted mainly of animal sacrifices. The animals had to be without any blemish, and a person who came to Jerusalem and wished to offer a sacrifice had to be certain that he was purchasing a sound animal. The priests, therefore, gave the privilege of selling sacrificial animals to a few chosen

Courtesy Pro-Jerusalem Society

THE CATTLE MARKET AS IT LOOKS TODAY

dealers, and permitted them to keep their sheep within the Temple area. Sacrificial doves, too, were kept on sale there. As Jews came from all parts of the world, each bringing his own coins, money changers sat at tables in the Temple court and exchanged the foreign coins for Judean money.

CLEARS TEMPLE OF TRADING

Jesus felt outraged at such use of God's house. He probably had never visited Jerusalem before, and was very greatly disappointed to see parts of the Temple converted into a market place.

Accordingly, Jesus ordered his followers to clear the court of all trading. He himself led in overturning the money-changers' tables. The frightened sacrificial animals stampeded in all directions. Doves flew about wildly. The guards were afraid to interfere, because the mobs at that time were usually armed. The common people felt certain that their deliverance from heathen bondage was at hand.

So long as Jesus remained in Galilee, he attracted little attention, and the leading men of the nation took slight notice of him. His first few days in Jerusalem, however, roused all responsible Jewish leaders against him.

All Jewish Parties Unite Against Jesus

All religious Jews were offended at his calling himself the Messiah. A simple carpenter from Galilee claimed to be "the Son of Man" which meant God's specially chosen one, or the "Son of God." His manner was so unlike that of any rabbi. He dared compare himself with Moses. He told the people that if they had faith in him, their sins would be forgiven. Which rabbi before him had been so arrogant? Who but God forgives sins? The rabbis considered him a blasphemer and guilty of an offence which was as serious as high treason.

SADDUCEES RESENT HIS TEMPLE ACTIVITY

The Sadducees were angered at Jesus because he usurped their power in the Temple. Picture a person coming into the Post Office or the City Hall, driving out the officials in charge, and directing how the business of the building should be conducted. The expelled officers could certainly have no love for him. In addition to driving them out, he abused them. He declared that when the Kingdom of God arrived, the Sadducees would not be admitted, but would suffer the worst of tortures instead. It would be worse for them on that day than for Sodom and Gommorah.

The Sadducees were disturbed for another reason. They feared that Jesus might head a rebellion against Rome. It was not unusual for a million persons to gather at Jerusalem for a festival, especially for the Passover. The Roman procurators always feared trouble on the occasions of the pilgrimages of Passover, Shabuoth and Succoth. At those times the procurators came to Jerusalem personally, and held large forces in readiness. The least rioting would give the Romans an excuse for massacre and pillage.

RABBIS ANGERED AT HIS SUPERIOR ATTITUDE

The Pharisaic rabbis, who could have had no objection to the teachings of Jesus, which differed very little from their own, found much to object to in his manner and in his treatment of them. Jesus appears to have believed that there were no righteous teachers besides himself. Jesus attacked all the Pharisaic rabbis. He called them fools and hypocrites, robbers of the poor and the widow; vipers, blind leaders of the blind. He said that they merely loved to display themselves in the market place and to receive all the honors, but that within, they were as lifeless as the grave. Jesus had spent but little time in Jerusalem. He may have heard that some men, called leaders among the Pharisees, were acting unjustly. He certainly did not know all the rabbis of his time. Had he heard of the great Hillel who was dead but a short time and whose teachings were so like his own? Would a messenger of God speak in such vile language of the rabbis, about the just and honest men who were teaching the nation how to lead righteous lives?

If, therefore, the rabbis could find no fault with the teachings of Jesus, they could certainly find many faults with his practice. Jesus had taught his disciples to do as the rabbis taught, but not as the rabbis did. The rabbis could have made the very same answer. "Do as Jesus teaches, but not as Jesus does." Jesus was teaching that one should love his enemy, that one might not even call another harsh names, yet he hated his opponents and called them vipers, fools, and hypocrites. He taught that people should not resist evil and should not use force. Yet, in the Temple, Jesus used force. Instead of arguing lovingly with the money-changers, he threw their tables over and drove them from the Temple.

The Pharisees, therefore, regarded Jesus as a person who might have been a very fine teacher if he had not pretended to be the Messiah. They said, too, that his teachings would endanger the Jewish nation. He cared only for those persons who would accept his teachings. All the others might be destroyed or suffer torture. As leaders of the Jewish people, therefore, they too could see more harm than good from his activity.

Leaders Rob Jesus of Popular Confidence

The Sadducees and the Pharisees together planned to destroy Jesus' popularity with the crowds. They decided to test Jesus, to see whether he really planned to head a revolution against Rome or not. That, indeed, was the main reason for his large following, for the Zealots who were awaiting a Messiah hoped that this Passover would free them of Roman bondage. Word spread through the crowds that the Messiah would be asked whether or not they were to continue paying their taxes to Rome. Everyone was eagerly waiting for his pronouncement, because the withholding of the taxes meant the outbreak of a revolution.

A delegation approached Jesus and asked him, "Master, is it lawful to pay the tax unto Caesar?" Jesus asked them to show him a coin. "Whose picture is this on the coin?" he asked. "Caesar's, of course," was their reply. "Then give unto Caesar the things which are Caesar's and unto God the things which are God's," replied Jesus.

When the people learned of his reply they were severely disappointed. He was not the Messiah. The masses fell away from him. The Zealots turned against him. The common people were now ready to attack him for his insults to their leaders.

Jesus' Last Seder Supper

It was Thursday, the day before the Passover. Many Jews were in the practice of observing their Seder on Thursday evening, a day before the Passover, if the Passover night was on Friday. Jesus, too, followed the custom. But Jesus feared that his enemies might arrest him during the night. He and his disciples, therefore, observed the Seder secretly in the upper chamber of a poor water-carrier's house. This was Jesus' last meal, and is known among the Christians as the Lord's last supper. There were matzoth and wine, which Jesus called his flesh and his blood. Today the Christians observe a ceremony called communion, wherein they eat a little wafer in memory of the matzoth, and drink some wine. These represent to them the body and the blood of Jesus.

After the Seder, Jesus and his party completed the reading of Haggadah, and sang the final psalms. Jesus, fearing that he might be discovered, left with two of his disciples for the Mount of Olives. Jesus felt that this Seder night might bring him sorrow. He begged his disciples to stay awake with him, but they could not keep awake and soon were soundly asleep. Jesus himself could not sleep. He prayed, instead, that the night pass in peace.

Jesus Arrested

Suddenly soldiers appeared—the guards of the high priest. They were led by Judas, who was one of the twelve disciples of Jesus. Judas having probably persuaded himself that Jesus was no Messiah, but an arch heretic who deserved no mercy, therefore prepared to turn him over to the authorities. Judas had arranged with the guards that he would point out Jesus by kissing him. Jesus was bound and taken before the Sanhedrin.

Jesus was brought to trial for heresy. Witnesses were called, but their testimony did not appear sufficient to condemn Jesus. The Sanhedrin then asked Jesus whether he was the Messiah. Jesus told them that he was and that they would very soon see him sitting at the right hand of God. At these words the members of the Sanhedrin rent their garments as in mourning, declaring that he had blasphemed God and decreed that he be turned over to the Roman governor with the recommendation that he be put to death.

Sentenced to Be Crucified

The Sanhedrin had not the power of sentencing people to death. The procurator alone could do that. The governor at the time was Pontius Pilate, a Roman officer known for his cruelty. Jesus was brought before Pilate who asked him, "Do you claim to be the King of the Jews?" "You have said it," answered Jesus. Pilate's decision was swift. A pretender to the throne of the Jews, without Roman authority, was a revolutionary, and received the severest penalty. The Roman governor could little understand the kind of kingdom that Jesus had in mind, and probably Jesus himself was not quite certain what it was to be. Pilate ordered that Jesus be crucified that same day.

Crucifixion was a cruel penalty which Romans alone used. A person on the cross suffered for hours, often for days, before he expired. Pilate was bent on using this extreme and cruel penalty, and was anxious to hasten the execution, so that he could set an example to others who might be tempted to make trouble during the holiday.

Crucifixion and Burial

The Roman soldiers to whom Jesus was turned over first desired to have their sport with the "King of the Jews." They dressed him in purple, and placed a crown of thorns upon his head. After dividing his garment among themselves, they led him out to be crucified. Jesus' cross was set up between those of two thieves, and over it, in mockery of the Jewish people, the soldiers wrote "Jesus, King of the Jews."

It was within a few hours of the Passover festival. Jewish practice demanded that dead bodies were not to be publicly exposed over night—certainly not on the most important festive night. A Jew, therefore, asked Pilate for permission to bury Jesus, and the permission was granted. Jesus was hastily placed in a tomb, and a stone rolled against it, till proper burial could be arranged after the feast.

At the news of what befell their leader, Jesus' followers fled in fear. There only remained a few women believers who were not considered important enough to attract public attention. These women remained behind to prepare the body fittingly for burial.

SPREAD OF BELIEF THAT JESUS HAD RISEN

Early Sunday morning at the break of dawn, the women came to the grave, with ointments and shrouds. To their amazement, they found the stone rolled away from the opening, and the body gone. Greatly frightened, they imagined that they saw some one clad in white who told them that Jesus had risen from the dead and would reappear to them shortly.

The women made haste to search out the other disciples and communicated the news to them. General rumor had it that the body had been taken out the night before and buried in accordance with Jewish custom. But the disciples of Jesus would not believe it. As they were hastening back to Galilee, out of reach of the Jerusalem officials, some of them saw Jesus in their dreams and spoke to him. There is nothing strange in seeing and speaking to dead persons in our dreams. But the disciples accepted it as a vision of God. They were certain now that Jesus would soon return.

They gathered as many believers in Jesus as they could find, and organized a society to wait for his second coming. James, a brother of Jesus, was chosen head of the group.

The Ebionim

This society consisted only of Jews. The members were as careful in the observance of the Jewish law as were other Jews. There was only one difference at first between the new sect and the other Jews. While the Jewish nation was still hoping for the Messiah, the Christian Jews believed that the Messiah (the Christ) had already come in the person of Jesus of Nazareth. True, he had died, but he would soon come again. The members of this society were so certain of the immediate coming of Jesus that every one who joined it had to sell all his property and turn the funds into the common treasury.

The society called itself "Ebionim," the poor ones. The members probably did little work, and devoted their energy to preaching. They tried to gain as converts to their group persons who, together with them, would give up earthly cares and await the Kingdom of Heaven.

Joined by Non-Jews

Jesus had taught that only Jews would enter the Kingdom of Heaven. Whoever, therefore, wished to be among the chosen, had to be a Jew. The apostles in their effort to gain converts appeared to succeed better among the heathen than among the Jews. In their efforts to convince people of the miracles they had seen and of the visions of Jesus which they had, they could persuade few Jews to believe the stories. The Messiah could not have come, since their suffering was greater than before. The non-Jews, who were becoming interested in the Jewish religion, gave much readier attention to the new preachers. The miracles, particularly, attracted them to the new faith, as we already saw in an earlier section.

But as non-Jewish converts were increasing in number, they were bringing in practices which the Jewish religion forbade. They were not careful with their food, or in laws of cleanliness. Since the Ebionim were still part of the Jewish people, the Sanhedrin sent out officers to inquire into the heresy and to punish the offenders in accordance with the law.

Saul—Paul of Tarsus

One of the officials thus sent by the Sanhedrin was Saul of Tarsus. Saul was the most severe of all the judges, sent against the new sect, and wherever he arrived, the new Christians felt his severity.

Saul who was given to trances, once had a dream

of Jesus, in which Jesus appeared to him and said, "Saul, why do you persecute me?"

When he awoke, Saul took the vision so much to heart that he turned from persecutor to member of the new faith. He changed his name to Paul, as a sign of his new life. Paul now became as active in behalf of his new religion as he had been in opposing it. In a short time he was among the leaders of the new group, and was accepted as an apostle.

Paul was given the special mission of preaching to the gentiles. He travelled through Asia Minor and through the cities of Greece, and although he encountered great opposition from the local Jews, he was very successful in making many converts. While the other apostles were making no progress, Paul's new converts were joining in large numbers. The reason for his enormous success was the fact that he excused the gentiles from the most difficult practices of Judaism, circumcision, and keeping the dietary law.

Paul Favors Changes in Law

There was bitter opposition to Paul on the part of the other disciples. The others were insisting that Jesus did not wish them to set aside any part of the law. Unless one was a firmly believing Jew one could not enter into Jesus' Kingdom.

Paul, anxious to retain his large following, presented a new argument. The old law, said he, was to last only until the Messiah should come. The Messiah had come, therefore the old law became void. Hereafter, anyone who believed in Jesus was a Jew whether he observed the law or not. Jews who did not believe in Jesus were no longer God's chosen people. God cast them off. The new believers were the only real Jews.

How long the struggle between Paul and the leaders of the Ebionim went on, we do not know. The Palestine society was poor, and the members depended for their livelihood upon the contributions of other congregations. Paul was most successful of all apostles in the sum which he raised, and therefore could not be dispensed with. In the meantime, the Jewish nation had entered upon the war of freedom against Rome. The members of the new Christian sect took no part in the war, and withdrew from Jerusalem, the center of Jewish life. This act naturally separated them from the main Jewish body. The heathen converts, in the meantime, were increasing by thousands, outnumbering the much smaller groups of Jewish-Christians. The Palestinian Jewish-Christians thus gradually passed out of importance and the place of leadership shifted to the chief city of the gentiles, Rome.

Separation of Christianity from Judaism

The differences between the new religion and Judaism were constantly becoming more pronounced. The belief in the Messiahship of Jesus alone would have sufficed to make the Jews feel that the new sect was not of its own kindred. With their nation reduced to slavery and their Temple in ashes, the thought of a Messiah already come was but a mockery to the Jews. But the Christians were moving ever further away from the spirit of Judaism. They surrendered the main belief of Judaism in one God, invisible and indescribable. Jesus, at first spoken of as the son of God was soon considered a god himself, the most important of the Christian gods. Besides Jesus, the 'son,' the Christians worshipped the Jewish god whom they called the Father, and a third being, the Holy Ghost. Thus, the Christians worshipped what they called 'The Trinity.'

Turning further from Judaism, the Christians made images of their god Jesus, and of other men and women, members of Jesus' family or his first followers. The latter were worshipped as saints and half-gods, another pagan custom. For in the Jewish religion, even the greatest of men, Moses, Abraham, or Samuel, were always considered merely as human beings. Christianity thus came to consist of a little Judaism mixed with paganism, and has kept much of its ancient nature to this day.

Present Day Christianity Influenced by Paul

The present religion of Christianity is really the result of the work of Paul and of the gentile converts. The main bond which held the new sect together was the belief in Jesus. The new Christians might or might not observe the Jewish laws, as they pleased. Everything in the religion now had to be rearranged and organized about the life of Jesus. Former holidays, Jewish and heathen, were taken into the new religion and given new meanings in connection with the life of Jesus.

For a long time after Jesus' death, his disciples believed that he would soon return to them. But the first generations of Christians passed away, and Jesus did not return. Gradually the belief in the immediate return of Jesus, which even Paul held, was given up. Instead Jesus was expected after a thousand years, the millenium. Books about Jesus and his teachings, about the Apostles and their activity, were collected into a new set of holy writings. The new Christians prized the old Jewish Bible too much to surrender it for the new books. They therefore accepted both collections, calling the Jewish Bible the Old Testament, and their new writings the New Testament.

RESUME

This is how Christianity grew out of Judaism, through Jesus and his disciples; particularly through Paul. The apostles of Christianity brought to the Greeks the moral teachings of the Bible and of the rabbis. Christianity, on its side, had nothing to offer the Jews. Few practical Jews could be persuaded to sell their possessions and wait till an executed man would rise from the dead. But the gentile world found much nobility even in the simplified Judaism offered by Paul. It accepted as much of Judaism as it could, and mixed it with many of its old superstitions. Out of the mixture arose the new religion, Christianity.

SUPPLEMENTARY WORK

Discuss or Debate the Following Questions

1. Would you have advised the Jews to relax some of their laws to make it easier for gentile converts to join them?
2. What are some of our present day superstitions?
3. Should Jews be glad that Christianity grew out of Judaism?
4. Do any people to-day still believe in religious or magic ways of healing the sick?
5. Why are Christians to-day anxious to convert others to their faith while Jews apparently are not?
6. A man says: "I am a good Jew at heart, though I do not observe any of the Jewish customs." Can he truly be a good Jew at heart under such conditions?
7. Since there are more Christians than Jews in the world to-day, and since there are many Christian sects which have given up the doctrine of the Trinity, why should not the Jews turn Christian?

Additional Readings
for teachers

Schürer, *op. cit.*, Part I, vol. I, pp. 166–256.

Schürer, *op. cit.*, Part I, vol. II, pp. 1–165, Part II, vol. II, pp. 128–187.

Margolis and Marx, *op. cit.*, pp. 177–188.

Klausner, J., *Jesus of Nazareth.*

Graetz, *op. cit.*, II, pp. 118–177, 190–199, 221–232.

Josephus, *op. cit.*, Bk. XVII, ix–xiii, Bk. XVIII, ii–vii, Bk. XX, ii, v, vi.

Riggs, *op. cit.*, pp. 232–257.

FOR PUPILS

Harris, *Thousand Years,* pp. 117–134.
Meyers, *op. cit.,* I, pp. 94–101.
Dubnow, *op. cit.,* II, pp. 94–97, 104–114.
Magnus, *op. cit.,* pp. 47–52, 53–57.

SECTION VII

THE WAILING WALL

The only remaining wall of the Temple enclosure.

HOW DID THE JEWISH STATE COME TO AN END?

PALESTINE LOSES ITS IMPORTANCE

WE are now coming to the end of the story of our ancestors during Second Temple days. We know, of course, that the story did end. If it had not ended, Palestine would have remained the largest Jewish settlement. But today New York City alone has one and a half times as many Jews as are found in the whole of Palestine. Most of the Jews who are in Palestine today have come only after the close of World War I. There were centuries when Palestine contained merely three or four thousand Jews.

The land, itself, moreover, was no longer what it had been in the prosperous days of our forefathers' independence. During the reign of the Hasmonean kings, several million persons lived comfortably in Palestine. At that time none of our modern inventions and fertilizing methods with which to increase the yield of the soil were known. The fruits of Palestine, its olives, dates, and figs, its grapes, and pomegranates, were famous in their world. Today the land is rocky. But after superhuman effort the land once more approaches Hasmonean fertility. When Jews first came to Palestine they found it marshy and treeless. They drained the swamps and converted them into good grain land. The part owned by the Arabs is still in large measure treeless. During the last eighteen hundred years Palestine has barely supported a half million Arabs. These have lived in poverty. Lack of food, and disease have diminished their numbers even during periods when other peoples were increasing in population.

How did this great change come about? What made the entire Jewish people leave its home land, and how did the land itself become a waste? We shall give only part of the answer. The entire course of events took many years. The Jews did not rise in a body and flee from their land. Nor were all the plantations suddenly ruined. But Palestine suffered a great misfortune from which it never recovered; the land slowly wasted away. Finally, Jewish Palestine disappeared and remained only the prayer-dream of the ages until our age made it real again.

The Great Catastrophe—A War Against Rome

We shall tell, in this section, about the great catastrophe which overtook our ancestors. It was a struggle against Rome, an attempt by our people to wrest its freedom from Rome. The war was fought between the years 67–70 C.E. Our ancestors failed, and Rome took a cruel revenge.

How rash, how hopeless for little Judea to fight great Rome! Look at this map. Here is the Roman Empire shaded. Judea is shown in solid black.

This tiny land risked a war against the largest

world empire. It was indeed a mad attempt, yet men
are often driven to dare death rather than to submit
to degrading slavery.

What Drove the Jews to War?

A whole nation does not embark upon such a dangerous enterprise hastily and thoughtlessly. Years and
years of suffering drives a people to despair until it
reaches the point when it feels that it has little to lose
even from failure.

We recall that after Archelaus was deposed by
Rome, Palestine was ruled directly by Roman governors or procurators. We described the rule of the
procurators in a previous section. For a short time it
appeared as though there would be a change in Jewish fortune. Agrippa I, a descendant of Mariamne, the
Hasmonean wife of Herod, gained favor at Rome.
The Roman Emperor appointed him king over the
northeastern districts of Transjordania, and later over
the entire Palestine. Agrippa I, who had been a reckless
spendthrift in his youth, proved a pious, wise, and patriotic king, devoted to the welfare of his people. He
lightened taxes. He prepared to strengthen the walls
of Jerusalem and sought to make alliances with neighboring kings, possibly in the hope of rebelling against
Rome. Agrippa could not accomplish much because
Rome was distrustful of his plans. Finally, after five
or six years of rule, Agrippa, while attending games at
Caesarea, was treacherously poisoned by enemies of
the Jewish people, who feared the new rise of Jewish

© "Migdal"

THE WALLS AROUND JERUSALEM

Notice gates, turrets and towers. The present walls are fairly modern, having been built by the Caliph Suleiman the Magnificent in the sixteenth century.

power. In 44 C.E., Judea was turned over to procurators again.

A son of Agrippa, called Agrippa II, was later given the rule of some districts in Northern Palestine. In addition, he was also appointed supervisor of the Temple at Jerusalem, with power to choose the high priest. But Agrippa II was more interested in his own comforts than in the welfare of his fellow Jews. He was popular neither with the priests nor with the Roman procurators. When we meet him again, he will be helping the Romans in their war against the Jews.

After the devoted Agrippa I, the rule of the procurators became harder to bear than before. The Roman procurators drove the Jewish nation to despair. We shall see how the Romans brought the Jewish people to rebellion by—

(a) Interference with their religion;

(b) Reducing a large part of the nation to beggary;

(c) Destroying the respect of the people for their government.

Interference with Religion

We have already told, in the previous section, how the Romans were constantly interfering with what the Jews considered sacred. We recall the attempt to bring the Roman eagles to Jerusalem. We remember also that the procurator retained the garments of the high priest.

Perhaps the most outstanding incident of Roman interference in Jewish religious life was the attempt of the insane emperor, Caligula, to have his statue set up and worshipped in the Temple.

CALIGULA DEMANDS WORSHIP AS GOD

The news that Rome planned to set up an idol reached Judea in early spring, at sowing time. The entire population of Judea, poor peasants risking the complete failure of their crops, left their fields and hastened to the Roman government seat in Syria to entreat the governor not to enforce the royal order. The governor feared to disobey the emperor, but neither could he withstand the entreaties of the thousands of petitioners gathered about him. Hoping that the Jews would disperse after a few days, the governor set out upon a trip of inspection, but the Jews followed after him. Weeks passed, the spring was already over, and many fields could no longer be planted, but the Jews persisted. After fifty days, the governor yielded. He knew that disobedience of the emperor would mean his death, but he could not resist the prayers of a whole people.

An order did indeed come from the emperor that the governor put himself to death. Fortunately, news arrived at the same time that the emperor had been murdered. This marked the end of his decrees.

SOLDIERS INSULT TEMPLE WORSHIPPERS

Such crises were not soon forgotten. The memory of them might have been permitted to die away if the

succeeding Roman generals had been more thoughtful.
Instead, insults continued. During the sacred festivals,
when thousands of pilgrims were worshipping at the
Temple, a soldier made indecent jokes about the worshippers. The Jews asked the procurator that the soldier be punished. Upon his refusal, a riot broke out,
in the course of which the Roman soldiers were ordered to attack the masses of worshippers. Thousands
died that day by Roman swords, and thousands more
were trampled by the crowds which tried to escape
through the Temple gates.

MASSACRE AT CAESAREA

Another incident which fanned the flames further occurred at Caesarea. That city had been built by Herod.
The majority of its residents were Jews, though
the Syrian Greeks also lived there in large numbers.
A dispute arose over the apportionment of power in
the city government between the Jews and the Syrian
Greeks. The matter was carried to the emperor's court
at Rome, where the Greeks succeeded in bribing the
Roman court to render the decision that hereafter the
Jews were to have no citizenship rights at all in Caesarea. The Jews were hurt at being deprived of citizen-
ship in one of their own cities, and angered by the
Syrians rejoicing over their victory.

A short time thereafter on a Sabbath morning, an
incident occurred which led to open bloodshed. A
Greek set up an altar at the head of a narrow alley
which led to the synagogue, and mockingly, sacrificed

THE STATE COMES TO AN END 315

doves on the altar as the Jews were going to prayer. Doves were used as a sacrifice for persons who had recovered from leprosy. The Egyptian anti-Semites had invented the story that the Jews were the descendants of lepers who were expelled from Egypt. This Greek was now aiming to insult the Jews by calling them lepers.

The young Jews resented the insult, and fell upon the offender. A fight began in which the entire population of Caesarea was soon involved. When it was clear that the Greeks were suffering the worst of the encounter, Roman soldiers were ordered out. At first, the soldiers tried to stop the fighting. But failing in that, they turned their weapons upon the Jews. Twenty thousand Jews are said to have lost their lives that day.

Some of the older men feared that in the rioting injury might be done to the synagogue. More concerned over the sacred scrolls than over their lives, these men removed the scrolls from the synagogue, and fled with them to a neighboring village fifteen miles away.

When quiet was at last restored, the procurator, Florus, began to inquire into the causes of the rioting. Instead of punishing the ones who began the disturbance, he meted out punishment to the Jews. Many more Jews were now executed. Even the persons who had removed the Torah-scrolls were punished for having acted without permission. The massacre of Caesarea was to the Jews what the Boston massacre was to the colonists in the American Revolution.

Impoverishment of Nation

The foregoing were some of the persecutions which the Jews suffered, mainly for religious causes, and which led them to make war against Rome. Had the nation been prosperous, it might have hesitated longer over going to war. But Roman rule had made a large part of the Jews indifferent, and reckless of life or fortune.

Let us picture the average Jewish farmer, struggling to earn a livelihood with the aid of his entire family. After the meager crop was harvested, he had to pay his tithe, one tenth, of all the produce, to the priest. Then came the publican who had to collect enough in taxes for the Roman Emperor, for the governor of the district, for the procurator, and for himself. The rabbis had condemned the acts of the publicans, and declared them sinful, but they could do nothing more. The poor man was left without enough to live on, and with little ambition to improve his farm. If he would raise a large crop, it would only mean that he would be obliged to pay higher taxes.

Years of famine were not unknown. When the crop was bad, all the income went to pay the taxes. The poor farmer was then forced to sell his land, and he tried to seek work as a laborer. He was not always certain of finding employment, and even when he did, his wages were very low—about a half dinar (ten cents) a day. He could no longer work together with his sons on his own farm; they had to find work for themselves.

DRIVES YOUNG INTO GANGS

The boys, left alone, often joined gangs. There were all sorts of gangs—patriotic secret clubs, patriotic terrorist clubs, and robber gangs. The patriotic organizations, the Zealots, preyed on Roman and Greek commerce. The terrorist gangs became known as Sicarii, men of the dagger. The Sicarii carried daggers under their clothes, and killed anyone whom they regarded as an enemy. The rich merchants of Jerusalem or the wealthy Jews, who were buying up the abandoned farms, were as hateful to the Sicarii as were the Romans themselves. Men were slain in broad daylight, in the middle of the market place. Thus, the poor risked their lives for booty. The rich were in constant danger because of their wealth.

The many caves and mountainous hiding places in Judea and Galilee made it impossible for the Romans to suppress banditry. When the bandits were caught they were tortured in a cruel manner. They were crucified in public view. Yet the death of their comrades only added new fury to the survivors.

The Roman procurators were more eager to suppress the patriotic organizations than to destroy the banded thieves. Procurator Florus, particularly, openly shared the loot with the thieves. He freed thieves from prison for a ransom, and permitted whole villages to be robbed that he might share in the spoils.

Roads were unsafe, commerce declined, and employment fell off. It was difficult for poor men to earn a livelihood. Thousands were already living the life of armed soldiers in secret camps. Thousands more were ready to do the same. What else was there to do? They had already lost their liberty, their property, their honor, and their freedom of worship. If a stroke against Rome might restore what they had lost, it was worth trying.

Destroying Respect for Local Jewish Government

For a long time the local Jewish government succeeded in persuading the nation to keep its peace. Again and again the elders at Jerusalem, the Sanhedrin, and the high priest, implored the people not to rise against Rome. But Rome was undermining the respect of the Jews for government. The head of the Jewish state was the high priest. The nation rightly expected that the high priest should act as was befitting the head of their religion. The chief priest was the nation's example of how men should live under the law.

But the high priests were chosen by Rome. Men were no longer selected for their priestly worth. The office was sold to priests of wealth, who paid large sums for it, and hoped to repay themselves at the cost of the people. The servants of the high priests invaded threshing floors and robbed the tithes that were intended for other priests. The poor priests starved while the rich found their posts so profitable that they were outbidding each other before the Roman procurators for the privilege of the office. Rival priestly families often had pitched battles in the streets of

Jerusalem. The successful high priest appointed his followers to all the important positions.

COMMON PEOPLE DESIRE TO SEIZE POWER

How could the nation honor such rule? The common man saw that might alone was supreme. If so, why should he not seize the powers of government himself, and rule the land in his own interests? He would expel Rome and its wealthy Jewish henchmen.[1] He would organize a real republic, a free state for the people.

The common people of Jerusalem were thus plotting to rebel against their own rulers as well as against Rome. The wealthy men of the party of the high priests as well as peace-loving citizens therefore feared and hated their rebel fellow-Jews more than they hated the Romans. They were in greater danger of their lives from the Jewish Sicarii than from the Romans. Their position was like that of the Tories during the American Revolution. Thus the nation was divided within itself, and was unable to profit by the guidance of its leaders and elders.

Jews Driven to Madness by Rome

You have undoubtedly noticed that when a person is greatly irritated, the slightest offense may drive him into a fit of temper. Often, in like manner, a whole people, enraged, loses its temper. Then it can no longer

---

[1] a slavish follower

think; it cannot reason. It strikes; it fights; it cannot listen to advice. It follows those leaders who are as headstrong as it is itself. It is a nation gone mad.

Rome drove the Jews to madness. Every fresh oppression, every new execution of a well known leader, every new slight to Jewish religious feeling, heightened the nation's anger. The massacre at Caesarea was still a red flame in the heart of Judea—and now came two incidents which started the great war.

Florus Demands Temple Gold—The Massacre

Florus, the Roman procurator, had been by far the most shameless robber whom Rome had sent to rule Jerusalem. Under him thieves had openly plundered cities and villages. Under him the massacre at Caesarea had taken place. Now Florus demanded that seventeen talents of sacred Temple gold (worth more than half a million dollars) be turned over to him.

The Jews might suffer all indignities [1] to themselves —they would permit no insult to their Temple. A large crowd assembled at the Temple mount, and openly denounced Florus. It was suggested that Florus must have become very poor and that a collection might be taken up for him. Someone began to pass around the Temple charity boxes, and the crowd, in sport, threw copper coins into them.

When Florus learned how he was made sport of by the Jews, he hastened to Jerusalem to avenge the slight to his dignity. He turned over a section of the city to

---

[1] insults

his soldiers to pillage and slay as they pleased. Old and young, rich and poor, fell before the fury of the Romans. Wealthy leaders of the people were publicly crucified. The terror continued till a large part of Jerusalem was covered with ruins and corpses.

Demand That Jews Greet Legions Begins War

After the Roman soldiers were tired of their killing, and quiet reigned again in the city, Florus sent for the leading men of Jerusalem. He upbraided them

ROMAN SOLDIERS

for what had happened, blaming them particularly for permitting the insults to his person. He then informed them that two companies of Roman soldiers were on their way to Jerusalem, and that he expected the population of Jerusalem to come out to greet them, as was the custom; otherwise, he would consider the Jews enemies of Rome.

The people stubbornly refused to humble themselves before the Roman soldiers. They were prepared to undergo any suffering rather than to do the wishes of the procurator. But the elders and the priests pleaded with them not to bring further calamity upon their Fatherland.

Finally, the people consented. On the next day the Jews assembled in large numbers to greet the soldiers. But it seemed that this was another pretext[1] on the part of Florus to anger the Jews. He was anxious for a rebellion; otherwise, he feared, he might have too much to account for at Rome. As the soldiers approached, the Jews offered the usual greetings, to which it was customary for the soldiers to respond. Instead, the soldiers passed by, completely disregarding the Jews. The crowd began to murmur and complain, whereupon the soldiers were ordered to attack the Jews. Taken entirely by surprise, the Jews broke into a wild panic and fled toward the city. Before they could reach the city, many had fallen by Roman swords, and many more were trampled to death crowding through the gates. But having gained their narrow streets, the Jews suddenly turned on the Romans. From housetops, from windows, and alleys, missiles began to fly at the soldiers. It was now the Romans' turn to flee. The war against Rome had started.

A REVOLUTION IN JERUSALEM

Having cleared the city of Roman soldiers, the mob felt itself master of Jerusalem. The anti-Roman party seized the control of the Temple and the Sanhedrin. The Sadducee officials were deposed. The peace-loving Pharisees of the school of Hillel were in disfavor. The Zealot Pharisees of the school of Shammai who called for war were now in authority.

---

[1] excuse

One of the first acts of the new government was to order all connections with Rome severed. No more taxes were to be paid, and even the sacrifices for the Roman emperor were to be discontinued. The heads of the school of Hillel attempted to protest. They urged that it had always been the custom to accept sacrifices from non-Jews. But the revolutionary leaders did not heed them.

The poor people celebrated the birth of the revolution in their own way. They set fire to the house of archives (the public records) where their debts were recorded. Then they set fire to the palaces of the rich.

Soldiers Fail to Suppress Rebellion

The legitimate [1] high priest and his officials did not surrender their authority without a struggle. They sent urgent calls for help to Florus and to King Agrippa II. We recall that Agrippa II, a son of Agrippa I, was given a small kingdom by Nero, north of the Jewish land. He also had the power of appointing the high priests in Judea. Florus was not anxious to interfere in Jerusalem as yet. He hoped that the rebellion would grow more serious. Agrippa did send soldiers to aid his high priest. For a time, the soldiers of Agrippa were getting the better of the rebels. Soon, however, there was the wood offering festival when Jews from all parts of the land brought gifts of wood to Jerusalem. The thousands of visitors from the provinces sided with the rebellion. There were among them, par-

---

[1] rightful

ticularly, many Sicarii. With their aid, the tide turned, and soon the Agrippians were pleading for mercy. Jerusalem was cleared of foreign enemies, and the rebellion felt secure.

Roman Army Is Routed

The Romans were now beginning to look upon the rebellion as serious. Cestius Gallus, the governor of the entire district of Syria, gathered a large army of about 30,000, and marched against Jerusalem. He had no doubt that he could make short work of the rebellion and, indeed, he encountered little difficulty on his march. But when he appeared before Jerusalem, he saw that the task would be much harder than he had imagined. It was very near the rainy season when the roads would be in bad condition, and his army would not be sure of its supplies. After a few days, he suddenly decided to retreat.

The road from Jerusalem is narrow, and flanked on both sides by steep, jagged mountain ranges. The Romans had barely gone a short way from the city, when they found themselves surrounded on all sides by an invisible foe. Spears and javelins cut down the Romans by the hundreds, while they could make no attempt even to defend themselves. The Roman retreat became a rout. The Romans left their baggage, their war engines, and their gold, and the soldiers' pay, and tried to escape. Only the coming of night helped the commander to flee with a small part of his troops. The Jews returned to Jerusalem, laden with booty. Jerusalem celebrated its victory over a real Roman army.

Preparation for War with Rome Begins

The revolutionary government now set out in earnest to prepare for the expected war with Rome. A new government was organized for the whole country. Judean governors were appointed for all the districts of Palestine. Everywhere active war preparations were started. Soldiers were drilled, food was gathered and new fortifications were erected.

APPROACHES TO JERUSALEM. THE VALLEY OF JEHOSHAPHAT

The Area of the Revolt

PHŒNICIA

Damascus

GALILEE

MT. Carmel

Dora

Cæsarea

SAMARIA

Sebaste

Apolonia

Antipatris

Jaffa

Jabneh

JUDEA

Beth Horon

Jerusalem

Herodium

Bethlehem

Beth-Zur

Hebron

Dead Sea

Masada

EDOM

Mediterranean Sea

Sea of Galilee

Yarmuk River

DECAPOLIS

Jordan River

Jabbok River

PEREA

Arnon River

NABATÆANS

MILES

Great activity was going on in Jerusalem. The walls surrounding the city were strengthened, and new walls and towers were built. Large cisterns were provided with water, and storehouses were filled with food. Jerusalem, in the heart of the mountains, now had three mighty walls with a large number of towers surrounding it. The people believed they could brave a siege for a long time.

Unfavorable Conditions within Jerusalem

Yet in spite of all effort, the war against Rome did not begin favorably. Things appeared calm outwardly, but the nation was not at all ready, nor could it ever be, for the people had no confidence in its rulers. All the offices of importance had been filled by men of wealth and nobility who had joined the rebellion. The poor people whose lot did not improve with the revolution blamed their misfortunes upon their new leaders whom they hated as much as they did the Romans. At any moment a civil war might break out within Jerusalem.

NO OUTSTANDING LEADER

There appeared no great leader whom all the people would follow. There were many factions, each with its own leader. The rebel priests had their leader, Eliezer, of the family of the high priest. The Zealots had several leaders, the outstanding one of whom was to be John of Giscala, a Galilean. The Sicarii had leaders of their own, the most famous of whom proved to be Simon bar Giora.

Each faction was suspicious of all the others, and every leader was stirring up his followers against the opposing leaders as bitterly as against Rome.

Under such conditions how might a nation expect to win any war, particularly, a war against Rome? Many who truly despised Rome could yet see no hope for success. The nation was divided. Whole cities were divided one against the other. Outwardly they were all loyal, but there was no certainty that they would really offer opposition to Rome.

EXAMPLE OF JOSEPHUS, GOVERNOR OF GALILEE

A good illustration is afforded by the situation in Galilee, the most important single district of Palestine. Galilee was the most prosperous section of the land, containing a large Jewish population in many fortified cities. The revolutionary parties, the Zealots, and the Sicarii, had their birth there. Yet the man who was chosen governor and commander in chief of the armies of Galilee was himself friendly to Rome, and never truly confident of winning. He was constantly hesitating between making war and surrendering.

This man, Josephus Ben Mattathias, later to become famous as the Jewish historian, was of a priestly family which traced its descent from the Hasmoneans. His Maccabean ancestry may have been responsible for his high post. He was a brilliant scholar; versed in Jewish learning as well as in the writings of the Greeks and the Romans. He had been on a mission to Rome, and therefore understood a little more clearly than other leaders the power of the enemy. Although he had no military experience to speak of, he was chosen to command a large army.

A leader of this sort could hardly inspire confidence among the local Zealot leaders for whom Josephus was too aristocratic. John of Giscala, the most popular of the Galilean leaders, a fiery Zealot who had equipped a company of soldiers at his own cost, considered Josephus an outright traitor, and stirred up the people against him. Josephus might have lost his office had he not cunningly set one city against another. There was much business jealousy between the Galilean cities. Josephus, instead of trying to make them forget their disputes, widened the divisions among them.

Under such conditions a great war was to begin.

JEWS LACK MILITARY SKILL

In general, the Jews possessed little military equipment and no military training. Everybody, at the time, used weapons, but the Jews were to face the most expert soldiers of the world. The Romans had engines of war which the Jews did not even know how to use.

MASSACRES IN HELLENISTIC CITIES

In addition to all these internal difficulties, external calamities [1] overtook the Jews. Jews from Palestine

---

[1] misfortunes

had settled in all surrounding Greek cities where they engaged in commerce, and formed formidable [1] competitors [2] to the Greeks.

The Romans now began to spread word that the Jews were plotting against all the gentiles. They instigated the Greeks to believe that the Jews wished to destroy them all and to annex their land to the Jewish States. Perhaps some Jews did actually hope that the Messiah was at hand and that the whole world would fall beneath his rule.

As a result, a wave of massacres spread throughout the Hellenistic cities. The Greeks attacked the Jews, and the Jews fell upon the Greeks. Everywhere Roman soldiers naturally sided with the Greeks. The most terrible massacre took place in Alexandria when over fifty thousand Jews were killed, and their entire quarter suffered pillage. In the cities of Transjordania, in Asia Minor, and on the coast, Jewish dead were counted by the tens of thousand. A madness had broken over the land. No one was spared; neither young nor old. Thus the Jewish war began.

The War in Galilee

Nero, aroused by the defeat of his general, Cestius Gallus, realized that a serious war would be waged in Judea. Accordingly, he assigned the task of subduing the Jews to his most famous general, Vespasian, and gave him an army of 60,000 picked soldiers.

---

[1] strong
[2] took much of the Greek business away

Vespasian, together with his son Titus, set out against Palestine. Vespasian's plan was first to reduce the North, Galilee, then to occupy the country about Jerusalem, and finally to attempt its conquest.

Battle at Jotapata

The Roman army appeared in Galilee, and after overrunning a few villages encamped before a small

VESPASIAN

Galilean city, Jotapata, where Josephus, the governor of Galilee, happened to be at the time. The city was strongly fortified, and prepared to give resistance to the Romans. Vespasian hardly thought that the small city would withstand the main Roman army. The Romans believed they would occupy Jotapata in a day or two by storming the gates or scaling the walls. But they were driven back with such heavy losses that Vespasian saw that a long siege would probably be necessary before achieving a victory.

The Romans then began to prepare for a siege. They threw up embankments, mounds on which to place their engines which threw large stones into the city. They also set about building towers higher than the city walls, from which their archers and slingers

THE BATTERING RAM

Worked by soldiers under the shed by means of ropes twisted as springs.

could shoot into the city. But when the embankments and towers were built, the Jews rushed out of the city and burned them. The Romans were obliged to build new towers which they covered with iron to make them fire proof. From their high position the Romans were now raining missiles into the city. The only hope for the Jews was to raise their walls higher. It would have been impossible for the Jews to build, being exposed to the Roman fire. But they cleverly spread fresh hides on poles as a cover for their heads. Stones, spears and arrows slid off the hides, and, under the eyes of the Romans, the wall rose above the Roman towers.

Seeing that their towers were now useless, the Romans decided to use the battering ram—a long log with an iron head of a ram. The ram's head hammered at one spot in the wall till the stones were bound to give way. The Jews lowered bags of chaff over the spot where the ram struck the wall, to deaden the thud of the ram. Finally, when the Romans succeeded in cutting these bags down, and when the ram made a breach in the wall, Vespasian found to his dismay, that a new wall had been erected immediately behind the opening and that he must begin anew.

Unfortunately the city had not enough water. So

scant was the supply, that the water had to be distributed by measure. The Romans saw, from their observation posts, how the Jews were in want of water, and planned to starve the city into surrender because of thirst. But the Jews decided to fool the Romans. They soaked clothes in water and let them drip over the walls. The Romans imagined that the Jews had enough water, and gave up the idea of settling to a long siege.

The Romans, impatient with their lack of success, again decided to attempt to take the city by storm. The plan was to scale the walls on ladders. The entire army advanced against the walls; the soldiers held their

STORMING A CITY

Notice the massed shields forming a protective roof, the tall towers for the archers, the battering rams and the engines for throwing missiles.

shields over their heads firmly, one next to the other, forming a roof of iron. The defenders tried the usual weapons, but spears and stones would do little damage to the massed shields. The Jews then resorted to boiling oil. The burning oil flowed through the joints of the armor, and the soldiers fell back, mad with pain. The Romans were forced to retreat again with heavy losses.

Fall of Jotapata and Surrender of Josephus

Jotapata finally fell through treachery. A deserter told the Roman general, Vespasian, that the city could easily be taken at the break of dawn. The defenders of the city reduced in number, tired from the constant fighting, and parched from thirst, were unable to stay awake all night. If the night passed quietly, they permitted themselves a nap at daybreak.

Vespasian thought he had nothing to lose by making the attempt. At early dawn a few soldiers stealthily ascended the walls, and found the Jewish guards fast asleep. The rest of the Roman army followed, and a general slaughter took place. The Romans, angered at the long resistance spared no one. Nor did the Zealots wish to be spared. They had vowed never to surrender, and they were ready to die fighting.

Josephus, the governor of Galilee, and about forty soldiers, hid for safety in an empty cistern. Josephus suggested that they surrender to the Romans, but his companions turned their swords at him and were ready to kill him. Josephus then advised that since they preferred to die by their own hand, they kill one another, and that they draw lots for the order in which they were to die. Josephus chanced to pick the last lot. When all the others were dead and only Josephus and one more were left, Josephus persuaded the last survivor that they both surrender to the Romans. Thereafter, throughout the rest of the war, Josephus accompanied the Romans, and urged the other cities to surrender. For that reason many Jewish historians consider Josephus a traitor.

End of the War in Galilee

We have told of one battle in Galilee to show how valiantly and desperately the untrained Jews were ready to make a stand against Rome. There were other cities in Galilee, but they were not all minded to fight for their freedom. Some of them, such as Tiberias and Tarechias, surrendered without a blow. These cities may have sincerely believed that the war was hopeless. Another city, Gamalla, encouraged by the example of Jotapata, did resist, and suffered the fate of Jotapata. Even after its walls fell the city did not ask for quarter. There was a high hill at the end of the city from which projected a precipice over a deep ravine below. The Jews climbed the hill and held the Romans at bay for some time. But suddenly a terrific storm arose, blowing toward the Jews. So fierce was the wind that the Jewish spears and javelins were carried back. The Jews despaired not merely because the Romans were gaining but because they believed that the storm was

an omen from God directed against them. Yet rather
than surrender, all the fighting men with their families threw themselves over the precipice, and were
dashed to pieces in the ravine below.

Gradually the Romans were occupying Galilee. Occasionally, a small village engaged the Romans in
battle. Many Galileans, patriotic Zealots, who were
unable to force a battle in their own city, fled to Jerusalem before the oncoming of the Romans. The most
famous of these bands was one under the leadership
of John of Giscala, whom we have already mentioned.
When the Romans advanced against Giscala, John
asked that they give him a day to decide upon surrender, and used that as an opportunity for escape.

Thus ended the war in Galilee. It had cost thousands of lives and hundreds of flourishing villages.
Had all of Galilee been united against Rome the war
would undoubtedly have lasted longer; it is doubtful whether the outcome would have been different.
The boldest spirits were either dead, or nursing revenge at Jerusalem. The more prosperous farmers and
merchants were happy to have saved what they could
from the catastrophe.[1] Galilee was beaten, but not
crushed. In fifty years it would be ready for a new
attempt for freedom.

JERUSALEM BEFORE THE SIEGE

Jerusalem was still untouched by the war, but other
troubles were in store for it. The city had accomplished

---

1 misfortune, destruction

its revolution. It had appointed new governors, a new high priest, and new members of the Sanhedrin. The new officers were drawn from members of the wealthy and noble classes who had joined the revolution.

The failure of the war in Galilee, particularly the surrender of Josephus, created great dissatisfaction among the poorer classes. Josephus, the aristocrat,[1] was branded as a traitor, and all other officers of the old nobility fell under suspicion. The populace feared that their new leaders were more concerned for their wealth and safety than for the national freedom. The many fugitives who were pouring into the city daily helped to increase the distrust of the aristocracy.

New Arrivals Seize Power

Gradually the new arrivals and their leaders began to exercise power independently of the city authorities. The fugitives from Galilee were soldiers, trained in arms, and could resist the regular city officials. The Zealots were becoming so uncontrollable that the high priest and his party decided to subdue them by force. The Zealots fled for safety to the Temple mount where they fortified themselves in the outer court. For a long time, neither side was able to make any headway. At last, the besieged Zealots persuaded the Idumean Jews to come to their aid. Twenty thousand Idumeans entered Jerusalem. With their assistance, the Zealots defeated the aristocratic party and seized control of

---

[1] rich man, member of the nobility

the government of Jerusalem. John of Giscala, head of the Zealots, became the actual ruler of the city. The Zealots now began a reign of terror against the aristocrats whom they accused of being opposed to the revolution. The poor soldiers, newcomers in Jerusalem from the villages, took the liberty of looting [1] homes and shops. It required a long time to establish order.

New Civil Wars—The Sicarii Gain Power

The disorders in Jerusalem aroused much opposition to John. The wealthy classes were the victims of the terror, while the extreme Sicarii accused John of not persecuting the enemies of the revolution vigorously enough. Only John's own followers were satisfied with him. Otherwise, there were rival leaders and rival parties, each opposed to John and his rule. Each party, too, was intent on establishing itself by force. One group of extreme Zealots seized the inner Temple court, and began a war against John. While this civil war was in progress, the aristocratic party organized an attack against John. Thus, the Temple mount was a ladder of battles. The aristocrats below attacked John in the center who was fighting the extreme Zealots above.

The Sicarii, made up of the poorest elements, were not participating actively in the civil war. The stronghold of the Sicarii was outside of Jerusalem, near Hebron. Simon bar Giora was gathering about him large numbers of followers. After his army had in-

---

[1] robbing

creased to 20,000, and after he had occupied the entire southern district, he next marched against Jerusalem. Simon found the city gates barred against him, and settled down to a siege outside of Jerusalem.

The aristocratic party, failing to gain over John, decided upon a desperate measure. They invited the Sicarii into the city to help them against the Zealot, John. The Sicarii were very glad to enter, but no sooner had they gained admittance to the city than they fell upon the party which had invited them. A new reign of terror and of looting began. When the Sicarii made themselves masters of Jerusalem, they next turned against John in the Temple Court.

Food and Supplies Destroyed in Civil Wars

John in the meantime had overcome his opponents in the upper Temple Court. Now there were two parties at war for the control of the city. Neither party was able to vanquish the other, but each made sallies and inflicted damage on the other. Each side tried hard to destroy the other's supplies. In those skirmishes, the large stores of food which had been prepared for the war with Rome, were set on fire. When both finally realized that they should have been fighting a common enemy, it was already too late to undo the harm.

Choice of New Emperor Delays Roman Advance

The Romans had left Jerusalem in peace for a while. There were troubles at Rome of greater interest to

Vespasian than the Jewish war. The Emperor Nero had been murdered, and his successor, too, was killed after a few months. The throne of Rome was thus vacant, and in accordance with Roman customs would be filled by some general nominated by the strongest army. The legion in Palestine promptly proclaimed their own Vespasian emperor. Several other generals were also named by their armies and Vespasian feared that he would have to fight his rivals before securing the royal purple. Vespasian was thus prepared to withdraw the army from Judea, if necessary. Unfortunately for the Jews, the throne was secured for Vespasian by friends in Italy. He was thus enabled to leave Judea with a small guard, entrusting the command of the war to his son, Titus.

© *Funk and Wagnalls*

"JUDEA NAVALIS"

Coin of Titus celebrating victory over Judea, the naval power.

THE WAR IN JUDEA

During the entire period of waiting, Vespasian was kept informed of what was going on in Jerusalem. He saw no danger in the delay. He believed, on the contrary, that he had much to gain by such a course. In the meantime he had busied himself by attacking the smaller cities in Judea. An expedition was also sent against Jaffa where the Jews had organized a large pirate fleet, and were preying upon Roman commerce. Through an accident of nature, the Jewish naval power was destroyed. A terrific storm drove the Jewish ships against the rocky shore, and since the entire coast was in Roman hands, the Jews could find no shelter. Thus the naval auxiliaries of Jerusalem were shattered. Jerusalem itself continued in the grip of civil war.

Jewish Parties Unite But Too Late

After Vespasian left for Italy, Titus began the advance against Jerusalem. Not until the Romans were in sight of the city did both sides hastily make peace. John of Giscala and Simon bar Giora agreed to lead the war jointly. But too much harm had already been done. The city's large food stores had been destroyed. Starvation was facing the city at the very outset of

Courtesy Dr. Nelson Glueck

ROCKY SEACOAST OF PALESTINE

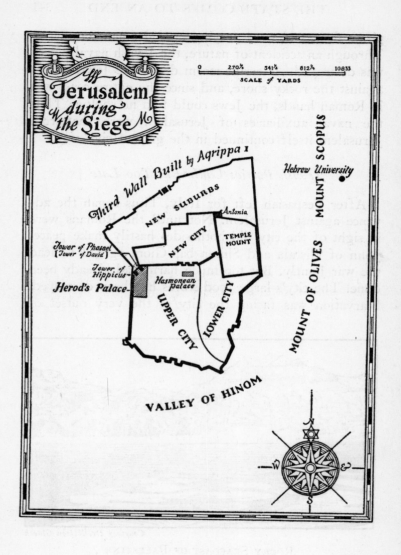

Jerusalem during the Siege

SCALE of YARDS
0   270¾   541½   812¾   1083⅓

Third Wall Built by Aqrippa I

NEW SUBURBS

Antonia

NEW CITY

TEMPLE MOUNT

Tower of Phasael
[Tower of David]

Tower of Hippicus

Herod's Palace

Hasmonean palace

UPPER CITY

LOWER CITY

Hebrew University

MOUNT SCOPUS

MOUNT OF OLIVES

VALLEY OF HINOM

N
W — E
S

the war. Many visitors had come for the Passover celebration, increasing the number of the defenders, but adding also to the numbers to be fed. Long before the city surrendered there was no more possibility of a successful defense.

Still the Romans found it no small task to take Jerusalem. Jerusalem was a powerfully fortified city. On three sides steep hills made it inaccessible. Only on the northern side could it be attacked, and there, the strong tower of Antonia, the fort which guarded the Temple, blocked the way. Three walls of enormous stones encircled the city.

Except for the lack of food, the defenders of Jerusalem felt quite equal to the Romans. The Jews were not afraid to come out from behind their walls. As the Roman outposts were preparing to build their camp, the Jews rushed forth and attacked them, and only the hasty aid of Titus saved the Romans' camp. Titus himself was wounded in one of these engagements.

Repulse Romans—Are Overcome by Famine

Titus began to erect battlements for his engines but when they were completed the Jews rushed out from behind their walls and set the battlements on fire. The Romans were forced to build new towers and battlements. They needed much timber for the work, and they cut down all the trees on the surrounding hills. When the new works were completed the Jews made a sally and destroyed them. The Romans had to bring new timber over a distance of twenty or more miles.

RUINS OF ANTONIA
The ancient fortress that defended the Temple.

But as the Romans were beginning to fear that the Jews were invincible,[1] news began to reach them of the food shortage in the city. Unfortunately, the hunger within the city was now too far at work. Food had become scarce, and whoever had any, hid it. Meals were eaten in underground cellars, for there was no longer enough food even for the fighting men. The soldiers began to raid homes, and took away whatever food supplies they found. The civil population was left to starve. The dead became so numerous in the city that it was no longer possible even to bury them. Thousands now attempted to desert to the Romans. Some were

---

[1] one who cannot be conquered

received but thousands of unfortunates were killed by the Roman soldiers, who searched them for hidden gold. Others, after their long fast, fell too suddenly upon coarse foods, and died of painful indigestion. The defenders of Jerusalem, moreover, stationed guards and executed any deserters whom they caught.

The deserters' tales of horror led the Romans to believe that Jerusalem would now fall an easy prey. Accordingly, they attempted to scale the wall with ladders. But the Romans were repulsed violently, and they saw that Jerusalem would yet withstand a long siege. At a council of war it was decided to erect a wall all about Jerusalem, to prevent any one from bringing food into the city. Jerusalem was now completely cut off. Then the battering rams began to hammer at the city walls.

The Walls Give Way

The famished defenders of Jerusalem were no longer able to halt the Romans. The first wall fell beneath the blows of the ram, then the second fell. Finally the third wall began to give way at Antonia, but the Romans found a new wall behind it. In the night Roman soldiers secretly scaled the last wall. The guards were unable to offer resistance. Antonia fell, and the Jews were driven back to the Temple.

Battlements were now set up against the walls surrounding the Temple area. The starving Jews tried to demolish the mounds, but were no longer able. But the Jews still held the Romans off in an all day battle, and kept them from gaining the Temple hill. The Romans set their rams against the walls, surrounding the Temple area, but the stones were so large that the ram could not shake them. At last Titus ordered that fire be set to the Temple gates.

The Temple Afire

The Jews had believed throughout the war that in the end God would come to their aid. Even when they saw the Temple gates aflame they did not give up hope. Every foot of the Temple mount was bitterly contested. Finally, as the Romans were pushing the

© *Publishers' Photo Service*

THE ARCH OF TITUS

Erected at Rome in honor of his victory over Judea. Showing his soldiers carrying away the Temple vessels—the Menorah, the table of Showbread and the silver trumpets.

© *Funk and Wagnalls*

JUDEA DEVICTA—DEFEATED JUDEA

Imperial Rome stepping on conquered Judea. From a coin struck by Vespasian to celebrate the victory.

Jews up the hill, a Roman soldier seized a burning firebrand and threw it into the Temple through the golden window. It was in the month of Ab, the middle of the Palestinian summer. There had been no rain for months and the Temple timbers readily caught fire. When the Jews saw their Temple in flames, their courage failed them. They feared that God's help would no longer arrive. They had fought desperately in defense of the House of God. Now they cried out in despair—and they knew that they had lost.

The Battle for the Upper City

The lower city now was in Roman hands. The city was set on fire, and the Roman soldiers looted the ruins. The war against Rome was practically over.

Yet, when Titus called upon the Jews to surrender, even now the Zealots refused to give themselves up to Rome. John and Simon offered to end the war if they would be permitted to march off with their followers into the wilderness. Titus, enraged, ordered a new attack against the upper city. Again there was a siege, and the worn out Jewish armies still held the Romans back for eighteen days.

Roman Vengeance

At last the upper city also fell. The Romans, angered because of the stubborn opposition, took their vengeance. Titus ordered the upper city to be burned to the ground. All survivors were assembled into the Temple

THE VICTORIOUS GLADIATORS SALUTING THE CÆSAR

area, and there the old, the weak, and the fighting men were killed. Many young men were sent as slaves to the mines of Egypt, while others were selected to be killed in the arenas by wild beasts or gladiators.

The End of John and Simon

John gave himself up to the Romans. Simon bar Giora hid in a cavern, but driven by hunger he emerged dressed in a white sheet, like a ghost. He was soon caught and taken prisoner.

Titus collected trophies to bring back to Rome where he was to celebrate his triumph. He took the sacred Temple furniture, the table of showbread, the candelabra, the altar, and the other smaller Temple vessels. He selected the handsomest of the Judean youths to march in his procession. John and Simon, too, were to be in the march, with ropes around their necks. John was to spend his remaining days in a Roman prison; Simon was executed after the triumph as a sacrifice to the war god.

THE END

Thus ended the Jewish uprising against Rome. Palestine was in ruins, and a million Jews had lost their lives. Throughout the slave markets of the Roman world, as far as distant Spain, Jewish slaves were bought cheaply.

This ends the story of our state in Palestine. Jews think of their past history not so much in terms of independent government as in terms of Temples. Even when Judea was under Persian or Roman rule, the Temple at Jerusalem was the symbol of our people's unity. With the Temple destroyed, another chapter in the history of our people is sealed.

Two great periods in the story of our people were now completed. The first lasted from the conquest of Canaan to the year 586 B.C.E. when our ancestors lost their independence and their first Temple. The second is the one which this book has told. And now the third and longest of the three periods is to begin. Would the Jewish people be able to continue without its independence and without its Temple? Neither Rome before the walls of Jerusalem nor our own forefathers making their last stand on the ramparts of the Holy City, could have foreseen the future.

The great teachers, however, did foresee and understand. They knew that the Jewish people was more than a state, and more than a body of worshippers gathered about a Temple and a priesthood. The Jewish people was a sacred union which, in the midst of a world of war and violence, attempted to proclaim one God and one humanity.

While Roman battering rams were shaking the walls of Jerusalem, and the doom of the Holy City seemed certain, a great teacher, Yohanan b. Zaccai, one of the illustrious pupils of Hillel, gave thought to the new symbol which might replace the Temple. Not a city nor a structure, but a book would hereafter be the symbol of Jewish unity, the flag of a scattered people. Secretly Yohanan b. Zaccai left Jerusalem and secured permission from Titus to organize a school for Jewish study at Jabneh. The house of study would replace the Temple and the teachers would constitute the priesthood. And thus we became a People of the Book, a people of schools and scholars. Spread throughout the world, and confronted with trials more severe than any which our forefathers had encountered, our Book proved stronger than any enemy.

Therefore we have been called "Am Olam, the Eternal People."

Now the third period of our history, the longest and most tragic, has ended. We are beginning the fourth period, a new era of independence of Israel, in its own home land. It was the supreme miracle that more than three-quarters of the nations of the world agreed to restore Israel's statehood. Despite that agreement, Israel had to fight a war to establish its claims. As soon as the war was over, even during the war itself, Israel established self-government of which we may well be proud. It has been proved that in order to set up a new government, even under conditions of war, it is not necessary to resort to dictatorships which now dominate a large part of the world, but that a true people's democracy may be counted upon to yield the greatest happiness to its people and to promote effectively the peace of the world.

May we hope that Israel's glorious day will now come as was foretold by our prophets of old.

SUPPLEMENTARY WORK

MAP EXERCISES

1. Draw an outline map of Palestine. Fill in the most important political divisions and locate one important city in each section.
2. On an outline map of Palestine locate at least five cities which are important in the war against Rome.

QUESTIONS FOR DISCUSSION AND DEBATE

1. Is it a good thing for the Jews that the Temple at Jerusalem was destroyed?
2. Were the Jews wise in going to war against Rome? Is it foolish to embrace a lost cause?
3. Is revolution ever justified, or do we now possess better ways of settling disagreements than through bloodshed?
4. Is it true that the more oppressive the government is the more rebellious are the subjects?
5. While the Jews were at war with Rome, was it right for anyone who opposed the war to join the Romans? Would we call Josephus particularly a traitor?
6. The Zealots had pledged to die by their own hand rather than to surrender to Rome. Was John of Giscala false to his pledge when he surrendered to the Romans, or can you see any reasons for excusing his conduct?

ADDITIONAL PROJECTS

1. Make a clay model of the city of Jerusalem, showing the site of the walls, the fortifications and the Tower of Antonia.

2. Make models of Roman war engines.
3. Record an imaginary conversation between two Romans in the course of which they mention the war in Judea.
4. Hold a mock trial at which Josephus is charged with treason.
5. Prepare a talk on the importance of the Temple in Jewish history.
6. Plan a program to commemorate the fall of the Jewish state.
7. Resolved that an unworthy government should not be respected.
8. Resolved that Roman oppression of Judea was more severe than British oppression of the thirteen American colonies.
9. Write an imaginary diary of a Jewish prisoner taken captive to Rome with Titus.

ADDITIONAL READINGS
FOR TEACHERS

Margolis and Marx, *op. cit.*, pp. 189–204.
Graetz, *op. cit.*, II, 233–320.
Josephus, *op. cit.*, Bks. XIX, i–ix, XX, i, vii–ix, xi. *The Wars of the Jews,* Preface, Bk. II, xiv–xviii.
Riggs, *op. cit.*, pp. 260–277.
Radin, *op. cit.*, chaps. xviii–xx.
Bailey and Kent, *op. cit.*, pp. 345–352.

FOR PUPILS

Harris, *Thousand Years,* pp. 147–178.
Meyers, *op. cit.*, I, pp. 105–116.
Dubnow, *op. cit.*, II, pp. 114–140.
Magnus, *op. cit.*, pp. 57–69.

INDEX

Aaron, 45, 115
Abraham, 301
Adar, 108
Adiabene, 257
African Natives, 84
Agriculture, 140
Agrippa I, 310, 312
Agrippa II, 312, 323
Ahriman, 54
Ahura Mazda, 54
Alcimus, 108, 110, 238
Alexander Janneus, 123; accession of, 126; wars of, 126; becomes Sadducee, 172; clashes with Pharisees, 172f.
Alexander, Son of Aristobulus, 196, 198
Alexander the Great, conquest of Palestine by, 63; kindness to Jews, 64, 65; Alexandria built in honor of, 65; death of, and result, 65; empire of, partitioned, 67, 140, 227, 230
Alexandra Salome, 123; reign of, 126, 174; replaces Sadducees by Pharisees, 175; last days of, 185f.
Alexandria: population, 229; occupation, 233; self-government, 235; Jews in, 330; massacre of Jews in, 330
Alexandrian Library, 236
Al Hanisim, 62

Alphabet, reform of, 49
Altar, 20, 101
America, 228
American Jews, 234
American Revolution, 84, 315, 319
Ammon, 24, 25, 35
Ammonites, 4, 44, 45
Amos, 11
Angels, 55
Anti-Semitism in Diaspora, 246f.
Antigonus b. Aristobulus, 200f.
Antioch, 113, 189, 210, 231
Antiochians, 86
Antiochus III, 81, 83
Antiochus IV, Roman influence upon, 83f.; interference in Judea by, and Syrian war, 84f.; after death of, 105f.
Antipas, Herod, see Herod Antipas
Antipater, 191f., 192, 195, 198f.
Antonia, 344, 345
Antony, Mark, 206
Apocrypha, 240f.
Apostles, the twelve, 285; flee at Jesus' execution, 298; succeed among gentiles, 299; in Christian writings, 302
Appolonius, 96
Arabia, King of, 192, 257
Arabs, 131, 308

High Priest *(Cont.)*
od, 205, 268; appointed by
procurator, 270; chosen by
Rome, 318
Hilkiah, 32
Hillel, personality of, 216, 273;
story of, 217f.; teachings of,
219f.; the lover of the Torah,
221; compared to Jesus, 291;
school of, 322, 323
Historical books, 51
History, Jewish, in Greek, 241
Holy Ghost, 301
Holy of Holies, 150, 197
Honey, 139
Horace, 256
Hosea, 11
Housing of poor, 40
Hycranus II, 123; accession of,
185; high priest, 191; and
Antipater, 191f.; and Pom-
pey, 193f.; and Herod, 199,
204; ransomed from Parthi-
ans, 204
Hyrcanus, John, *see* John Hyr-
canus
Iberia (Spain), 188
Idol worship, attacked by proph-
et, 16f.; abolished in Judea,
24; Greek, demolished at
Temple, 101; ridiculed in
Egypt, 247
Idumeans, 337
Images of Jesus, 301
Immigrants, Jews as, 233
Individual responsibility for Sin,
13f.
Intermarriage, 23, 28, 30, 34f.,
40, 42
Interpretation of Law, severity

* For new State of Israel, *see* page 371.

Interpretation of Law *(Cont.)*
of Ezra in, 39, 44f.; dispute
over, 162f.; by Sadducees,
164f.; by Pharisees, 167f.
Isaiah, 11, 16
Isaiah, Second, 16
*Israel, and God, 10f.; not pun-
ished for sins of fathers, 14
Jaffa, in Hasmonean times, 131;
Roman expedition sent out
against, 340; Jewish fleet destroyed at, 341
James, brother of Jesus, 297
Janneus, Alexander, *see* Alexander Janneus
Jason (Joshua), 84f.; usurps office of Onias, 85f.; contrib-
utes to Greek games, 86; replaced by Menelaus, 86; orders massacre of party of
Menelaus, 88; flight of, 89,
205, 238
Jeremiah, flees to Egypt, 4; letter of, 6
Jericho, in Hasmonean times,
131; palm district of, 139
Jerusalem, exiles return to, 20;
in restored Judea, 22; flight
from, 28; fortified by Nehemiah, 36f.; repopulated by
Nehemiah, 41; under Pto-
lemy I, ruler of Egypt, 65;
under Hellenists, 84f., 104;
occupied by Judas, 101; sieges
of, under John, 125; population of, 131; religious capital,
144; besieged by Antipater,
192; occupied by Romans,
194f.; Romans withdraw
from, 195; almost destroyed

Michael, 55
Middle Ages, 246
Migrations of Jews, 227
Miracle, of Chanukah, 116f.
Mizpah, 98
Moab, 24, 25; punished by
  Judas, 105
Moabite, 4, 22, 28, 38, 42, 44,
  45
Modin, 94
Mohammedanism, 255
Monday, 49
Money changers, 289
Monotheism, in Jewish religion,
  151; surrendered by Christi-
  anity, 301
Moses, 12, 31, 40, 43, 47, 48,
  290, 301
Mount Gerizim, see Gerizim,
  Mount
Mount of Olives, 294
Munzab, King, 257
Nabatean Arab, 206
Nablus, 52, 53
Nahardea, 229
Nasi, 219
Nazareth, 278, 281
Nazarite, 72, 74
Nebo, 11
Nebuchadnezzar, King, 3, 6, 93,
  229
Nehemiah, governor, 35ff.; re-
  turn of, 42f.; reforms of, es-
  tablished, 45; book of, 51;
  reforms of, undone, 90; life
  a century after, 154
Nero, 323, 330
New Moon, 24
New Testament, 302
New York City, 307

Nezivin, 229
Nicanor, 98, 108
Nicanor Day, 108
Nile, 230
Non-Jews in Palestine in Has-
  monean times, 130
North Africa, 233
Number of returned exiles, 18
Occupations in Hasmonean
  times, 135, 140, 142
Octavian (Augustus Caesar),
  206, 208
Oils, 137, 138
Old Testament, 302
Olives, Mount of, 137
Onias III, high priest, 84; ac-
  cused of treachery, 85; death
  of, 87f.; descendants of, in
  Egypt, 238
Onias IV, 238
Orphans, care of, 154
Pagan customs in Christianity,
  301
Palestine, change in life of, under Greeks, 67ff.; unsettled
  conditions of, 77; interest in
  past of, 127f.; geography of,
  127ff.; result of colonization
  of, 182; differences between
  Ancient and Modern, 127ff.;
  under the Hasmonean kings,
  128f.; population of, 130;
  census of 1926 of, 130;
  when Jews first left, 227f.;
  loses its importance, 307;
  agriculture of, past and present, 307f.; population of, in
  19th century, 308
Palestinian, settlers, 128; merchants, 135; products, 137f.;

In the days of the
second temple